YOUR $100,000 CAREER PLAN

Match Your Personality to a Six-Figure Job

Laurence Shatkin, Ph.D.

jist Works
America's Career Publisher

YOUR $100,000 CAREER PLAN

Match Your Personality to a Six-Figure Job

© 2009 by JIST Publishing

Published by JIST Works, an imprint of JIST Publishing
7321 Shadeland Station, Suite 200
Indianapolis, IN 46256-3923

Phone: 800-648-JIST   Fax: 877-454-7839
E-mail: info@jist.com   Web site: www.jist.com

Some Other Books by the Author

Quick Guide to College Majors and Careers

90-Minute College Major Matcher

150 Best Recession-Proof Jobs

Great Jobs in the President's Stimulus Plan

Quantity discounts are available for JIST products. Please call 800-648-JIST or visit www.jist.com for a free catalog and more information.

Visit www.jist.com for information on JIST, free job search information, tables of contents and sample pages, and ordering information on our many products.

Acquisitions Editor: Susan Pines
Development Editor: Stephanie Koutek
Cover Designer: Lynn Miller
Interior Designer and Layout: Toi Davis
Cover Image: © Jacob Wackerhausen/iStockphoto
Proofreaders: Paula Lowell, Jeanne Clark
Indexer: Joy Dean Lee

Printed in the United States of America
14 13 12 11 10 09   9 8 7 6 5 4 3 2 1

Library of Congress Cataloging-in-Publication Data
Shatkin, Laurence.
Your $100,000 career plan : match your personality to a six- figure job / Laurence Shatkin.
    p. cm.
Includes index.
ISBN 978-1-59357-668-4 (alk. paper)
1. Occupations--United States. 2. Vocational guidance--United States.
I. Title. II. Title: Your one hundred thousand dollar career plan.
HF5382.5.U5S4647 2009
650.1--dc22

                                    2009006042

All rights reserved. No part of this book may be reproduced in any form or by any means, or stored in a database or retrieval system, without prior permission of the publisher except in the case of brief quotations embodied in articles or reviews. Making copies of any part of this book for any purpose other than your own personal use is a violation of United States copyright laws. For permission requests, please contact the Copyright Clearance Center at www.copyright.com or (978) 750-8400.

We have been careful to provide accurate information throughout this book, but it is possible that errors and omissions have been introduced. Please consider this in making any career plans or other important decisions. Trust your own judgment above all else and in all things.

Trademarks: All brand names and product names used in this book are trade names, service marks, trademarks, or registered trademarks of their respective owners.

ISBN 978-1-59357-668-4

Plan Your Path to a High-Paying Job

Would you continue to do your job even if you won the lottery? If so, more power to you. But for most of us, income is an important reason for working, and the higher the income, the better we feel about our jobs. Roughly 6 percent of American workers earn $100,000 or more per year. Why not you?

This book identifies more than 100 occupations that pay six figures to a significant number of workers. It explains where the highest-paying positions are, in terms of both industries and geographical locations.

But which six-figure jobs might be right for *you?* One important key is your personality. This book includes an assessment to help you understand where your personality fits into a structure that is used by many career development professionals. With this knowledge, you can decide which of 10 career tracks best suits your personality and learn how to navigate that career track to a six-figure job.

For each career track and personality type, you'll see what high school preparation is appropriate, what college majors are a good fit, and what strategies experienced workers can pursue to maximize their earnings. You'll also learn about the six-figure jobs associated with that career track.

Finally, you'll learn job-finding techniques that are much more productive than help-wanted ads or Web-based job-matching sites. You'll also learn tips for negotiating salary, so when you get hired (or seek a raise) you can improve your chances of being paid six figures.

Some Things You Can Do with This Book

- Develop long-term plans for education, training, or work experience that will put you in reach of a six-figure job.

- Develop strategies for maximizing your income in your present occupation.

- Find ways to shift to a new occupation that uses your accumulated experience and your network of contacts.

- Prepare for a job search or salary negotiations using proven techniques developed by the experts.

These are a few of the many ways you can use this book. We hope you find it as interesting to browse as we did to put together. We have tried to make it easy to use and as interesting as occupational information can be.

When you are done with this book, pass it along or tell someone else about it. We wish you well in your career and in your life.

Credits and Acknowledgments: While the author created this book, it is based on the work of many others. The occupational information is based on data obtained from the U.S. Department of Labor and the U.S. Census Bureau. These sources provide the most authoritative occupational information available. Some of the noneconomic job-related information is derived from the Occupational Outlook Handbook, 2008–2009 Edition, published by the U.S. Department of Labor. Other noneconomic job-related information is derived from the O*NET database, which was developed by researchers and developers under the direction of the U.S. Department of Labor. They, in turn, were assisted by thousands of employers who provided details on the nature of work in the many thousands of job samplings used in the database's development. The version of the O*NET database used for this book was the most recent, release 13. The staff of the U.S. Department of Labor deserve thanks and praise for their efforts and expertise in providing such rich sources of data. The taxonomy of college majors (the Classification of Instructional Programs) is from the U.S. Department of Education.

© JIST Works

Summary of Major Sections

Introduction. A short overview to help you better understand and use the book. *Starts on page 1.*

Chapter 1—How Personality Can Be the Key to Your $100,000 Job. Explains the six personality types identified by John L. Holland and why they are a useful way of looking at careers. *Starts on page 15.*

Chapter 2—What's Your Personality Type? Take an Assessment. Helps you discover your personality type with a short, easy-to-complete assessment. *Starts on page 22.*

Chapter 3—Your Career Plan for a $100,000 Job. Helps you choose a career track that can lead to a six-figure job. *Starts on page 32.*

Chapter 4—What Career Track Matches You? A Checklist. Focuses on the work-related characteristics of the tracks and provides an alternative way to choose a career track. *Starts on page 55.*

Chapters 5–14—Ten Career Tracks to a $100,000 Job. Explains each of 10 career tracks that can lead to high-paying jobs, shows strategies that each of the six personality types can use to get on this career track and achieve six-figure earnings, provides key facts about the related jobs and summarizes their characteristics, and presents opportunities for workers to branch out from this career track to another track. *Starts on page 62.*

Chapter 15—The $100,000 Job Hunt. Outlines strategies for clarifying job goals, finding jobs that aren't advertised, and maximizing your salary both in a new job and in your present job. *Starts on page 260.*

Table of Contents

© JIST Works

Chapter 6—The Bachelor's-in-Business Career Track to a $100,000 Job

© JIST Works

Chapter 8—The Engineering Career Track to a $100,000 Job 109

Chapter 9—The Entrepreneurial Career Track to a $100,000 Job..125

© JIST Works

Chapter 10—The Information Technology Career Track to a $100,000 Job 155

Chapter 11—The Managerial Career Track to a $100,000 Job...171

© JIST Works

Chapter 12—The Professional Career Track to a $100,000 Job 200

© JIST Works

Chapter 13—The Scientific Career Track to a $100,000 Job 225

© JIST Works

Chapter 14—The Technician/Artisan Career Track to a $100,000 Job 241

© JIST Works

© JIST Works

Introduction

This book is designed to show you how to prepare for and get a job that pays six figures. Even if you eventually fall short of making a salary that exceeds $100,000, the strategies in this book point the way to high-paying jobs. And, unlike most other books about achieving wealth, this one is based on the *personality theory* that many career development professionals use with their clients. That's why this book can help you aim for a high-paying career that suits your interests and skills.

This introduction explains how to use this book. It provides details about how the 138 six-figure jobs included in the book were selected and matched to personality types. It identifies sources of the information about the jobs and suggests how you should interpret the facts presented in chapters 5 through 14.

Who This Book Is For and What It Covers

Many of the six-figure jobs included in this book take years of preparation: education, training, work experience, or some combination of these. Therefore, the broadest range of options in this book is available to young people who are still planning their college education. On the other hand, the book also includes many jobs that are options for people to consider later in their careers. Some careers are open to people who are willing to get some additional education at the graduate or professional level. Other careers are open to people with work experience—or just a combination of good ideas and business savvy.

The book covers 10 *career tracks:* broad preparation pathways, each of which can lead you to various six-figure jobs. Because the book is rooted in the RIASEC personality theory of John L. Holland, it helps you understand your personality type and explains how people with different personalities can choose an appropriate career track and navigate that track toward a high-paying career.

How to Use This Book

Different readers will use this book in different ways. Probably one of the following ways will be right for you.

People Who Are Deciding On a Career Goal

Are you a young person who has not yet decided on a college major and a career goal? Are you an experienced worker who wants to make a career change? Or have you been out of the workforce for some years and want to re-enter with a new goal? If any of these profiles resembles you, you may want to use the book this way:

- Read chapter 1 to understand the connection between your personality and your career options. Then, take the assessment in chapter 2 to clarify your primary personality type and one or two secondary types.

- In chapter 3, use what you've learned about your personality to choose one or more career tracks that might suit you. If you're still not sure about your personality type, or if you want an additional way of choosing a career track, use the checklist in chapter 4 to choose a career track that meets your preferences for various features of work.

- Chapters 5 through 14 are each devoted to one career track. When you have made a tentative choice of one or more tracks, turn to the appropriate chapter. Learn a way to navigate the track that suits your personality type, explore the high-paying jobs that the track can lead to, see how to maximize your earnings in this track, and find what other tracks can be exit routes from the track, possibly to even higher earnings.

People Who Are Already Moving Toward a Career Goal or in a Career

Are you a college student and wondering how you will use your education after you get your degree? Are you in the military or another training program and planning how to use your newly acquired skills to earn a high income? Or are you a seasoned worker and want to use your experience to move into a six-figure job? If any of these profiles resembles you, you may want to use the book this way:

- If you're familiar with the RIASEC personality types, skip this bullet point. Otherwise, read chapter 1 to understand the connection between your personality and your career choices. Then, take the assessment in chapter 2 to clarify your primary personality type and one or two secondary types.

- Find a chapter from 5 through 14 that describes your present career track or the one you seem to be headed for. Look at the career goals

© JIST Works

that are consistent with your personality type. If your present career or career goal is not a good fit for your personality, note which goals are. If your present career or career goal *is* a good fit, note other interesting career goals that also may suit you. Pay attention to the actions you would need to take to change your career goal while remaining in that track. Also note the section called "Achieving Six Figures in the *x* Track," which may suggest a strategy you can use to propel your career toward higher earnings.

- If none of the career goals in your present track suits you, use chapters 3 and 4 to choose a different track that might be a better fit. Then explore the track in the appropriate chapter from 5 to 14.

People Who Want Higher Pay in Their Present Career

- Maybe you're in the right occupation but your present *job* is a dead end, with few chances for raises or advancement. To earn six figures, you're going to need to find a job with more opportunity. Chapter 15 has suggestions for job-hunting strategies that the experts find most successful.

- Chapter 15 also suggests tactics that you can use when you negotiate with your boss about a raise.

Where the Information Comes From

The information in this book comes from two major government sources:

- **The U.S. Department of Labor:** The U.S. Department of Labor's O*NET database includes information on about 950 occupations and is now the primary source of detailed information on occupations. One of the information topics the O*NET covers is the personality types that are discussed in this book. The Labor Department updates the O*NET on a regular basis, and this book is based on the most recent one available, release 13. As it happens, in release 13 the data about personality types has been completely revised and updated. Information about earnings, growth, and number of openings—not included in the O*NET—is derived from sources at the U.S. Department of Labor's Bureau of Labor Statistics (BLS). The Occupational Employment Statistics survey provided reliable figures on earnings, and the Employment Projections program provided the nation's best figures on job growth and openings. Many of the recommendations for preparation pathways to occupations were based on information from the 2008–2009 edition of the *Occupational Outlook Handbook*.

- **The U.S. Department of Education:** The names of college majors included in this book are taken from the Classification of Instructional Programs (CIP), a system developed by the U.S. Department of Education. The links from CIP college majors to occupations are based on a crosswalk developed by the National Crosswalk Service Center.

Of course, information in a database format can be boring and even confusing, so this book organizes and presents the government data in easy-to-understand formats.

How the $100,000 Jobs Were Selected

There are no occupations in which *everyone* earns over $100,000. In fact, of the 825 occupations for which the BLS reports income, only 26 have median earnings in six figures—and keep in mind that this median figure, by definition, means that half of the workers earn less. On the other hand, the purpose of this book is to show you how to be an exceptional earner, so it made sense to include occupations in which a six-figure paycheck is attainable by a small but significant group of workers.

Therefore, three kinds of jobs were selected to make up the 138 job titles included in this book:

- **Six-Figure Occupations:** In these 65 occupations, at least 25 percent of the workers earn more than $100,000. For example, Political Scientists was included, even though its median earnings are only $91,580, because the highest-paid 25 percent of the workers earn more than $118,310.

- **Six-Figure Niche-Industry Jobs:** In these 63 occupations, at least 10 percent of the workers in the best-paying industries earn more than $100,000. Only industries in which that 10 percent represents more than 1,000 workers were considered. For example, Civil Engineers was included, even though its median earnings are only $71,710, because 13,195 workers in the Professional, Scientific, and Technical Services industry earn more than $114,100 and 2,731 workers in the Manufacturing industry earn more than $103,480. On the

© JIST Works

other hand, Marine Engineers and Naval Architects was not included because, although the best-paid 10 percent of the workers in four industries earn six figures, the largest high-paid workforce in question numbers only 351 workers.

- **Six-Figure Niche-Location Jobs:** In these 10 occupations, at least 10 percent of the workers in the best-paying metropolitan areas earn more than $100,000. Only metro areas in which that 10 percent represents more than 500 workers were considered. For example, Cost Estimators was included, even though its median earnings are only $54,920, because 958 workers in the New York area earn more than $105,130 and 683 workers in the Chicago area earn more than $101,180. On the other hand, Interior Designers was not included because, although the best-paid 10 percent of workers in 10 metro areas earn six figures, the largest high-paid workforce in question numbers only 374 workers.

How the Career Tracks Were Created

The ten career tracks included in this book were created to serve as a convenient way to do career planning. People who prepare for jobs in a particular career track tend to take similar high school courses and get a similar level of postsecondary education. In the less diverse career tracks, such as the Engineering track, students take similar courses while in college (at least for the first two years) and pursue similar extracurricular activities. The Professional track is considerably more diverse. Students in this track may be classified by their college coursework and extracurricular activities into two different groups—those preparing for a career in health and those preparing for law. Nevertheless, both kinds of Professional-track students need to complete several years of professional school and pass a licensure exam, so in many ways their experiences are similar. The Technician/ Artisan career track is highly diverse and admittedly serves partly as a catch-all for jobs that don't fit into any other track.

Several jobs are linked to two career tracks, and it might make sense to link some jobs to three. Track assignments were limited to two in order to reduce the amount of redundant information in the book.

Keep in mind that the jobs listed for each career track do not exhaust all the possible six-figure career options within that track. For example, the Managerial track does not include Food Service Managers, because not even 10 percent of these workers earn $100,000. However, there probably

5

are a few six-figure positions in this occupation. So it is possible that you may enter one of these career tracks and decide to specialize in an occupation *not* listed here, yet still end up earning six figures. If so, you are a truly exceptional worker, and your outstanding skills and determination are admirable.

Instead of trying to account for every possible career choice, the career tracks in this book are designed to cover the most likely options for earning $100,000.

Understand the Limits of the Data in This Book

This book uses the most reliable and up-to-date information available on earnings, projected growth, number of openings, and other topics. The earnings data came from the U.S. Department of Labor's Bureau of Labor Statistics. This is highly reliable data obtained from a very large U.S. working population sample by the Bureau of Labor Statistics. It tells us the average annual pay received as of May 2007 by people in various job titles (actually, it is the median annual pay, which means that half earned more and half less). As you look at these figures, keep in mind that they are estimates. The same is true for the figures on rate of job growth and annual job openings.

Understand that a problem with such data is that it describes an average. Just as there is no precisely average person, there is no such thing as a statistically average example of a particular job. This book partially addresses this problem by reporting, in the facts about jobs, information about the highest-paying industries and metro areas. But even within a single industry or geographic region you'll find great differences in earnings. Workers with more experience or specialized knowledge usually earn more than new recruits and those with only an average understanding of their field.

The figures for job growth and number of openings are projections by labor economists—their best-informed forecasts of what we can expect between now and 2016. They are not guarantees. A catastrophic economic downturn, war, or technological breakthrough could change the actual outcome.

Finally, don't forget that the job market consists of both job openings and job *seekers*. The figures on job growth and openings don't tell you how many people will be competing with you to be hired. The Department

© JIST Works

of Labor does not publish figures on the supply of job candidates, so this book cannot tell you about the level of competition you can expect. Competition is an important issue that you should research for any tentative career goal. The *Occupational Outlook Handbook* provides informative statements for many occupations. You should speak to people who educate or train tomorrow's workers; they probably have a good idea of how many graduates find rewarding employment and how quickly. People in the workforce also can provide insights into this issue. Use your critical thinking skills to evaluate what people tell you. For example, educators or trainers may be trying to recruit you, whereas people in the workforce may be trying to discourage you from competing. Get a variety of opinions to balance out possible biases.

So, in reviewing the information in this book, please understand the limitations of the data. You need to use common sense in career decision making as in most other things in life.

Data Complexities

For those of you who like details, the following section presents some of the complexities inherent in this book's sources of information and how they were resolved. You don't need to know this to use the book, so jump to the next section of the introduction if details bore you.

The 138 jobs in this book were selected on the basis of economic data, and you'll find information on earnings, size of the workforce, projected growth, and number of job openings for each job in chapters 5 through 14. Getting this information and making it understandable is not a simple task.

Earnings

The employment security agency of each state gathers information on earnings for various jobs and forwards it to the U.S. Bureau of Labor Statistics. This information is organized in standardized ways by a BLS program called Occupational Employment Statistics, or OES. To keep the earnings for the various jobs and regions comparable, the OES screens out certain types of earnings and includes others, so the OES earnings used in this book represent straight-time gross pay exclusive of premium pay. More specifically, the OES earnings include the job's base rate; cost-of-living allowances; guaranteed pay; hazardous-duty pay; incentive pay,

© JIST Works

including commissions and production bonuses; on-call pay; and tips. They do not include back pay, jury duty pay, overtime pay, severance pay, shift differentials, nonproduction bonuses, or tuition reimbursements. Also, self-employed workers are not included in the estimates, and they can be a significant segment in certain occupations (especially those in the Entrepreneurial track).

Highly Paid Workforce

As noted earlier in this introduction, none of the 138 occupations in this book pays *every* worker $100,000. The niche jobs, especially, offer six-figure earnings to only a small group of workers. Within the set of facts for each occupation in chapter 5 through 14, you'll find a statement about the size of this highly paid workforce.

The BLS does not provide a figure for exactly how many people in each occupation earn more than $100,000, but it is possible to get a rough idea. For each occupation covered by the OES salary survey, the BLS provides five figures that represent various dollar levels within the total distribution of earnings among the workforce: the first decile (10 percent earn less, 90 percent more); the first quartile (25 percent earn less, 75 percent more); the median (half earn less, half more); the third quartile (75 percent earn less, 25 percent more); and the ninth decile (90 percent earn less, 10 percent more). In the "Highly Paid Workforce" statement for each job, you'll find one of these figures—the one closest to $100,000—and the number of workers that it represents. For example, for Mechanical Engineers, it states, "Out of a total salaried workforce of 222,330, 22,233 people (10%) earn more than $108,740." If none of the figures is close to $100,000, you'll find the *two* figures that bracket $100,000. These figures, together with the figures for job growth and number of openings, can give you an idea of how much opportunity there is for six-figure work in this occupation.

Projected Growth and Number of Job Openings

This information comes from the Office of Occupational Statistics and Employment Projections, a program within the Bureau of Labor Statistics that develops information about projected trends in the nation's labor market for the next 10 years. The most recent projections available cover the years from 2006 to 2016. The projections are based on information about people moving into and out of occupations. The BLS used data from various sources in projecting the growth and number of openings

© JIST Works

for each job title—some data came from the Census Bureau's Current Population Survey and some came from an OES survey. The BLS economists assumed a steady economy unaffected by a major war, depression, or other upheaval. They also assumed that recessions may occur during the decade covered by these projections, as would be consistent with the pattern of business cycles we have experienced for several decades. However, because their projections cover 10 years, the figures for job growth and openings are intended to provide an average of both the good times and the bad times.

The Department of Labor provides a single figure (22.9%) for the projected growth of 38 postsecondary teaching jobs and also provides a single figure (237,478) for the projected annual job openings for these 38 jobs—18 of which are included in this book. Because these college-teaching jobs are related to very different interests—from engineering to business to agriculture to sociology—and because separate *earnings* figures are available for each of the 38 jobs, it made sense to provide separate job-openings figures for each of these jobs. If the trends of the last several years continue, none of these jobs can be expected to grow or take on workers at a faster rate than the other 37. Therefore, it is reasonable to assume that all of these college-teaching jobs share the same rate of job growth, 22.9%, and it made sense to compute separate figures for their projected job openings by dividing the total (237,478) into 38 parts, each of which is proportional in size to the current workforce of the job.

Perhaps you're wondering why this book presents figures on both job growth and number of openings. Aren't these two ways of saying the same thing? Actually, you need to know both. Consider the occupation Industrial-Organizational Psychologists, which is projected to grow at the impressive rate of 21.3 percent. There should be lots of opportunities in such a fast-growing job, right? Not exactly. This is a tiny occupation, with only about 1,900 people currently employed, so even though it is growing rapidly, it will not create many new jobs (about 100 per year). Now consider General and Operations Managers. Because of the decline of manufacturing, this occupation is growing at the sluggish rate of 1.5 percent. Nevertheless, this is a huge occupation that employs almost 1.75 million workers, so even though its growth rate is unimpressive, it is expected to take on more than 100,000 new workers each year as existing workers retire, die, or move on to other jobs. That's why you should pay attention to both of these economic indicators when you consider which of these six-figure jobs offer you the best opportunities.

© JIST Works

Information About Each Track

Chapters 5 through 14 explain how you can reach a six-figure job by pursuing one of 10 career tracks. The *Occupational Outlook Handbook* was the most important source of information for the recommendations about what courses and majors to take, what extracurricular activities to pursue, and what career ladders are open to experienced workers. Professional associations provided some additional information.

Characteristics of the Six-Figure Jobs

For each career track described in chapters 5 through 14, you'll find a list of the characteristics of the related six-figure jobs (that is, the jobs described in detail at the end of the chapter). The top five characteristics are presented for each of six topics: Highest-Level Skills, Highest-Level Work Activities, Most Important Knowledges, Most Important Work Contexts, Most Important Work Needs, and Most Important Work Styles. For each topic, the highest-rated characteristic is ordered first, with the remaining four listed in descending order by their ratings. For skills and work activities, the ratings are based on the difference between the skill or activity rating for required *level of mastery* and the mean rating for all occupations on this skill or activity. For the other topics, the value of the *importance* rating is used instead. The ratings for the jobs are derived from the O*NET database; they are weighted averages, meaning that within each track the jobs with the largest workforce size have the biggest influence on the list of characteristics.

Job Descriptions

At the end of each chapter on the career tracks, you'll find a brief but information-packed description for each of the six-figure jobs associated with that track. The descriptions are divided into Six-Figure Occupations, Six-Figure Niche-Industry Jobs, and Six-Figure Niche-Location Jobs and are presented in alphabetical order within each group.

The descriptions are based on the most current information from a variety of government sources and are designed to be easy to understand. The sample that follows—with an explanation of each of its component parts—will help you better understand and use the descriptions.

© JIST Works

Job Title
↓

Law Teachers, Postsecondary

Teach courses in law. Includes both teachers primarily engaged in teaching and those who do a combination of both teaching and research.

Personality Code → **Personality Code:** SIE

College Majors: Law (LL.B., J.D.); Legal Studies, General. ←**College Majors**

Median Annual Earnings: $87,730

Highly Paid Workforce: Out of a total salaried workforce of 12,610, 6,305 people (50%) earn more than $87,730 and 3,153 (25%) earn more than $125,120.

Economic Data Elements → **Annual Job Growth Through 2016:** 22.9%

Average Annual Job Openings Through 2016: 2,169

Best-Paying Industries: Educational Services.

Best-Paying Metro Areas: Washington-Arlington-Alexandria, DC-VA-MD-WV.

- **Job Title:** This is the job's title as defined by the Standard Occupational Classification (SOC) scheme, which is used by all branches of government to report information about occupations. Each SOC occupation is linked to one or more occupations in the O*NET database, and the definition presented here is derived from the O*NET job it most closely resembles. This definition can provide a quick notion of whether or not the job interests you.

- **Personality Code:** For each job, the O*NET database identifies its three most closely related personality types, and the initials for those types appear here. The initials are drawn from the letters R (for Realistic), I (for Investigative), A (for Artistic), S (for Social), E (for Enterprising), and C (for Conventional). In some cases, only one or two types are considered relevant. When a job is linked to more than one O*NET job, the personality type is based on the average of the RIASEC ratings of the related jobs. Chapter 1 explains what these personality types are and how they can help with career planning.

- **College Majors:** As explained earlier in this introduction, the majors related to the occupation are identified by a crosswalk created by the National Crosswalk Service Center and are derived from the Classification of Instructional Programs (CIP). This information can help with college planning. For example, if you are already in college or are planning to enroll in a particular college, you may want to check to be sure that one of these majors is available. If you have not yet made college plans, you may want to find a college that offers one of these majors and examine the description of the course requirements on the college's Web site. This information can help you decide whether the major is one you will enjoy and be successful in. Note that the names of the majors listed here may not correspond exactly to the names of majors offered at any particular college. For example, the major "Political Science and Government, General," may be offered under the name "Political Science" or "Government."

- **Economic Data Elements:** The information on median earnings, highly paid workforce, job growth, annual openings, best-paying industries, and best-paying metro areas comes from various government databases, as explained earlier in this introduction. Use the figures on median earnings and on the high-paid workforce to gauge how common or rare six-figure jobs are within this occupation. In some cases, a large fraction of the workforce is earning more than $100,000; in other cases, only a small group earns at that level, so to join them you would need to relocate to a few high-paying areas or acquire unusual skills. Note that even an occupation with a large fraction of six-figure earners may offer few job opportunities; for (an extreme) example, the entire workforce of Prosthodontists consists of 380 workers, so even though 75% of them are earning more than $122,440, that well-paid group numbers only 285 people, and only 54 job openings are expected each year in all of the United States. Your odds would be much better if you were to set your sights on being a Dentist, General, of which 63,945 workers earn more than $100,040 and for which 7,106 job openings are expected each year.

Getting all the information included in the job descriptions was not a simple process, and it is not always perfect, but you can be confident that the descriptions are based on the best and most recent sources of data available.

© JIST Works

Sources of Additional Information

The job descriptions in chapters 5 through 14 are only a first step in career exploration. When you are ready to investigate careers in greater detail, here are a few resources that will be helpful in getting additional information on the jobs listed in this book.

Print References

- *O*NET Dictionary of Occupational Titles:* Revised on a regular basis, this book provides good descriptions for all jobs listed in the U.S. Department of Labor's O*NET database. There are 950 job descriptions at all levels of education and training, plus lists of related job titles in other major career information sources, educational programs, and other information. Published by JIST.

- *Enhanced Occupational Outlook Handbook:* Updated regularly, this book provides thorough descriptions for 270 major jobs in the current *Occupational Outlook Handbook,* brief descriptions for the O*NET jobs that are related to each, brief descriptions of thousands of more-specialized jobs from the *Dictionary of Occupational Titles,* and other information. Published by JIST.

Internet Resources

- **The U.S. Department of Labor Bureau of Labor Statistics Web site:** The Department of Labor Bureau of Labor Statistics Web site (http://www.bls.gov) provides a lot of career information, including links to other Web pages that provide information on the jobs covered in this book. This Web site is a bit formal and, well, confusing, but it will take you to the major sources of government career information if you explore its options.

- **O*NET site:** Go to http://online.onetcenter.org/ for the full set of information from the O*NET database. The Crosswalk Search linked to this page allows you to enter any job title used in this book and see the related O*NET jobs.

- **CareerOneStop:** This site (http://www.careeronestop.org/) is operated by the Minnesota Department of Labor on behalf of the U.S. Department of Labor and provides access to state and local information about occupations. It also can identify a one-stop career center near you that can help you find local job openings and providers of education and training.

Thanks

Thanks for reading this introduction. You are surely a more thorough person than those who jumped into the book without reading it, and you will probably get more out of the book as a result.

© JIST Works

Chapter 1

How Personality Can Be the Key to Your $100,000 Job

Why Use Personality to Choose a Career?

Many psychological theorists and practicing career counselors believe that you will be most satisfied and productive in a career if it suits your personality. There are two main aspects of a job that determine whether it is a good fit:

- The nature of the work tasks and the skills and knowledge you use on the job must be a good match for the things you like to do and the subjects that interest you. For example, if you like to help other people and promote learning and personal development and if you like communication more than working with things or ideas, then a career in social work might be one that you enjoy and do well.

- The people you work with must share your personality traits so that you feel comfortable and can accomplish good work in their company. For an example of the opposite, think of how a person who enjoys following set procedures and working with data and detail might feel if forced to work with a group of conceptual artists who constantly seek self-expression and the inspiration for unconventional new artistic ideas.

One of the advantages of using personality as a key to career choice is that it is *economical*—it provides a tidy summary of many aspects of people and of careers. It doesn't require that you think separately about every skill, working condition, work style, and category of knowledge you might like or dislike in their work. Nor does it require you to put occupations under a microscope and evaluate how well each job offers each of these separate features. Instead, it views people and careers from 40,000 feet. When you compare yourself or a job to certain basic personality types, you encounter much less complexity. With fewer ideas and facts to sort through and consider, you can focus quickly on a small set of occupations that are most likely to satisfy you.

Describing Personality Types

You've probably heard people's personalities described in various ways: "grouch," "drama queen," "fuddy-duddy," "charmer," or "clown," among others. Most of these personality types apply to social situations rather than to work. To be useful in career choice, a set of personality types should have these characteristics:

- They should differentiate well between kinds of work.

- They should differentiate well between people.

- They should be broad enough that a small number of these categories can cover the whole universe of jobs and people.

- They should have neutral connotations, neither negative nor positive.

The RIASEC Personality Types

During the 1950s, the career guidance researcher John L. Holland was trying to find a meaningful new way to arrange the output of an interest inventory and relate it to occupations. He devised a set of six personality types that would meet the criteria listed in the previous section, and he called them Realistic, Investigative, Artistic, Social, Enterprising, and Conventional. (The acronym *RIASEC* is a convenient way to remember them.)

These terms may not be immediately clear to you, but they should be easier to understand after you read the following table, which shows how they apply to both people and work.

© JIST Works

PERSONALITY TYPE	HOW IT APPLIES TO PEOPLE	HOW IT APPLIES TO WORK
Realistic	Realistic personalities like work activities that include practical, hands-on problems and solutions. They enjoy dealing with plants; animals; and real-world materials such as wood, tools, and machinery. They enjoy outside work. Often they do not like occupations that mainly involve doing paperwork or working closely with others.	Realistic occupations frequently involve work activities that include practical, hands-on problems and solutions. They often deal with plants; animals; and real-world materials such as wood, tools, and machinery. Many of the occupations require working outside and do not involve a lot of paperwork or working closely with others.
Investigative	Investigative personalities like work activities that have to do with ideas and thinking more than with physical activity. They like to search for facts and figure out problems mentally rather than to persuade or lead people.	Investigative occupations frequently involve working with ideas and require an extensive amount of thinking. These occupations can involve searching for facts and figuring out problems mentally.
Artistic	Artistic personalities like work activities that deal with the artistic side of things, such as forms, designs, and patterns. They like self-expression in their work. They prefer settings where work can be done without following a clear set of rules.	Artistic occupations frequently involve working with forms, designs, and patterns. They often require self-expression, and the work can be done without following a clear set of rules.
Social	Social personalities like work activities that assist others and promote learning and personal development. They prefer to communicate more than to work with objects, machines, or data. They like to teach, to give advice, to	Social occupations frequently involve working with, communicating with, and teaching people. These occupations often involve helping or providing service to others.

(continued)

© JIST Works

(continued)

Personality Type	How It Applies to People	How It Applies to Work
	help, or otherwise to be of service to people.	
Enterprising	Enterprising personalities like work activities having to do with starting up and carrying out projects, especially business ventures. They like persuading and leading people and making decisions. They like taking risks for profit. These personalities prefer action rather than thought.	Enterprising occupations frequently involve starting up and carrying out projects. These occupations can involve leading people and making many decisions. They sometimes require risk taking and often deal with business.
Conventional	Conventional personalities like work activities that follow set procedures and routines. They prefer working with data and details rather than with ideas. They prefer work in which there are precise standards rather than work in which you have to judge things by yourself. These personalities like working where the lines of authority are clear.	Conventional occupations frequently involve following set procedures and routines. These occupations can include working with data and details more than with ideas. Usually there is a clear line of authority to follow.

© JIST Works

Holland went further by arranging these six personality types on a hexagon.

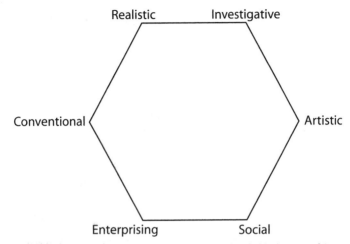

Figure 1: Holland's hexagon of personality types. (After Holland, A Theory of Vocational Choice, *1959.)*

He used this diagram to explain that people tend to resemble one type primarily, but they may also have aspects of one or more adjacent types. Each personality type tends to have little in common with the types on the opposite side of the hexagon. Therefore, for example, a person might be primarily Investigative, with an additional but smaller resemblance to the Realistic type. Such a person would be described by the two-letter code IR and might be well suited to work as a Chemical Engineer or a Veterinarian (both coded IR). This person would have little in common with an Enterprising personality type and likely would not be very happy or productive as a Training and Development Manager (coded ES). But this person could get along well with both Investigative and Realistic personalities and, to a lesser extent, with Artistic personalities.

Since Holland developed this model, hundreds of researchers and practitioners have investigated the RIASEC framework and have applied it to real-life decisions and situations. Many career decision-making assessments have been created to help people determine what personality types best describe them. You can find one such assessment in chapter 2 of this book.

Although the RIASEC scheme does a good job of covering the whole world of work, the symmetrical hexagon shape used to illustrate it may be a little misleading because, when you count the different jobs in our economy and the number of people working in those jobs, you'll find that some sectors of the hexagon are much more heavily populated than others. For example, there are about twice as many people working in jobs that are considered Realistic as there are people working in Social jobs.

The distribution of jobs on the hexagon is even more lopsided when we consider only the $100,000 jobs covered by this book:

PERSONALITY TYPE	NUMBER OF $100,000 JOBS IN THIS BOOK
Realistic	7
Investigative	48
Artistic	6
Social	21
Enterprising	46
Conventional	10

You should not be troubled by this lack of symmetry in the RIASEC model (even if you are an Artistic type). It simply reflects the nature of the United States economy, in which people who work in business, the professions, academia, science, and engineering tend to command higher wages. If you are not interested in these fields, don't get depressed; some people who work in Realistic and Artistic jobs earn six figures, and this book can help you focus on the jobs these people hold.

No theory can perfectly describe the infinite variety of personalities to be found in our culture and the messy distribution of jobs that a free economy produces. You should note that the RIASEC scheme for describing personality types is not the only one that is used in career decision-making. However, it is the most popular and most thoroughly researched one, so it is the best one to use in this book.

Other Assessments with RIASEC Output

Apart from the assessment in chapter 2 of this book, you may want to use any of these free assessments to explore your personality type in RIASEC terms:

© JIST Works

- The O*NET Computerized Interest Profiler (for Windows), which you can download at www.onetcenter.org/CIP.html (the assessment in Part II is based on it)

- The Career Interests Game, in the University of Missouri's Career Center at http://career.missouri.edu/students/explore/thecareerinterestsgame.php

- The Work Interest Quiz at www.myfuture.com/toolbox/workinterest.html

You also have a number of options if you are willing to pay a fee. For example, you can access John Holland's own Self-Directed Search at www.self-directed-search.com.

Keep in mind that although all of these assessments produce outputs with RIASEC codes and some of them also link these codes to occupations, they will not necessarily produce the exact same output. Assessment of personality is not as exact a science as, say, chemistry. Neither is the task of linking personalities to occupations.

You should not regard the output of any personality assessment as the final word on what career will suit you best. Use a variety of approaches to decide what kind of person you are and narrow down the kinds of work you enjoy. Actual work experience is probably the best way to test a tentative choice.

An Alternative to the RIASEC Approach

If the RIASEC approach does not appeal to you, or if you get inconclusive results from the assessment in chapter 2, you may want to try the checklists in chapter 3. This exercise focuses on various characteristics of the $100,000 jobs in the 10 career tracks and provides another way to narrow down your choice.

Highlights of Chapter 1

- Personality types are an economical way to describe yourself and various career options so you can judge whether a job is a good fit for you (and vice versa).

- The six personality types identified by John L. Holland are the ones most widely used by counselors and career development professionals.

Chapter 2

What's Your Personality Type? Take an Assessment

In this chapter, you can take a Personality Type Inventory that will help you determine your primary RIASEC personality type and perhaps one or two secondary RIASEC personality types. It asks if you like or dislike various activities and then lets you score your responses. You can use your scores in the following chapters of the book to identify specific highly rewarding jobs to explore.

It's easy to use the Personality Type Inventory—just turn the page and follow the directions beginning with Step 1. This is not a test, so there are no right or wrong answers. There is also no time limit for completing this inventory.

If someone else will be using this book, you should photocopy pages 24–29 and mark your responses on the photocopy.

Note: This inventory is based on the O*NET Interest Profiler, Version 3.0, developed by the U.S. Department of Labor (DOL). The DOL's edition consists of several components, including the Interest Profiler Instrument, Interest Profiler Score Report, and Interest Profiler O*NET Occupations Master List. The DOL provides a separate Interest Profiler User's Guide with information on the profiler's development and validity as well as tips for professionals using it in career counseling. Additional information on these items is available at www.onetcenter.org, which is maintained by the DOL. This Personality Type Inventory is a version of the DOL's O*NET Interest Profiler that uses its work activity items and scoring system but has shorter directions, format changes, and additional content.

Restrictions for use: This and any other form of the O*NET Interest Profiler should be used for career exploration, career planning, and vocational counseling purposes only, and no other use has been authorized or is valid. Results should not be used for employment or hiring decisions or for applicant screening for jobs or training programs. Please see the DOL's separate "O*NET User's Agreement" on p. i of the document at http://www.onetcenter.org/dl_tools/CIP.pdf for additional details on restrictions and use. The word "O*NET" is a trademark of the U.S. Department of Labor, Employment and Training Administration.

Step 1: Respond to the Statements

Carefully read each work activity (items 1 through 180). For each item, fill in just one of the three circles as follows:

If you think you would LIKE the activity, fill in the circle containing the L, like this:

If you think you would DISLIKE the activity, fill in the circle containing the D, like this:

If you are UNSURE whether you would like the activity, fill in the circle with the ?, like this:

As you respond to each activity, don't consider whether you have the education or training needed for it or how much money you might earn if it were part of your job. Simply fill in the circle based on whether you would like, would dislike, or aren't sure about the activity.

After you respond to all 180 activities, you'll score your responses in Step 2.

© JIST Works

Would you LIKE the activity or DISLIKE the activity, or are you UNSURE?

1. Build kitchen cabinets   (L) (?) (D)
2. Guard money in an armored car   (L) (?) (D)
3. Operate a dairy farm   (L) (?) (D)
4. Lay brick or tile   (L) (?) (D)
5. Monitor a machine on an assembly line   (L) (?) (D)
6. Repair household appliances   (L) (?) (D)
7. Drive a taxicab   (L) (?) (D)
8. Install flooring in houses   (L) (?) (D)
9. Raise fish in a fish hatchery   (L) (?) (D)
10. Build a brick walkway   (L) (?) (D)
11. Assemble electronic parts   (L) (?) (D)
12. Drive a truck to deliver packages to offices and homes   (L) (?) (D)
13. Paint houses   (L) (?) (D)
14. Enforce fish and game laws   (L) (?) (D)
15. Operate a grinding machine in a factory   (L) (?) (D)
16. Work on an offshore oil-drilling rig   (L) (?) (D)
17. Perform lawn care services   (L) (?) (D)
18. Assemble products in a factory   (L) (?) (D)
19. Catch fish as a member of a fishing crew   (L) (?) (D)
20. Refinish furniture   (L) (?) (D)
21. Fix a broken faucet   (L) (?) (D)
22. Do cleaning or maintenance work   (L) (?) (D)
23. Maintain the grounds of a park   (L) (?) (D)
24. Operate a machine on a production line   (L) (?) (D)
25. Spray trees to prevent the spread of harmful insects   (L) (?) (D)
26. Test the quality of parts before shipment   (L) (?) (D)
27. Operate a motorboat to carry passengers   (L) (?) (D)
28. Repair and install locks   (L) (?) (D)
29. Set up and operate machines to make products   (L) (?) (D)
30. Put out forest fires   (L) (?) (D)

_____ 6 _____ **Page Score for R**

© JIST Works

Would you LIKE the activity or DISLIKE the activity, or are you UNSURE?

31. Study space travel	Ⓛ	⑦	Ⓓ
32. Make a map of the bottom of an ocean	Ⓛ	⑦	Ⓓ
33. Study the history of past civilizations	Ⓛ	⑦	Ⓓ
34. Study animal behavior	Ⓛ	⑦	Ⓓ
35. Develop a new medicine	Ⓛ	⑦	Ⓓ
36. Plan a research study	Ⓛ	⑦	Ⓓ
37. Study ways to reduce water pollution	Ⓛ	⑦	Ⓓ
38. Develop a new medical treatment or procedure	Ⓛ	⑦	Ⓓ
39. Determine the infection rate of a new disease	Ⓛ	⑦	Ⓓ
40. Study rocks and minerals	Ⓛ	⑦	Ⓓ
41. Diagnose and treat sick animals	Ⓛ	⑦	Ⓓ
42. Study the personalities of world leaders	Ⓛ	⑦	Ⓓ
43. Conduct chemical experiments	Ⓛ	⑦	Ⓓ
44. Conduct biological research	Ⓛ	⑦	Ⓓ
45. Study the population growth of a city	Ⓛ	⑦	Ⓓ
46. Study whales and other types of marine life	Ⓛ	⑦	Ⓓ
47. Investigate crimes	Ⓛ	⑦	Ⓓ
48. Study the movement of planets	Ⓛ	⑦	Ⓓ
49. Examine blood samples using a microscope	Ⓛ	⑦	Ⓓ
50. Investigate the cause of a fire	Ⓛ	⑦	Ⓓ
51. Study the structure of the human body	Ⓛ	⑦	Ⓓ
52. Develop psychological profiles of criminals	Ⓛ	⑦	Ⓓ
53. Develop a new way to better predict the weather	Ⓛ	⑦	Ⓓ
54. Work in a biology lab	Ⓛ	⑦	Ⓓ
55. Invent a replacement for sugar	Ⓛ	⑦	Ⓓ
56. Study genetics	Ⓛ	⑦	Ⓓ
57. Study the governments of different countries	Ⓛ	⑦	Ⓓ
58. Do research on plants or animals	Ⓛ	⑦	Ⓓ
59. Do laboratory tests to identify diseases	Ⓛ	⑦	Ⓓ
60. Study weather conditions	Ⓛ	⑦	Ⓓ

_____ 20 _____ **Page Score for I**

25

Would you LIKE the activity or DISLIKE the activity, or are you UNSURE?

61. Conduct a symphony orchestra ⓛ ⑦ Ⓓ
62. Write stories or articles for magazines Ⓛ ⑦ Ⓓ
63. Direct a play ⓛ ⑦ Ⓓ
64. Create dance routines for a show ⓛ ⑦ Ⓓ
65. Write books or plays Ⓛ ⑦ Ⓓ
66. Play a musical instrument ⓛ ⑦ Ⓓ
67. Perform comedy routines in front of an audience ⓛ ⑦ Ⓓ
68. Perform as an extra in movies, plays, or television shows ⓛ ⑦ Ⓓ
69. Write reviews of books or plays ⓛ ⑦ Ⓓ
70. Compose or arrange music ⓛ ⑦ Ⓓ
71. Act in a movie Ⓛ ⑦ Ⓓ
72. Dance in a Broadway show ⓛ ⑦ Ⓓ
73. Draw pictures Ⓛ ⑦ Ⓓ
74. Sing professionally Ⓛ ⑦ Ⓓ
75. Perform stunts for a movie or television show ⓛ ⑦ Ⓓ
76. Create special effects for movies Ⓛ ⑦ Ⓓ
77. Conduct a musical choir ⓛ ⑦ Ⓓ
78. Act in a play ⓛ ⑦ Ⓓ
79. Paint sets for plays ⓛ ⑦ Ⓓ
80. Audition singers and musicians for a musical show ⓛ ⑦ Ⓓ
81. Design sets for plays ⓛ ⑦ Ⓓ
82. Announce a radio show ⓛ ⑦ Ⓓ
83. Write scripts for movies or television shows Ⓛ ⑦ Ⓓ
84. Write a song ⓛ ⑦ Ⓓ
85. Perform jazz or tap dance ⓛ ⑦ Ⓓ
86. Direct a movie ⓛ ⑦ Ⓓ
87. Sing in a band Ⓛ ⑦ Ⓓ
88. Design artwork for magazines ⓛ ⑦ Ⓓ
89. Edit movies ⓛ ⑦ Ⓓ
90. Pose for a photographer ⓛ ⑦ Ⓓ

_____8_____ **Page Score for A**

© JIST Works

Would you LIKE the activity or DISLIKE the activity, or are you UNSURE?

91. Teach an individual an exercise routine   Ⓛ   ⑦   Ⓓ
92. Perform nursing duties in a hospital   Ⓛ   ⑦   Ⓓ
93. Give CPR to someone who has stopped breathing   Ⓛ   ⑦   Ⓓ
94. Help people with personal or emotional problems   Ⓛ   ⑦   Ⓓ
95. Teach children how to read   Ⓛ   ⑦   Ⓓ
96. Work with mentally disabled children   Ⓛ   ⑦   Ⓓ
97. Teach an elementary school class   Ⓛ   ⑦   Ⓓ
98. Give career guidance to people   Ⓛ   ⑦   Ⓓ
99. Supervise the activities of children at a camp   Ⓛ   ⑦   Ⓓ
100. Help people with family-related problems   Ⓛ   ⑦   Ⓓ
101. Perform rehabilitation therapy   Ⓛ   ⑦   Ⓓ
102. Do volunteer work at a nonprofit organization   Ⓛ   ⑦   Ⓓ
103. Help elderly people with their daily activities   Ⓛ   ⑦   Ⓓ
104. Teach children how to play sports   Ⓛ   ⑦   Ⓓ
105. Help disabled people improve their daily living skills   Ⓛ   ⑦   Ⓓ
106. Teach sign language to people with hearing disabilities   Ⓛ   ⑦   Ⓓ
107. Help people who have problems with drugs or alcohol   Ⓛ   ⑦   Ⓓ
108. Help conduct a group therapy session   Ⓛ   ⑦   Ⓓ
109. Help families care for ill relatives   Ⓛ   ⑦   Ⓓ
110. Provide massage therapy to people   Ⓛ   ⑦   Ⓓ
111. Plan exercises for disabled students   Ⓛ   ⑦   Ⓓ
112. Counsel people who have a life-threatening illness   Ⓛ   ⑦   Ⓓ
113. Teach disabled people work and living skills   Ⓛ   ⑦   Ⓓ
114. Organize activities at a recreational facility   Ⓛ   ⑦   Ⓓ
115. Take care of children at a day-care center   Ⓛ   ⑦   Ⓓ
116. Organize field trips for disabled people   Ⓛ   ⑦   Ⓓ
117. Assist doctors in treating patients   Ⓛ   ⑦   Ⓓ
118. Work with juveniles on probation   Ⓛ   ⑦   Ⓓ
119. Provide physical therapy to people recovering from an injury   Ⓛ   ⑦   Ⓓ
120. Teach a high school class   Ⓛ   ⑦   Ⓓ

_____12_____ **Page Score for S**

© JIST Works

Would you LIKE the activity or DISLIKE the activity, or are you UNSURE?

121. Buy and sell stocks and bonds   Ⓛ   ⑦   **Ⓓ**
122. Manage a retail store   Ⓛ   ⑦   **Ⓓ**
123. Sell telephone and other communication equipment   Ⓛ   ⑦   **Ⓓ**
124. Operate a beauty salon or barbershop   Ⓛ   ⑦   **Ⓓ**
125. Sell merchandise over the telephone   Ⓛ   ⑦   **Ⓓ**
126. Run a stand that sells newspapers and magazines   Ⓛ   ⑦   **Ⓓ**
127. Give a presentation about a product you are selling   **Ⓛ**   ⑦   Ⓓ
128. Buy and sell land   Ⓛ   **⑦**   Ⓓ
129. Sell compact discs at a music store   Ⓛ   ⑦   **Ⓓ**
130. Run a toy store   Ⓛ   ⑦   **Ⓓ**
131. Manage the operations of a hotel   **Ⓛ**   ⑦   Ⓓ
132. Sell houses   Ⓛ   **⑦**   Ⓓ
133. Sell candy and popcorn at sports events   Ⓛ   ⑦   **Ⓓ**
134. Manage a supermarket   Ⓛ   ⑦   Ⓓ
135. Manage a department within a large company   **Ⓛ**   ⑦   Ⓓ
136. Sell a soft drink product line to stores and restaurants   Ⓛ   **⑦**   Ⓓ
137. Sell refreshments at a movie theater   Ⓛ   ⑦   **Ⓓ**
138. Sell hair-care products to stores and salons   Ⓛ   ⑦   **Ⓓ**
139. Start your own business   **Ⓛ**   ⑦   Ⓓ
140. Negotiate business contracts   **Ⓛ**   ⑦   Ⓓ
141. Represent a client in a lawsuit   **Ⓛ**   ⑦   Ⓓ
142. Negotiate contracts for professional athletes   **Ⓛ**   ⑦   Ⓓ
143. Be responsible for the operation of a company   **Ⓛ**   ⑦   Ⓓ
144. Market a new line of clothing   Ⓛ   ⑦   **Ⓓ**
145. Sell newspaper advertisements   Ⓛ   ⑦   **Ⓓ**
146. Sell merchandise at a department store   Ⓛ   ⑦   **Ⓓ**
147. Sell automobiles   Ⓛ   ⑦   **Ⓓ**
148. Manage a clothing store   Ⓛ   ⑦   **Ⓓ**
149. Sell restaurant franchises to individuals   Ⓛ   ⑦   **Ⓓ**
150. Sell computer equipment in a store   Ⓛ   ⑦   **Ⓓ**

_____8_____ **Page Score for E**

© JIST Works

Would you LIKE the activity or DISLIKE the activity, or are you UNSURE?

151. Develop a spreadsheet using computer software   (L) (?) (D)

152. Proofread records or forms   (L) (?) (D)

153. Use a computer program to generate customer bills   (L) (?) (D)

154. Schedule conferences for an organization   (L) (?) (D)

155. Keep accounts payable/receivable for an office   (L) (?) (D)

156. Load computer software into a large computer network   (L) (?) (D)

157. Transfer funds between banks using a computer   (L) (?) (D)

158. Organize and schedule office meetings   (L) (?) (D)

159. Use a word processor to edit and format documents   (L) (?) (D)

160. Operate a calculator   (L) (?) (D)

161. Direct or transfer phone calls for a large organization   (L) (?) (D)

162. Perform office filing tasks   (L) (?) (D)

163. Compute and record statistical and other numerical data   (L) (?) (D)

164. Generate the monthly payroll checks for an office   (L) (?) (D)

165. Take notes during a meeting   (L) (?) (D)

166. Keep shipping and receiving records   (L) (?) (D)

167. Calculate the wages of employees   (L) (?) (D)

168. Assist senior-level accountants in performing bookkeeping tasks   (L) (?) (D)

169. Type labels for envelopes and packages   (L) (?) (D)

170. Inventory supplies using a hand-held computer   (L) (?) (D)

171. Develop an office filing system   (L) (?) (D)

172. Keep records of financial transactions for an organization   (L) (?) (D)

173. Record information from customers applying for charge accounts   (L) (?) (D)

174. Photocopy letters and reports   (L) (?) (D)

175. Record rent payments   (L) (?) (D)

176. Enter information into a database   (L) (?) (D)

177. Keep inventory records   (L) (?) (D)

178. Maintain employee records   (L) (?) (D)

179. Stamp, sort, and distribute mail for an organization   (L) (?) (D)

180. Handle customers' bank transactions   (L) (?) (D)

_____5_____ Page Score for C

© JIST Works

Step 2: Score Your Responses

Do the following to score your responses:

1. **Score the responses on each page.** On each page of responses, go from top to bottom and add the number of "L"s you filled in. Then write that number on the "Page Score" line at the bottom of the page. Go on to the next page and do the same there.

2. **Determine your primary interest area.** Which Page Score has your highest score: **R, I, A, S, E,** or **C?** Enter the letter for that personality type on the line below.

   My Primary Personality Type: $\underline{\text{I}}$

   You will use your Primary Personality Type *first* to explore careers. (If two Page Scores are tied for the highest scores or are within 5 points of each other, use both of them for your Primary Personality Type. You are equally divided between two types.)

   > R = Realistic
   > I = Investigative
   > A = Artistic
   > S = Social
   > E = Enterprising
   > C = Conventional

3. **Determine your secondary interest areas.** Which Page Score has your next highest score? Which has your third highest score? Enter the letters for those areas on the line below.

   My Secondary Personality Types: $\underline{\text{S}}$ $\underline{\text{A+E}}$

   (If you do not find many occupations that you like using your Primary Personality Type, you can use your Secondary Personality Types to look at more career options. You also can look for jobs that combine both types.)

Step 3: Find Career Tracks and $100,000 Jobs That Suit Your Personality Type

Turn to chapter 3 and look at the career tracks and $100,000 jobs that are listed for your primary and secondary personality types. Don't rule out a job just because the title is not familiar to you, and don't rule out a career track just because you have not previously thought about pursuing it.

© JIST Works

When you find career tracks and job titles that interest you or that you want to learn more about, turn to chapters 5 through 14, which cover 10 career tracks. In each chapter, you'll see strategies for reaching six-figure jobs that are appropriate for various Primary and Secondary Personality Types.

Highlights of Chapter 2

- This fast inventory can help you identify a primary personality type—and perhaps one or two secondary types—so you can narrow down your career options and focus on those that align best with your interests.

- The results of the inventory will also help you make best use of chapters 3 and 5–14 of this book, which are organized by personality types.

© JIST Works

Chapter 3

Your Career Plan for a $100,000 Job

In this chapter you're going to use what you now know about your personality to decide on a career track that ideally will lead you to a six-figure job. The career track you choose may take several years to lead you to your monetary goal, and there are no guarantees that it will bring you a six-figure paycheck. But all the tracks are based on the real experiences of people who have succeeded at this ambition. Why not you?

Choosing a Career Track by RIASEC Type

The following chart summarizes the relationships between career tracks and RIASEC types. (The rest of this chapter provides greater detail, including names of occupations.)

SECONDARY TYPE	PRIMARY PERSONALITY TYPE					
	R	**I**	**A**	**S**	**E**	**C**
R	*	Information Technology; Engineering; Professional; Scientific	*	Academic; Professional	Entrepreneurial; Technician/ Artisan	*
I	Technician/ Artisan	*	Technician/ Artisan	Academic	Managerial; Professional	Information Technology; Bachelor's-in-Business
A	*	Scientific	*	Academic	Distributive; Managerial	*

Secondary Type	PRIMARY PERSONALITY TYPE					
	R	**I**	**A**	**S**	**E**	**C**
S	*	Professional	*	*	Bachelor's-in-Business; Distributive; Entrepreneurial; Managerial; Professional; Technician/Artisan	*
E	*	Entrepreneurial; Scientific; Bachelor's-in-Business	Technician/Artisan	Academic	*	Bachelor's-in-Business; Distributive
C	Technician/Artisan	Information Technology; Engineering; Entrepreneurial; Scientific	*	Academic; Information Technology; Professional	Bachelor's-in-Business; Distributive; Entrepreneurial; Managerial; Technician/Artisan	*

* *Very few or no significant opportunities for six-figure jobs*

For each of the six RIASEC personality types, the following sections of this chapter show appropriate career tracks and the six-figure jobs associated with them. **Find the section that covers your primary personality type,** as determined by the assessment in chapter 2, by another assessment, or by your own insights into your personality. Then look for the career tracks and jobs associated with that primary personality type and with any secondary personality types you feel apply to you.

For example, if you believe that Social is your primary personality type and Investigative is a significant secondary type that describes you, turn to the section about the Social type, read the general discussion of career tracks for the Social type and then find the subsection about suggested career tracks and six-figure jobs for the Social-Investigative (SI) type. You may also want to look at the subsections for other personality types combined with the Social type. If you're unsure whether Social or Investigative describes you best, you may also want to turn to the section about the

Investigative type and find the subsection about the Investigative-Social (IS) type. After making a tentative choice of a career track, turn to the later chapter (5–14) that describes that career track in detail. You may want to compare two or more career tracks to confirm or second-guess your tentative choice.

You also can narrow down your choice of a career track by filling out the checklist in chapter 4.

You don't have to make an unshakable commitment to any career track. Some of the career tracks have similar early stages, so you may be able to postpone making a choice by taking steps that will get you started on two or more tracks simultaneously. And that's just one kind of fork you may find in your road. Sometimes one track may lead you to another track. For example, you might pursue a career in the Bachelor's-in-Business track and acquire enough skills and experience in a particular job and industry to be able to enter the Managerial track. Or you may decide some day to seek a job that doesn't promise six figures. These career tracks can lead to many kinds of work satisfaction other than just high income. The key to success (in its largest sense) is being always open to new career ideas as your needs and priorities change and as new opportunities present themselves.

At the end of this chapter is a table showing which chapter later in the book covers each track in detail.

A Note About the Jobs Linked to the Personality Types

In this chapter you'll find several jobs listed for each combination of primary and secondary RIASEC types. The ratings in the Department of Labor's O*NET database determined which jobs were assigned to each type. Other researchers may make somewhat different assignments, so you should not assume that the connection between jobs and types is an exact science. Consider several or all of the secondary types associated with your primary type.

You will find two types of six-figure jobs listed: Titles are listed as **occupations** if the highest-earning 25% of the workforce earns more than $100,000 and as **niche jobs** if the highest-earning 10% of those working in one or more particular industries or metropolitan areas earns more than $100,000. Some of these occupations and niche jobs may not be familiar to you, but in the chapters on the career tracks you'll find definitions of all related job titles, together with figures that can help you estimate their earning potential.

© JIST Works

Career Plans for Realistic People

The Realistic personality type has very limited opportunities for six-figure jobs, but you can still realize this goal if you're imaginative, persistent, highly talented, or lucky or have some combination of these features.

In the salary survey results from the Bureau of Labor Statistics (BLS), only two occupations with Realistic as their primary personality type have median earnings in the six-figure range. (These two occupations are the first two listed in the next table.) The unfortunate truth is that Realistic jobs tend to pay low wages. In fact, the approximately 300 Realistic occupations surveyed by the Bureau of Labor Statistics have an average median wage of just a little under $30,000. (That's a weighted average, giving more weight to the jobs with a larger workforce.)

Some niche jobs of the Realistic type do offer opportunities to earn six figures. For example, the 24,000 Transportation Inspectors (type RCI) working in all industries have average earnings of only $51,440. However, the 10,000 Transportation Inspectors working in Government average $103,910.

Also, a large number of occupations and niche jobs with six-figure potential have Realistic as their *secondary* personality type, which means that Realistic workers are likely to feel at ease with many of the work tasks, settings, and co-workers associated with these high-paying jobs. You will be able to find these secondarily Realistic jobs by looking under other primary types—for example, Investigative-Realistic or Enterprising-Realistic.

In the following listings, the Technician/Artisan career track dominates.

The Realistic-Investigative Type

Occupation	RIASEC Code	Track
Airline Pilots, Copilots, and Flight Engineers	RCI	Technician/Artisan
Oral and Maxillofacial Surgeons	RSI	Professional

Niche Job	RIASEC Code	Track
Civil Engineers	RIC	Engineering
Commercial Pilots	RIE	Technician/Artisan

(continued)

(continued)

Niche Job	RIASEC Code	Track
Electricians	RIC	Technician/ Artisan
Transportation Inspectors	RCI	Technician/ Artisan

The Realistic-Artistic Type

This combination of types offers almost no opportunities for six-figure earnings. Consider combining the Realistic or Artistic type with some other type.

The Realistic-Social Type

Six-figure job opportunities compatible with this type are limited. You may want to focus on other combinations with the Realistic type, or you may want to emphasize the Social type, in which case you should skip to that section of this chapter, especially the subsection about the Social-Realistic type.

Occupation	RIASEC Code	Track
Oral and Maxillofacial Surgeons	RSI	Professional

The Realistic-Enterprising Type

Niche Job	RIASEC Code	Track
Commercial Pilots	RIE	Technician/ Artisan

The Realistic-Conventional Type

Occupation	RIASEC Code	Track
Airline Pilots, Copilots, and Flight Engineers	RCI	Technician/ Artisan

© JIST Works

NICHE JOB	RIASEC CODE	TRACK
Civil Engineers	RIC	Engineering
Electricians	RIC	Technician/ Artisan
Transportation Inspectors	RCI	Technician/ Artisan

Career Plans for Investigative People

Investigative occupations tend to pay well; their weighted average earnings are $77,541, higher than the average for any other RIASEC type. The Investigative personality type is compatible with many occupations in science, high technology, and health care that have six-figure potential. Several Investigative niche jobs also provide opportunities for six-figure earnings.

In the following listings, the Scientific, Professional, Engineering, and Information Technology career tracks dominate. In the chapters about these career tracks, you'll see that most Investigative jobs with six-figure potential require at least a bachelor's degree and often considerably more education and training.

The Investigative-Realistic Type

OCCUPATION	RIASEC CODE	TRACK
Aerospace Engineers	IR	Engineering
Anesthesiologists	IRS	Professional
Astronomers	IAR	Scientific
Biochemists and Biophysicists	IAR	Scientific
Chemical Engineers	IR	Scientific
Computer and Information Scientists, Research	IRC	Information Technology
Computer Hardware Engineers	IRC	Engineering
Computer Software Engineers, Applications	IRC	Information Technology; Engineering

(continued)

© JIST Works

(continued)

OCCUPATION	RIASEC CODE	TRACK
Computer Software Engineers, Systems Software	ICR	Information Technology; Engineering
Dentists, General	IRS	Professional
Electronics Engineers, Except Computer	IR	Engineering
Engineering Teachers, Postsecondary	IRS	Academic
Geoscientists, Except Hydrologists and Geographers	IR	Scientific
Internists, General	ISR	Professional
Nuclear Engineers	IRC	Engineering
Obstetricians and Gynecologists	ISR	Professional
Optometrists	ISR	Professional
Orthodontists	IRS	Professional
Petroleum Engineers	IRC	Engineering
Physicists	IR	Scientific
Podiatrists	ISR	Professional
Prosthodontists	IR	Professional
Surgeons	IRS	Professional
NICHE JOB	**RIASEC CODE**	**TRACK**
Chemists	IRC	Scientific
Computer Systems Analysts	ICR	Information Technology
Electrical Engineers	IR	Engineering
Environmental Engineers	IRC	Engineering
Environmental Scientists and Specialists, Including Health	IRC	Scientific
Materials Engineers	IRE	Engineering
Mechanical Engineers	IRC	Engineering
Medical Scientists, Except Epidemiologists	IRA	Scientific

© JIST Works

NICHE JOB	RIASEC CODE	TRACK
Network and Computer Systems Administrators	ICR	Information Technology
Veterinarians	IR	Professional

The Investigative-Artistic Type

OCCUPATION	RIASEC CODE	TRACK
Astronomers	IAR	Scientific
Biochemists and Biophysicists	IAR	Scientific
Industrial-Organizational Psychologists	IEA	Scientific
Mathematicians	ICA	Scientific
Political Scientists	IAS	Scientific
Psychiatrists	ISA	Professional

NICHE JOB	RIASEC CODE	TRACK
Clinical, Counseling, and School Psychologists	ISA	Professional
Medical Scientists, Except Epidemiologists	IRA	Scientific

The Investigative-Social Type

OCCUPATION	RIASEC CODE	TRACK
Anesthesiologists	IRS	Professional
Dentists, General	IRS	Professional
Engineering Teachers, Postsecondary	IRS	Academic
Family and General Practitioners	IS	Professional
Internists, General	ISR	Professional

(continued)

© JIST Works

(continued)

Occupation	RIASEC Code	Track
Obstetricians and Gynecologists	ISR	Professional
Optometrists	ISR	Professional
Orthodontists	IRS	Professional
Pediatricians, General	IS	Professional
Pharmacists	ICS	Professional
Podiatrists	ISR	Professional
Psychiatrists	ISA	Professional
Surgeons	IRS	Professional
Niche Job	**RIASEC Code**	**Track**
Clinical, Counseling, and School Psychologists	ISA	Professional

The Investigative-Enterprising Type

Occupation	RIASEC Code	Track
Economists	ICE	Scientific; Entrepreneurial
Industrial-Organizational Psychologists	IEA	Scientific
Niche Job	**RIASEC Code**	**Track**
Industrial Engineers	ICE	Engineering
Management Analysts	IEC	Bachelor's-in-Business; Entrepreneurial
Market Research Analysts	IEC	Bachelor's-in-Business; Entrepreneurial
Materials Engineers	IRE	Engineering
Operations Research Analysts	ICE	Entrepreneurial; Scientific

© JIST Works

The Investigative-Conventional Type

OCCUPATION	RIASEC CODE	TRACK
Computer and Information Scientists, Research	IRC	Scientific; Information Technology
Computer Hardware Engineers	IRC	Engineering
Computer Software Engineers, Applications	IRC	Engineering; Information Technology
Computer Software Engineers, Systems Software	ICR	Engineering; Information Technology
Economists	ICE	Scientific; Entrepreneurial
Mathematicians	ICA	Scientific
Nuclear Engineers	IRC	Engineering
Petroleum Engineers	IRC	Engineering
Pharmacists	ICS	Professional

NICHE JOB	RIASEC CODE	TRACK
Chemists	IRC	Scientific
Computer Programmers	IC	Information Technology
Computer Systems Analysts	ICR	Information Technology
Environmental Engineers	IRC	Engineering
Environmental Scientists and Specialists, Including Health	IRC	Scientific
Industrial Engineers	ICE	Engineering
Management Analysts	IEC	Bachelor's-in-Business; Entrepreneurial
Market Research Analysts	IEC	Bachelor's-in-Business; Entrepreneurial
Mechanical Engineers	IRC	Engineering
Network and Computer Systems Administrators	ICR	Information Technology

(continued)

© JIST Works

(continued)

NICHE JOB	RIASEC CODE	TRACK
Network Systems and Data Communications Analysts	IC	Information Technology
Operations Research Analysts	ICE	Scientific; Entrepreneurial

Career Plans for Artistic People

Every field of art includes some people who, through exceptional talent and persistence, are able to earn high incomes. However, Artistic jobs tend to pay low wages and be highly competitive. Some of them (for example, Actors or Dancers) pay so irregularly that the Bureau of Labor Statistics does not publish annual earnings figures for them. Although six-figure earners are rare among fine artists, workers who use Artistic interests and skills for commercial purposes have greater opportunities for high income. Most of the following listings are for the Technician/Artisan career track.

Only one of the six-figure occupations has Artistic as its primary personality type: Art Directors, which is described in the Managerial career track (chapter 11) and also in the Technician/Artisan track (chapter 14). In addition, a handful of niche jobs are listed in the following tables. However, several six-figure occupations and niche jobs may be found that have Artistic as their *secondary* personality type—for example, look in the subsections for the Social-Artistic and Enterprising-Artistic types.

The Artistic-Realistic Type

Almost no occupations or reasonably large niche jobs match this type. You should consider other Artistic types or perhaps the Realistic type.

The Artistic-Investigative Type

NICHE JOB	RIASEC CODE	TRACK
Architects, Except Landscape and Naval	AI	Professional
Film and Video Editors	AEI	Technician/ Artisan
Writers and Authors	AEI	Technician/ Artisan

© JIST Works

The Artistic-Social Type

No occupations or reasonably large niche jobs match this type. You should consider other Artistic types or perhaps the Social-Artistic type.

The Artistic-Enterprising Type

OCCUPATION	RIASEC CODE	TRACK
Art Directors	AE	Technician/ Artisan

NICHE JOB	RIASEC CODE	TRACK
Editors	AEC	Technician/ Artisan
Film and Video Editors	AEI	Technician/ Artisan
Writers and Authors	AEI	Technician/ Artisan

The Artistic-Conventional Type

Almost no occupations or reasonably large niche jobs match this type. You should consider other Artistic types or perhaps the Conventional type.

NICHE JOB	RIASEC CODE	TRACK
Editors	AEC	Technician/ Artisan

Career Plans for Social People

The 107 Social occupations covered by the BLS have average earnings of only $37,021. Only five Social occupations are among the six-figure earners. However, several six-figure niche jobs have Social as their primary type; almost all of them are associated with the Academic career track.

You also may find six-figure occupations and niche jobs under the Investigative-Social and Enterprising-Social types.

© JIST Works

The Social-Realistic Type

NICHE JOB	RIASEC CODE	TRACK
Agricultural Sciences Teachers, Postsecondary	SIR	Academic
Chemistry Teachers, Postsecondary	SIR	Academic
Physical Therapists	SIR	Professional
Physician Assistants	SIR	Professional

The Social-Investigative Type

OCCUPATION	RIASEC CODE	TRACK
Atmospheric, Earth, Marine, and Space Sciences Teachers, Postsecondary	SI	Academic
Biological Science Teachers, Postsecondary	SI	Academic
Economics Teachers, Postsecondary	SI	Academic
Health Specialties Teachers, Postsecondary	SI	Academic
Law Teachers, Postsecondary	SIE	Academic

NICHE JOB	RIASEC CODE	TRACK
Agricultural Sciences Teachers, Postsecondary	SIR	Academic
Business Teachers, Postsecondary	SEI	Academic
Chemistry Teachers, Postsecondary	SIR	Academic
Computer Science Teachers, Postsecondary	SIC	Academic; Information Technology
Foreign Language and Literature Teachers, Postsecondary	SAI	Academic

© JIST Works

NICHE JOB	RIASEC CODE	TRACK
History Teachers, Postsecondary	SIA	Academic
Mathematical Science Teachers, Postsecondary	SIA	Academic
Physical Therapists	SIR	Professional
Physician Assistants	SIR	Professional
Physics Teachers, Postsecondary	SI	Academic
Psychology Teachers, Postsecondary	SIA	Academic
Registered Nurses	SIC	Professional
Sociology Teachers, Postsecondary	SIA	Academic

The Social-Artistic Type

NICHE JOB	RIASEC CODE	TRACK
Foreign Language and Literature Teachers, Postsecondary	SAI	Academic
History Teachers, Postsecondary	SIA	Academic
Mathematical Science Teachers, Postsecondary	SIA	Academic
Political Science Teachers, Postsecondary	SEA	Academic
Psychology Teachers, Postsecondary	SIA	Academic
Sociology Teachers, Postsecondary	SIA	Academic

© JIST Works

The Social-Enterprising Type

Occupation	RIASEC Code	Track
Law Teachers, Postsecondary	SIE	Academic

Niche Job	RIASEC Code	Track
Business Teachers, Postsecondary	SEI	Academic
Political Science Teachers, Postsecondary	SEA	Academic

The Social-Conventional Type

Niche Job	RIASEC Code	Track
Computer Science Teachers, Postsecondary	SIC	Academic; Information Technology
Registered Nurses	SIC	Professional

Career Plans for Enterprising People

The 92 Enterprising occupations tracked by BLS have average earnings of $49,112. Nevertheless, the Enterprising personality type is associated with many six-figure jobs, both as a dominant personality type and a secondary type. Enterprising jobs are linked to all career tracks except Academic and Professional.

The Enterprising-Realistic Type

Occupation	RIASEC Code	Track
Sales Engineers	ERI	Engineering; Distributive
Engineering Managers	ERI	Managerial; Entrepreneurial
Construction Managers	ERC	Managerial; Entrepreneurial

© JIST Works

NICHE JOB	RIASEC CODE	TRACK
First-Line Supervisors/ Managers of Construction Trades and Extraction Workers	ERC	Technician/ Artisan
First-Line Supervisors/ Managers of Mechanics, Installers, and Repairers	ECR	Technician/ Artisan

The Enterprising-Investigative Type

OCCUPATION	RIASEC CODE	TRACK
Administrative Law Judges, Adjudicators, and Hearing Officers	EIS	Professional
Computer and Information Systems Managers	ECI	Information Technology; Managerial
Engineering Managers	ERI	Managerial; Entrepreneurial
Lawyers	EI	Professional
Natural Sciences Managers	EI	Managerial; Scientific
Sales Engineers	ERI	Engineering; Distributive

The Enterprising-Artistic Type

OCCUPATION	RIASEC CODE	TRACK
Advertising and Promotions Managers	EAC	Managerial; Distributive
Public Relations Managers	EA	Managerial; Entrepreneurial

© JIST Works

(continued)

NICHE JOB	RIASEC CODE	TRACK
Advertising Sales Agents	ECA	Distributive
Public Relations Specialists	EAS	Bachelor's-in-Business

The Enterprising-Social Type

OCCUPATION	RIASEC CODE	TRACK
Administrative Law Judges, Adjudicators, and Hearing Officers	EIS	Professional
Agents and Business Managers of Artists, Performers, and Athletes	ES	Distributive; Entrepreneurial
Compensation and Benefits Managers	ECS	Managerial; Entrepreneurial
Education Administrators, Postsecondary	ECS	Managerial
General and Operations Managers	ECS	Managerial; Entrepreneurial
Judges, Magistrate Judges, and Magistrates	ES	Professional
Personal Financial Advisors	ECS	Bachelor's-in-Business; Entrepreneurial
Training and Development Managers	ES	Managerial; Entrepreneurial

NICHE JOB	RIASEC CODE	TRACK
Education Administrators, Elementary and Secondary School	ESC	Managerial
Employment, Recruitment, and Placement Specialists	ESC	Bachelor's-in-Business; Entrepreneurial
First-Line Supervisors/ Managers of Non-Retail Sales Workers	ECS	Managerial; Distributive

© JIST Works

NICHE JOB	RIASEC CODE	TRACK
First-Line Supervisors/ Managers of Police and Detectives	ESC	Technician/Artisan
Flight Attendants	ESC	Technician/Artisan
Insurance Sales Agents	ECS	Distributive; Entrepreneurial
Medical and Health Services Managers	ECS	Managerial; Entrepreneurial
Public Relations Specialists	EAS	Bachelor's-in-Business

The Enterprising-Conventional Type

OCCUPATION	RIASEC CODE	TRACK
Advertising and Promotions Managers	EAC	Managerial; Bachelor's-in-Business
Air Traffic Controllers	EC	Technician/Artisan
Chief Executives	EC	Managerial; Entrepreneurial
Compensation and Benefits Managers	ECS	Managerial; Entrepreneurial
Computer and Information Systems Managers	ECI	Information Technology; Managerial
Construction Managers	ERC	Managerial; Entrepreneurial
Education Administrators, Postsecondary	ECS	Managerial
Financial Managers	EC	Managerial; Entrepreneurial
General and Operations Managers	ECS	Managerial; Entrepreneurial
Industrial Production Managers	EC	Managerial; Entrepreneurial

(continued)

© JIST Works

(continued)

OCCUPATION	RIASEC CODE	TRACK
Marketing Managers	EC	Managerial
Personal Financial Advisors	ECS	Bachelor's-in-Business; Entrepreneurial
Purchasing Managers	EC	Managerial; Entrepreneurial
Real Estate Brokers	EC	Distributive; Entrepreneurial
Sales Managers	EC	Managerial
Securities, Commodities, and Financial Services Sales Agents	EC	Distributive; Entrepreneurial

NICHE JOB	RIASEC CODE	TRACK
Administrative Services Managers	EC	Managerial; Entrepreneurial
Advertising Sales Agents	ECA	Distributive
Education Administrators, Elementary and Secondary School	ESC	Managerial
Employment, Recruitment, and Placement Specialists	ESC	Bachelor's-in-Business; Entrepreneurial
Financial Examiners	EC	Bachelor's-in-Business; Entrepreneurial
First-Line Supervisors/ Managers of Construction Trades and Extraction Workers	ERC	Technician/ Artisan
First-Line Supervisors/ Managers of Mechanics, Installers, and Repairers	ECR	Technician/ Artisan
First-Line Supervisors/ Managers of Non-Retail Sales Workers	ECS	Distributive

© JIST Works

Niche Job	RIASEC Code	Track
First-Line Supervisors/ Managers of Police and Detectives	ESC	Technician/ Artisan
Flight Attendants	ESC	Technician/ Artisan
Insurance Sales Agents	ECS	Distributive; Entrepreneurial
Logisticians	EC	Bachelor's-in-Business; Entrepreneurial
Medical and Health Services Managers	ECS	Managerial; Entrepreneurial
Property, Real Estate, and Community Association Managers	EC	Managerial; Entrepreneurial
Real Estate Sales Agents	EC	Distributive; Entrepreneurial
Sales Representatives, Wholesale and Manufacturing, Technical and Scientific Products	EC	Distributive
Transportation, Storage, and Distribution Managers	EC	Entrepreneurial

Career Plans for Conventional People

Jobs in which the Conventional personality type dominates are usually comparatively low-paying. The 94 Conventional occupations tracked by the BLS average $30,563. Nevertheless, you can find one occupation (Actuaries) with six-figure potential and a few high-paying niche jobs of this type. These jobs are linked to several different career tracks. You may want to look at the Enterprising-Conventional and Investigative-Conventional types for additional rewarding career options.

© JIST Works

The Conventional-Realistic Type

Only highly limited six-figure career opportunities are associated with this combination of types. You may consider looking at the suggestions for the Realistic-Conventional type.

NICHE JOB	RIASEC CODE	TRACK
Computer Specialists, All Other	CIR	Information Technology

The Conventional-Investigative Type

OCCUPATION	RIASEC CODE	TRACK
Actuaries	CIE	Scientific

NICHE JOB	RIASEC CODE	TRACK
Accountants and Auditors	CEI	Bachelor's-in-Business; Entrepreneurial
Computer Specialists, All Other	CIR	Information Technology
Database Administrators	CI	Information Technology
Financial Analysts	CIE	Bachelor's-in-Business

The Conventional-Artistic Type

This combination of types offers almost no opportunities for six-figure earnings. Consider combining the Conventional or Artistic types with some other type.

The Conventional-Social Type

This combination of types offers highly limited opportunities for six-figure earnings. Consider combining the Conventional or Social types with some other type.

NICHE JOB	RIASEC CODE	TRACK
Loan Officers	CES	Bachelor's-in-Business

© JIST Works

The Conventional-Enterprising Type

OCCUPATION	RIASEC CODE	TRACK
Actuaries	CIE	Scientific

NICHE JOB	RIASEC CODE	TRACK
Accountants and Auditors	CEI	Bachelor's-in-Business; Entrepreneurial
Cost Estimators	CE	Engineering; Technician/Artisan
Financial Analysts	CIE	Bachelor's-in-Business
Loan Officers	CES	Bachelor's-in-Business
Purchasing Agents, Except Wholesale, Retail, and Farm Products	CE	Distributive
Sales Representatives, Wholesale and Manufacturing, Except Technical and Scientific Products	CE	Distributive

Have You Settled on a Career Track?

If you feel you have a good idea which career track is likely to suit you (maybe more than one), skip to the appropriate chapter(s) from the following list:

Academic Track	chapter 5
Bachelor's-in-Business Track	chapter 6
Distributive Track	chapter 7
Engineering Track	chapter 8
Entrepreneurial Track	chapter 9
Information Technology Track	chapter 10
Managerial Track	chapter 11
Professional Track	chapter 12
Scientific Track	chapter 13
Technician/Artisan Track	chapter 14

© JIST Works

Still Not Sure About Which Track to Choose?

Go on to chapter 4 and fill out the checklist there. It will help you narrow down your choices.

Highlights of Chapter 3

- In this chapter, you can use a combination of primary and secondary personality types to identify career tracks and six-figure jobs that may suit you.

- The career tracks identified here are keyed to later chapters of the book.

© JIST Works

Chapter 4

What Career Track Matches You? A Checklist

This chapter provides another way of selecting a career track that may be a good match for your interests and attitudes. It's not a formal assessment, but it is based on the characteristics of the six-figure jobs included in this book, as described in the O*NET database and as organized into 10 career tracks.

Read each statement that follows and decide whether or not you agree with it. If you agree with a statement, circle all the capital letters to the right of the statement. If you disagree **strongly** with a statement, cross out all the capital letters. If you feel neutral about a statement or disagree only mildly with it, leave the capital letters alone. (If someone else will be using this book, write the letters and crossed-out letters on a separate sheet of paper.) Answer as truthfully as you can.

Statements About Work

I WANT A JOB WHERE I OFTEN... (CIRCLE NO MORE THAN **6** SETS OF LETTERS; CROSS OUT NO MORE THAN **6**)

estimate the characteristics of products, events, or information	S
evaluate how information meets standards	B
provide consultation and advice to others	BES
provide personal care to others	P
communicate with persons outside the organization	DE
interact with computers	BIN
coordinate the work and activities of others	T
think creatively	AIN
analyze data or information	ABEINS

(continued)

(continued)

I want a job where I often... (circle no more than 6 sets of letters; cross out no more than 6)

document or record information	P
draft, lay out, and specify technical devices, parts, and equipment	NT
guide, direct, and motivate subordinates	MT
identify objects, actions, and events	P
process information	BINS
deal with external customers	BDEMP
interpret the meaning of information for others	AS
update and use relevant knowledge	IP
monitor and control resources	EM
perform for or work directly with the public	DP
establish and maintain interpersonal relationships	D
resolve conflicts and negotiate with others	DEM
sell to or influence others	D
schedule work and activities	MT
staff organizational units	M
train and teach others	A
help others to improve their knowledge or skills	A
develop and build teams	T

I want a job that requires me to... (circle no more than 5 sets of letters; cross out no more than 5)

analyze information and use logic	ABINS
be open to change	AI
set challenging goals and work towards them	A
watch gauges, dials, or other indicators of machine operation	T
determine how money will be spent to get the work done	BDEM
make decisions carefully, because errors have serious results	P
be pleasant with others on the job	N

© JIST Works

I WANT A JOB THAT REQUIRES ME TO... (CIRCLE NO MORE THAN 5 SETS OF LETTERS; CROSS OUT NO MORE THAN 5)

use scientific rules and methods to solve problems	ANS
be sensitive to others' needs and feelings	AP
compete against other workers	D
control operations of equipment or systems	T
take on responsibilities and challenges	DEIMS
work in close physical proximity to other people	P
lead, take charge, and offer opinions and direction	MT
talk to others to convey information effectively	AP
write computer programs	BINS
be persistent in the face of obstacles	D
accept criticism and deal calmly and effectively with stress	BEPT
spend most of the workday sitting	BEINS

I WANT A JOB THAT LETS ME... (CIRCLE NO MORE THAN 4 SETS OF LETTERS; CROSS OUT NO MORE THAN 4)

make use of my individual abilities	INPS
get a feeling of accomplishment	AP
have opportunities for advancement	B
give directions and instructions to others	ABEMNT
plan my work with little supervision	BDEIMST
try out my own ideas	AIMNS
get recognition for the work I do	DS
make decisions on my own	DEIMNST
do things for other people	AP
be looked up to by others in my company and my community	ANP
have something different to do every day	DT
have good working conditions	BDEIM
do public speaking	A

© JIST Works

I WANT A JOB IN WHICH I USE THESE KINDS OF KNOWLEDGE (CIRCLE NO MORE THAN 4 SETS OF LETTERS; CROSS OUT NO MORE THAN 4):

Administration and Management	DEM
Biology	PS
Building and Construction	T
Chemistry	S
Clerical Practices	BEM
Computers and Electronics	IN
Customer and Personal Service	D
Design	INT
Economics and Accounting	BDEM
Education and Training	A
Engineering and Technology	INST
English Language	A
History and Archeology	A
Law and Government	B
Mathematics	DINS
Mechanical Devices	T
Medicine and Dentistry	P
Personnel and Human Resources	BEM
Philosophy and Theology	A
Physics	NS
Production and Processing	T
Psychology	P
Sales and Marketing	BDEM
Sociology and Anthropology	AP
Telecommunications	I
Therapy and Counseling	P

© JIST Works

Scoring Your Responses

Now, look at all the letters you have circled and crossed out.

COUNT THE NUMBER OF TIMES YOU HAVE *CIRCLED* EACH LETTER AND WRITE IT HERE:	COUNT THE NUMBER OF TIMES YOU HAVE *CROSSED OUT* EACH LETTER AND WRITE IT HERE:	SUBTRACT THE SECOND NUMBER FROM THE FIRST AND WRITE THE DIFFERENCE HERE:
A _____	A̶ _____	_____ Academic Track
B _____	B̶ _____	_____ Bachelor's-in-Business Track
D _____	D̶ _____	_____ Distributive Track
E _____	E̶ _____	_____ Entrepreneurial Track
I _____	I̶ _____	_____ Information Technology Track
M _____	M̶ _____	_____ Managerial Track
N _____	N̶ _____	_____ Engineering Track
P _____	P̶ _____	_____ Professional Track
S _____	S̶ _____	_____ Scientific Track
T _____	T̶ _____	_____ Technician/Artisan Track

Connecting Your Scores to Career Tracks

Now that you have tallied your scores, you can identify the career tracks that have the features that you want and don't have the features that you want to avoid.

If one or two tracks score much higher than all the others...

These are probably the tracks you should consider most seriously. See the table at the end of this chapter that lists which chapters cover these tracks.

If the results of this chapter conflict with the results of chapter 3...

Each of the chapters may be indicating different aspects of your preferences, so consider all the tracks suggested. You may have conflicting work needs and may need to make trade-offs, giving up certain satisfactions in your work to get other satisfactions.

If no score stands out from the others...

Be guided by the results you got from chapter 3.

If no track stands out in either this chapter or chapter 3...

This may mean you don't have strong feelings about your preferences. Look at all the chapters describing the tracks. What you read there may help you choose one track as your tentative goal. As you advance along this track, periodically take stock of your progress and your level of satisfaction.

Chapters That Cover Each Track

Academic Track	chapter 5
Bachelor's-in-Business Track	chapter 6
Distributive Track	chapter 7
Engineering Track	chapter 8
Entrepreneurial Track	chapter 9
Information Technology Track	chapter 10
Managerial Track	chapter 11
Professional Track	chapter 12
Scientific Track	chapter 13
Technician/Artisan Track	chapter 14

© JIST Works

Highlights of Chapter 4

- This chapter invites you to consider a wide range of job characteristics that you may like or dislike.

- Based on your preferences, you can identify career tracks that you can explore in detail in the following chapters of the book.

© JIST Works

Chapter 5

The Academic Career
Track to a $100,000 Job

The Academic career track leads to work in postsecondary teaching.

Postsecondary teachers instruct students in a wide variety of academic and vocational subjects beyond the high school level. Most of these students are working toward a degree, but many others are studying for a certificate or to improve their knowledge or career skills. In addition to teaching, postsecondary teachers, particularly those at four-year colleges and universities, also do a significant amount of research in the subject they teach. They must also keep up with new developments in their field and may consult with government, business, nonprofit, and community organizations.

A major goal in the traditional academic career is attaining tenure. The process of attaining tenure can take approximately seven years of moving up the ranks from instructor to assistant professor to associate professor to professor. Colleges and universities usually hire new tenure-track faculty as instructors or assistant professors under term contracts. At the end of the period, their record of teaching, research, and overall contribution to the institution is reviewed and tenure may be granted if the review is favorable. Those denied tenure usually must leave the institution. Tenured professors cannot be fired without just cause and due process.

The number of tenure-track positions is declining as institutions seek flexibility in dealing with financial matters and changing student interests. Institutions rely more heavily on limited-term contracts and part-time, or adjunct, faculty, thus shrinking the total pool of tenured faculty. Limited-term contracts, typically lasting two to five years, may be terminated or extended when they expire but generally do not lead to the granting of tenure. In addition, some institutions have limited the percentage of faculty who can be tenured.

Some people who hold a day job in a nonacademic career track do part-time work as an adjunct faculty member, typically by teaching night classes. They do so to supplement their daytime earnings, to impart their accumulated wisdom to students, or to begin a transition to the Academic track. In fact, more than one-quarter of postsecondary teachers work part time. Almost none are self-employed.

Note that the preparation for the Academic career track does not usually focus on equipping you with teaching skills, although you may learn some from experience as a graduate teaching assistant. In fact, this preparation route is very similar to that of someone on the Scientific or Professional track, to which you can change at any time.

Your Strategy for Getting on the Academic Career Track

All Personality Types

You will need to earn a doctoral or professional degree in a subject to teach it at the postsecondary level. It is possible to teach in college with a master's degree, but a doctorate is normally required for a six-figure position.

High school students can prepare by taking college-prep courses in whatever subject they plan to teach, plus courses in supporting skills such as math, writing, or public speaking. Gain experience through related summer jobs, extracurricular activities, or volunteer work.

As a *college student,* you should major in the subject you intend to teach. Alternatively, you can minor in this subject as an undergraduate and focus on it in graduate or professional school. Summer jobs or internships related to the subject will give you helpful experience.

Experienced workers with skills learned in the workplace may move from another career track into a college teaching career, provided they earn a master's or doctoral degree. (Many in the Scientific, Engineering, or Professional track already have an advanced degree.) It also helps to have experience doing research and, ideally, a portfolio of published articles documenting your research. Work experience in industry may make it easier for you to find consulting work or later to return to a nonacademic track.

Realistic

None of the 18 Academic jobs included in this book has Realistic as its primary personality type, but three postsecondary teaching jobs have it as a secondary type because it is relevant to the subject matter being taught: agricultural sciences, chemistry, and engineering. Best earning prospects are in teaching engineering or chemistry.

High school students aiming for any of these career goals should take college-prep science courses, plus math through at least pre-calculus. Try to get summer jobs in a scientific or agricultural setting. Science fair competitions also can provide valuable research experience.

College students may be able to do research projects under the supervision of faculty. Science- or agriculture-related summer jobs or internships can also be useful. After you obtain your doctorate, you may want to do additional postdoctoral research to gain experience and skill in a high-paying specialization.

Experienced workers from a scientific or agricultural setting may find their connections with industry useful for obtaining research grants and consulting work, for teaching students real-world skills, or for providing students with job connections.

Investigative

Of the 18 Academic jobs included in this book, only one (Political Science Teachers, Postsecondary) does not have Investigative as a secondary personality type, and one (Engineering Teachers, Postsecondary) has this as its primary type. Investigative people enjoy research-related tasks, and these are essential parts of the educational preparation and work roles for almost all college teaching occupations.

As a *college student,* you may not need to major in the subject you intend to teach; you may be able to minor in this subject as an undergraduate and focus on it in graduate school. This is particularly true for subjects, such as health specializations and law, in which you must earn a professional degree.

Experienced workers in high-paying fields in other career tracks are the most likely to be able to command high salaries as academics.

© JIST Works

Artistic

Several postsecondary teaching jobs have Artistic as a secondary personality type. Mostly these are specializations in the humanities, which demand the ability to write well or to appreciate literature. One exception is Mathematical Science Teachers, Postsecondary, who use the creative thinking processes associated with the Artistic type.

High school students should take humanities courses and develop their writing skills. Those intending to specialize in math should take the most advanced math courses available.

College students should major in English, foreign language, history, mathematics, political science, psychology, or sociology and should strive for an excellent academic record. If possible, you should try to get experience doing research under the supervision of a faculty member. For almost all of these majors, unless you go on to graduate or professional school, income opportunities outside of college teaching are considerably less lucrative. (Mathematics is an exception.) Those studying psychology should get a good grounding in statistics.

Experienced workers may not have much advantage in some of these subjects. But in other cases, high-level practical experience in the subject—for example, in cryptography, psychological counseling, or running a political campaign—may help you get a high-paying faculty position.

Social

All of the postsecondary teaching jobs except one have Social as their primary personality type. (The exception is Engineering Teachers, Postsecondary, which is coded IRS.) Teaching involves working with people and being interested in their learning.

Because the selection of Social college teaching jobs is so diverse, there is no specific advice that is worth adding to the suggestions listed previously for all personality types.

Enterprising

Three academic jobs have Enterprising as a secondary personality type; they teach the subjects business, law, and political science.

High school students interested in business can take related subjects such as accounting; perhaps more important would be summer work in a business setting. Those interested in law and political science should take humanities courses that improve their writing and research skills.

College students majoring in business should be sure to take courses that will enable them not just to conduct business but to do research. For example, they should study economics, statistics, and business research methods. Those planning to teach law can major in almost anything as undergraduates as long as they take courses that help them improve their writing skills. After completing law school, you should take the bar exam even if you intend to teach law rather than practice it.

Experienced workers can bring many real-life insights to teaching and may be able to command higher salaries than those who have only book learning.

Conventional

The Conventional personality type is not usually associated with college teaching, but it is a secondary type for those who teach computer science.

High school students should take the most advanced computer science courses available and should pursue this interest as a hobby.

College students should major in computer science and get a good grounding in theory as well as how-to. Note that this major also prepares you for the Information Technology career track.

Experienced workers in computer technology are likely to earn more in industry than in academia, but college teaching is an option for those who have a master's.

Achieving Six Figures in the Academic Track

The best-paying academic jobs are in fields that offer high-paying nonacademic jobs, such as medicine, law, engineering, and business. However, even if it is too late for you to specialize in one of these fields, there are other ways to maximize your earnings in academia.

Research is better rewarded than teaching, so concentrate your energies on doing research and publishing your findings. Present papers at conferences and build your scholarly reputation. An outstanding scholar may be appointed to an endowed chair, which is paid for by a fund outside of the university's regular budget and therefore is usually better compensated.

© JIST Works

If your skills and area of concentration are in high demand by industry, you may be able to supplement your academic earnings with paid consulting work for companies or foundations. Another strategy is to get a grant from a foundation, or sometimes a company, to conduct a research project of interest to the funding organization. If it is a large grant that requires you to coordinate the work of several academics and research assistants, plus perhaps some equipment and materials, you can receive additional compensation for managing the grant. Some academics who are able to get these grants and consulting engagements on a regular basis create a research center within the university, typically with a name such as "Institute for x Studies" or "Center for Studies in x." The research staff and facilities are maintained continuously, rather than for a one-shot project, and the academic who administers the center can command a better salary.

A few academics who are specialists in a topic that is of interest to the reading public earn extra income by writing for publication in the popular press. Others enhance their earnings by authoring a textbook for their subject or by writing test questions for a certification examination.

Moving On to Other Career Tracks

People with advanced degrees often move back and forth between the Academic career track and the Professional, Scientific, or Information Technology tracks. Moving out of academia is easiest for those with expertise in a field with commercial potential. Moving into academia is easiest for those who have a track record of research or expertise in a specialization that students are eager to learn about.

College faculty usually are expected to do committee work in addition to teaching and research. Those who have ability and interest in such work may be asked to chair their department and thus move into the Managerial track. Further advancement along that track may lead to working as a dean or, eventually, college president. At four-year institutions, such advancement requires a doctoral degree. At two-year colleges, a doctorate is helpful but not usually required, except for advancement to some top administrative positions.

College teachers can sometimes move into the Entrepreneurial track by forming a company to pursue commercial applications of a promising line of research. Some faculty make initial contacts with outside investors by persuading them to fund research within the university.

Characteristics of Six-Figure Academic Jobs

Highest-Level Skills

Science; Instructing; Writing; Speaking; Learning Strategies.

Highest-Level Work Activities

Training and Teaching Others; Interpreting the Meaning of Information for Others; Coaching and Developing Others; Thinking Creatively; Analyzing Data or Processing Information.

Most Important Knowledges

Education and Training; English Language; Philosophy and Theology; Sociology and Anthropology; History and Archeology.

Most Important Work Contexts

Electronic Mail; Face-to-Face Discussions; Freedom to Make Decisions; Structured versus Unstructured Work; Indoors, Environmentally Controlled.

Most Important Work Needs

Authority; Social Service; Creativity; Achievement; Social Status.

Most Important Work Styles

Dependability; Integrity; Analytical Thinking; Independence; Initiative.

Facts About Six-Figure Academic Jobs

The Bureau of Labor Statistics does not provide job-growth figures for individual college-teaching jobs; it gives the figure of 22.9% for all of them.

© JIST Works

Six-Figure Occupations

(At least 25% of the workers earn more than $100,000.)

Atmospheric, Earth, Marine, and Space Sciences Teachers, Postsecondary

Teach courses in the physical sciences, except chemistry and physics. Includes both teachers primarily engaged in teaching and those who do a combination of both teaching and research.

Personality Code: SI

College Majors: Acoustics; Astronomy; Astrophysics; Atmospheric Sciences and Meteorology, General; Atomic Physics; Geochemistry; Geochemistry and Petrology; Geology/Earth Science, General; Geophysics and Seismology; Hydrology and Water Resources Science; Meteorology; Nuclear Physics; Paleontology; Planetary Astronomy and Science; Plasma and High-Temperature Physics; Science Teacher Education/General Science Teacher Education; Solid State and Low-Temperature Physics; Theoretical and Mathematical Physics; others.

Median Annual Earnings: $73,280

Highly Paid Workforce: Out of a total salaried workforce of 9,030, 2,258 people (25%) earn more than $100,010.

Annual Job Growth Through 2016: 22.9%

Average Annual Job Openings Through 2016: 1,553

Best-Paying Industries: Educational Services.

Best-Paying Metro Areas: No metro area has a large number of six-figure workers.

Biological Science Teachers, Postsecondary

Teach courses in biological sciences. Includes both teachers primarily engaged in teaching and those who do a combination of both teaching and research.

Personality Code: SI

College Majors: Anatomy; Animal Physiology; Biochemistry; Biology/Biological Sciences, General; Biometry/Biometrics; Biophysics; Biotechnology; Botany/Plant Biology; Cell/Cellular Biology and Histology; Ecology; Entomology; Evolutionary Biology; Immunology; Marine

Biology and Biological Oceanography; Microbiology, General; Molecular Biology; Neuroscience; Nutrition Sciences; Parasitology; Pharmacology; Plant Genetics; Plant Pathology/Phytopathology; Toxicology; Virology; Zoology/Animal Biology; others.

Median Annual Earnings: $71,780

Highly Paid Workforce: Out of a total salaried workforce of 52,560, 13,140 people (25%) earn more than $102,930.

Annual Job Growth Through 2016: 22.9%

Average Annual Job Openings Through 2016: 9,039

Best-Paying Industries: Educational Services.

Best-Paying Metro Areas: Boston-Cambridge-Quincy, MA-NH; Houston–Sugar Land–Baytown, TX; Los Angeles–Long Beach–Santa Ana, CA; Philadelphia-Camden-Wilmington, PA-NJ-DE-MD.

Economics Teachers, Postsecondary

Teach courses in economics. Includes both teachers primarily engaged in teaching and those who do a combination of both teaching and research.

Personality Code: SI

College Majors: Applied Economics; Business/Managerial Economics; Development Economics and International Development; Econometrics and Quantitative Economics; Economics, General; Economics, Other; International Economics; Social Science Teacher Education.

Median Annual Earnings: $75,300

Highly Paid Workforce: Out of a total salaried workforce of 12,840, 3,210 people (25%) earn more than $101,100.

Annual Job Growth Through 2016: 22.9%

Average Annual Job Openings Through 2016: 2,208

Best-Paying Industries: Educational Services.

Best-Paying Metro Areas: No metro area has a large number of six-figure workers.

Engineering Teachers, Postsecondary

Teach courses pertaining to the application of physical laws and principles of engineering for the development of machines, materials, instruments,

© JIST Works

processes, and services. Includes teachers of subjects such as chemical, civil, electrical, industrial, mechanical, mineral, and petroleum engineering. Includes both teachers primarily engaged in teaching and those who do a combination of both teaching and research.

Personality Code: IRS

College Majors: Aerospace Engineering; Agricultural Engineering; Chemical Engineering; Computer Engineering; Construction Engineering; Electrical, Electronics and Communications Engineering; Environmental Engineering; Forest Engineering; Industrial Engineering; Manufacturing Engineering; Materials Engineering; Mechanical Engineering; Metallurgical Engineering; Mining and Mineral Engineering; Nuclear Engineering; Petroleum Engineering; Transportation and Highway Engineering; Water Resources Engineering; others.

Median Annual Earnings: $79,510

Highly Paid Workforce: Out of a total salaried workforce of 32,360, 8,090 people (25%) earn more than $105,720.

Annual Job Growth Through 2016: 22.9%

Average Annual Job Openings Through 2016: 5,565

Best-Paying Industries: Educational Services.

Best-Paying Metro Areas: New York–Northern New Jersey–Long Island, NY-NJ-PA; Philadelphia-Camden-Wilmington, PA-NJ-DE-MD; Washington-Arlington-Alexandria, DC-VA-MD-WV.

Health Specialties Teachers, Postsecondary

Teach courses in health specialties, such as veterinary medicine, dentistry, pharmacy, therapy, laboratory technology, and public health.

Personality Code: SI

College Majors: Allied Health and Medical Assisting Services, others; Art Therapy; Audiology and Speech-Language Pathology; Biostatistics; Cardiovascular Technology; Chiropractic; Clinical Laboratory Science/ Medical Technology/Technologist; Dental Hygiene; Dentistry; Electrocardiograph Technology; Massage Therapy; Medical Radiologic Technology; Nuclear Medical Technology; Occupational Health and Industrial Hygiene; Perfusion Technology; Pharmacy; Physical Therapy; Respiratory Care Therapy; Surgical Technology; Veterinary Medicine.

© JIST Works

Median Annual Earnings: $80,700

Highly Paid Workforce: Out of a total salaried workforce of 114,070, 57,035 people (50%) earn more than $80,700 and 28,518 (25%) earn more than $125,220.

Annual Job Growth Through 2016: 22.9%

Average Annual Job Openings Through 2016: 19,617

Best-Paying Industries: Educational Services; Health Care and Social Assistance.

Best-Paying Metro Areas: Baltimore-Towson, MD; Boston-Cambridge-Quincy, MA-NH; Cincinnati-Middletown, OH-KY-IN; College Station–Bryan, TX; Columbus, OH; Dallas–Fort Worth–Arlington, TX; Detroit-Warren-Livonia, MI; Houston–Sugar Land–Baytown, TX; Kansas City, MO-KS; Los Angeles–Long Beach–Santa Ana, CA; Minneapolis–St. Paul–Bloomington, MN-WI; New York–Northern New Jersey–Long Island, NY-NJ-PA; Oklahoma City, OK; San Francisco–Oakland–Fremont, CA; St. Louis, MO-IL; Washington-Arlington-Alexandria, DC-VA-MD-WV.

Law Teachers, Postsecondary

Teach courses in law. Includes both teachers primarily engaged in teaching and those who do a combination of both teaching and research.

Personality Code: SIE

College Majors: Law (LL.B., J.D.); Legal Studies, General.

Median Annual Earnings: $87,730

Highly Paid Workforce: Out of a total salaried workforce of 12,610, 6,305 people (50%) earn more than $87,730 and 3,153 (25%) earn more than $125,120.

Annual Job Growth Through 2016: 22.9%

Average Annual Job Openings Through 2016: 2,169

Best-Paying Industries: Educational Services.

Best-Paying Metro Areas: Washington-Arlington-Alexandria, DC-VA-MD-WV.

© JIST Works

Six-Figure Niche-Industry Jobs

(At least 10% of workers in the best-paying industries earn more than $100,000.)

Agricultural Sciences Teachers, Postsecondary

Teach courses in the agricultural sciences. Includes teachers of agronomy, dairy sciences, fisheries management, horticultural sciences, poultry sciences, range management, and agricultural soil conservation. Includes both teachers primarily engaged in teaching and those who do a combination of both teaching and research.

Personality Code: SIR

College Majors: Agricultural and Food Products Processing; Agricultural Business and Management, General; Agricultural Production Operations, General; Agriculture, General; Agronomy and Crop Science; Animal Husbandry and Production; Aquaculture; Farm/Farm and Ranch Management; Food Science; Horticultural Science; Landscaping and Groundskeeping; Ornamental Horticulture; Plant Protection and Integrated Pest Management; Poultry Science; Range Science and Management; Soil Science and Agronomy, General; others.

Median Annual Earnings: $78,460

Highly Paid Workforce: Out of a total salaried workforce of 10,700, 2,675 people (25%) earn more than $98,260 and 1,070 (10%) earn more than $123,140.

Annual Job Growth Through 2016: 22.9%

Average Annual Job Openings Through 2016: 1,840

Best-Paying Industries: Educational Services.

Business Teachers, Postsecondary

Teach courses in business administration and management, such as accounting, finance, human resources, labor relations, marketing, and operations research. Includes both teachers primarily engaged in teaching and those who do a combination of both teaching and research.

Personality Code: SEI

College Majors: Accounting; Actuarial Science; Business Administration and Management, General; Business Statistics; Entrepreneurial Studies; Finance, General; Financial Planning and Services; Franchising and

Franchise Operations; Human Resources Management; Insurance; International Business; Investments and Securities; Labor and Industrial Relations; Management Science, General; Marketing Management, General; Marketing Research; Public Finance; Purchasing, Procurement, and Contracts Management; others.

Median Annual Earnings: $64,900

Highly Paid Workforce: Out of a total salaried workforce of 67,700, 16,925 people (25%) earn more than $93,540 and 6,770 (10%) earn more than $125,400.

Annual Job Growth Through 2016: 22.9%

Average Annual Job Openings Through 2016: 11,643

Best-Paying Industries: Educational Services.

Chemistry Teachers, Postsecondary

Teach courses pertaining to the chemical and physical properties and compositional changes of substances. Work may include instruction in the methods of qualitative and quantitative chemical analysis. Includes both teachers primarily engaged in teaching and those who do a combination of both teaching and research.

Personality Code: SIR

College Majors: Analytical Chemistry; Chemical Physics; Chemistry, General; Chemistry, Other; Geochemistry; Inorganic Chemistry; Organic Chemistry; Physical and Theoretical Chemistry; Polymer Chemistry.

Median Annual Earnings: $63,870

Highly Paid Workforce: Out of a total salaried workforce of 19,800, 4,950 people (25%) earn more than $88,490 and 1,980 (10%) earn more than $122,080.

Annual Job Growth Through 2016: 22.9%

Average Annual Job Openings Through 2016: 3,405

Best-Paying Industries: Educational Services.

Computer Science Teachers, Postsecondary

Teach courses in computer science. May specialize in a field of computer science, such as the design and function of computers or operations and

© JIST Works

research analysis. Includes both teachers primarily engaged in teaching and those who do a combination of both teaching and research. (Also included in the Information Technology career track.)

Personality Code: SIC

College Majors: Computer and Information Sciences, General; Computer Programming/Programmer, General; Computer Science; Computer Systems Analysis/Analyst Training; Information Science/Studies.

Median Annual Earnings: $62,020

Highly Paid Workforce: Out of a total salaried workforce of 33,840, 8,460 people (25%) earn more than $88,390 and 3,384 (10%) earn more than $116,460.

Annual Job Growth Through 2016: 22.9%

Average Annual Job Openings Through 2016: 5,820

Best-Paying Industries: Educational Services.

English Language and Literature Teachers, Postsecondary

Teach courses in English language and literature, including linguistics and comparative literature.

Personality Code: SAI

College Majors: American Literature (Canadian); American Literature (United States); Comparative Literature; Creative Writing; English Composition; English Language and Literature, General; English Language and Literature/Letters, Other; English Literature (British and Commonwealth); Technical and Business Writing.

Median Annual Earnings: $54,000

Highly Paid Workforce: Out of a total salaried workforce of 60,910, 6,091 people (10%) earn more than $100,110.

Annual Job Growth Through 2016: 22.9%

Average Annual Job Openings Through 2016: 10,475

Best-Paying Industries: Educational Services.

Foreign Language and Literature Teachers, Postsecondary

Teach courses in foreign (i.e., other than English) languages and literature.

Personality Code: SAI

College Majors: Arabic Language and Literature; Chinese Language and Literature; Classics and Classical Languages, Literatures, and Linguistics, General; Foreign Languages, Literatures, and Linguistics, others; French Language and Literature; German Language and Literature; Italian Language and Literature; Japanese Language and Literature; Russian Language and Literature; Spanish Language and Literature; others.

Median Annual Earnings: $53,610

Highly Paid Workforce: Out of a total salaried workforce of 25,100, 2,510 people (10%) earn more than $105,170.

Annual Job Growth Through 2016: 22.9%

Average Annual Job Openings Through 2016: 4,317

Best-Paying Industries: Educational Services

History Teachers, Postsecondary

Teach courses in human history and historiography.

Personality Code: SIA

College Majors: American History (United States); Asian History; Canadian History; European History; History and Philosophy of Science and Technology; History, General; History, Other; Public/Applied History and Archival Administration.

Median Annual Earnings: $59,160

Highly Paid Workforce: Out of a total salaried workforce of 20,760, 2,076 people (10%) earn more than $105,090.

Annual Job Growth Through 2016: 22.9%

Average Annual Job Openings Through 2016: 3,570

Best-Paying Industries: Educational Services.

© JIST Works

Mathematical Science Teachers, Postsecondary

Teach courses pertaining to mathematical concepts, statistics, and actuarial science and to the application of original and standardized mathematical techniques in solving specific problems and situations.

Personality Code: SIA

College Majors: Algebra and Number Theory; Analysis and Functional Analysis; Applied Mathematics; Business Statistics; Geometry/Geometric Analysis; Logic; Mathematical Statistics and Probability; Mathematics and Statistics, Other; Mathematics, General; Mathematics, Other; Statistics, General; Topology and Foundations.

Median Annual Earnings: $58,560

Highly Paid Workforce: Out of a total salaried workforce of 44,560, 4,456 people (10%) earn more than $108,900.

Annual Job Growth Through 2016: 22.9%

Average Annual Job Openings Through 2016: 7,663

Best-Paying Industries: Educational Services.

Physics Teachers, Postsecondary

Teach courses pertaining to the laws of matter and energy. Includes both teachers primarily engaged in teaching and those who do a combination of both teaching and research.

Personality Code: SI

College Majors: Acoustics; Atomic/Molecular Physics; Elementary Particle Physics; Nuclear Physics; Optics/Optical Sciences; Physics, General; Physics, Other; Plasma and High-Temperature Physics; Solid State and Low-Temperature Physics; Theoretical and Mathematical Physics.

Median Annual Earnings: $70,090

Highly Paid Workforce: Out of a total salaried workforce of 12,530, 3,133 people (25%) earn more than $95,270 and 1,253 (10%) earn more than $125,730.

Annual Job Growth Through 2016: 22.9%

Average Annual Job Openings Through 2016: 2,155

Best-Paying Industries: Educational Services.

© JIST Works

Political Science Teachers, Postsecondary

Teach courses in political science, international affairs, and international relations. Includes both teachers primarily engaged in teaching and those who do a combination of both teaching and research.

Personality Code: SEA

College Majors: American Government and Politics (United States); Political Science and Government, General; Political Science and Government, Other; Social Science Teacher Education.

Median Annual Earnings: $63,100

Highly Paid Workforce: Out of a total salaried workforce of 14,160, 3,540 people (25%) earn more than $84,870 and 1,416 (10%) earn more than $116,010.

Annual Job Growth Through 2016: 22.9%

Average Annual Job Openings Through 2016: 2,435

Best-Paying Industries: Educational Services.

Psychology Teachers, Postsecondary

Teach courses in psychology, such as child, clinical, and developmental psychology, and psychological counseling. Includes both teachers primarily engaged in teaching and those who do a combination of both teaching and research.

Personality Code: SIA

College Majors: Clinical Psychology; Cognitive Psychology and Psycholinguistics; Community Psychology; Comparative Psychology; Counseling Psychology; Developmental and Child Psychology; Educational Psychology; Experimental Psychology; Industrial and Organizational Psychology; Marriage and Family Therapy; Personality Psychology; Physiological Psychology/Psychobiology; Psychology Teacher Education; Psychology, General; Psychometrics and Quantitative Psychology; School Psychology; Social Psychology; others.

Median Annual Earnings: $60,610

Highly Paid Workforce: Out of a total salaried workforce of 30,590, 3,059 people (10%) earn more than $107,280.

© JIST Works

Annual Job Growth Through 2016: 22.9%

Average Annual Job Openings Through 2016: 5,261

Best-Paying Industries: Educational Services.

Sociology Teachers, Postsecondary

Teach courses in sociology. Includes both teachers primarily engaged in teaching and those who do a combination of both teaching and research.

Personality Code: SIA

College Majors: Social Science Teacher Education; Sociology.

Median Annual Earnings: $58,160

Highly Paid Workforce: Out of a total salaried workforce of 16,130, 1,613 people earn more than $109,600.

Annual Job Growth Through 2016: 22.9%

Average Annual Job Openings Through 2016: 2,774

Best-Paying Industries: Educational Services.

Six-Figure Niche-Location Jobs

None.

Chapter 6

The Bachelor's-in-Business Career Track to a $100,000 Job

The Bachelor's-in-Business career track leads to work in specialized business roles.

These workers learn about a particular business function as part of a bachelor's degree program, usually in a major that specializes in that function. In some cases they may get a general business management degree and learn their specialization on the job. A small number of fast learners who lack a business degree may learn the required skills while working on a different, related job.

Some of them work in a business that specializes in serving their specialized role for other businesses—for example, in an accounting, market research, or staffing firm. More often they work in a departmental role that is not the core mission of their employer. Although they do not need to be informed about every aspect of the business, they may improve their usefulness by increasing their knowledge of other departments and of the industry as a whole. They also need to stay abreast of new developments in their specialization. Those who acquire outstanding skills, work in a hot industry sector, or live in a high-wage region may earn six figures.

Your Strategy for Getting on the Bachelor's-in-Business Career Track

Realistic

None of the 11 Bachelor's-in-Business jobs included in this book has Realistic as its primary or secondary personality type. If this career track appeals to you and you are willing and able to complete the degree requirements, you may want to seek a specialized business job within an industry that is linked to the Realistic type, such as construction or manufacturing.

Investigative

This section focuses on the two Bachelor's-in-Business jobs for which Investigative is the primary personality type: Market Research Analysts and Management Analysts. (For the two jobs for which Investigative is a secondary type—Financial Analysts and Accountants and Auditors—see the **Conventional** section of this chapter.)

High school students interested in these two jobs should take college-prep courses, especially math and computer science. Business courses are not as important, but a summer job in a business environment would be useful experience.

College students should choose the appropriate major and be sure to study more than the minimum requirements in math and statistics. Participation in business-related student activities and summer jobs in the business world plus an internship in your business specialization are all helpful.

Management Analysts (also sometimes called consultants), especially those who are self-employed, generally need to hold a master's degree or be *experienced workers* in an industry so their advice is credible. Those with less relevant education or experience may be hired by a consulting company and learn about the industry over several years by providing research support for analysts. A master's degree is also useful for Market Research Analysts who aspire to technical positions, and it can serve as a credential for those who want to find consulting work.

Artistic

Only one of the 11 Bachelor's-in-Business jobs included in this book has Artistic as a secondary personality type: Public Relations Specialists.

High school students should take college-prep courses, including advanced English courses or others that develop writing skill. Running the publicity campaign for a student activity would be valuable experience.

College students should major in public relations, journalism, advertising, or communication. Writing for a student publication (print or Web-based) or publicizing student activities can provide material for a portfolio. You may want to join the local chapter of the Public Relations Student Society of America. If you have demonstrated communications skills, a major in a field related to a specific industry such as finance, health care, or engineering may prepare you for a job in public relations for that industry.

Experienced workers with a portfolio of articles can sometimes be hired for public relations without a bachelor's degree in business. You may be given a formal training program or may perform beginner's tasks in the department, such as assembling files of press clippings, answering calls from the press and the public, compiling invitation lists and details for press conferences, or researching facts that senior staff can use in press releases.

Social

Four of the 11 Bachelor's-in-Business jobs have Social as a secondary personality type. These jobs involve extending business services to the public: financial advice, recruiting, loans, or public relations. For specific suggestions regarding Personal Financial Advisors and Employment, Recruitment, and Placement Specialists, see the **Enterprising** section of this chapter. For Loan Officers, see the **Conventional** section. For Public Relations Specialists, see the **Artistic** section. If you're not sure which of these functions might interest you most, you may hedge your bets by choosing one appropriate business major while also taking several courses in a different specialization. During high school and college, summer work in business settings that deal with the public can be helpful.

Enterprising

All 11 Bachelor's-in-Business jobs have Enterprising as a primary or secondary personality type. For specific suggestions regarding Public Relations Specialists, see the **Artistic** section of this chapter. For Accountants and Auditors, Credit Analysts, and Loan Officers, see the **Conventional** section. Management Analysts are discussed in the **Investigative** section. This section covers Employment, Recruitment, and Placement Specialists; Financial Examiners; Logisticians; and Personal Financial Advisors.

High school students may take one or two business-related subjects such as accounting, but college-prep courses are more important for reaching the goal of a bachelor's degree. Your achievement in math courses is an important indicator of your aptitude for many business specializations. Summer work in a business setting is helpful.

© JIST Works

College students have several specialized business majors to choose from. They can postpone making a choice by majoring in general business management or by minoring in a second specialization. Summer jobs or an internship in the targeted specialization will give you experience and also a network of contacts. If you intend to be a financial advisor, you should learn as much as you can about student financial aid even if you do not need to receive it; also, make a habit of following the stock market, perhaps by tracking a portfolio of imaginary investments. Those aiming to work in personnel or market research should take a combination of courses in the social sciences, business, and psychology. For market research, additional courses in statistics and survey design are particularly relevant. A master's in business administration in your intended specialization can accelerate your advancement to a high-paying job.

Experienced workers who are knowledgeable about one of these business specializations and perhaps have other skills (such as working with the public) can sometimes enter these occupations without a bachelor's degree. Personal Financial Advisors generally need a few years of work experience and study beyond the bachelor's to take the exam for certification, an important credential. Those who want to be licensed to sell securities must maintain a relationship with a large securities firm, even if they are self-employed, so that they may qualify for the appropriate licensure. Selling insurance requires additional licensure. Employment, Recruitment, and Placement Specialists may advance to manage a human resources department, but they may attain even higher earnings by starting up a recruiting firm, as described in chapter 10, about the Entrepreneurial track.

Conventional

All but one of the Bachelor's-in-Business jobs has Conventional as a primary or secondary personality type. This section focuses on those four jobs for which it is the primary type: Accountants and Auditors, Credit Analysts, Financial Analysts, and Loan Officers. In these jobs, the main purpose is to ensure that business dealings follow correct, standard procedures so that laws are upheld, the parties involved are fully informed, and company policies can be carried out consistently. For example, they make sure that their company's earnings and liabilities are stated clearly or that a lending institution has good information about the creditworthiness of borrowers. Those who combine this attention to detail with an Investigative flair may excel as Financial Analysts.

© JIST Works

High school students should focus on college-prep courses, especially math and computers, but they may also take one or two business-related courses. More important is summer work in a business setting, especially one that deals with information and business computer applications.

College students should major in finance or accounting. A master's in one of these subjects will improve the earning prospects of Financial Analysts and Accountants and Auditors. Summer jobs and internships in data-related businesses are especially valuable experiences.

New hires are taught the specific procedures of their company after being hired. For example, Loan Officers learn how to guide loan applicants through the application process and how to research an applicant's credit history. *Experienced workers* sometimes can learn the skills for one of these specializations by taking an administrative job within the targeted functional area, perhaps entering data into computer systems, handling phone calls and correspondence, or assisting consumers with paperwork. Many high-paying jobs in accounting and auditing require you to be a Certified Public Accountant (CPA). In most states, the coursework required to prepare for the CPA exam is equivalent to a master's degree, and many universities offer this degree as part of the program. Financial Analysts need to educate themselves continuously about conditions in the financial markets. As they acquire a track record of expertise in providing advice on investment decisions, they may advance to be portfolio managers or fund managers, supervising a team of analysts. The most outstanding of these workers can command superstar earnings. Those analysts who want to work as consultants may seek certification by the Institute of Management Consultants USA.

Achieving Six Figures in the Bachelor's-in-Business Track

The usual strategy for advancing in the Bachelor's-in-Business track is to build up your expertise in your business specialization by a combination of long-term experience and advanced coursework. In most specializations, a professional organization is available to provide training and certify your expertise, but you need to accumulate a record of accomplishments that confirms your paper credentials. Fortunately, business achievements in these specializations can usually be quantified in terms such as dollars saved or market share captured, so make sure your successes are displayed on your resume and don't be shy about referring to them when you network or interview.

© JIST Works

One of the best-paying ways to use your expertise, no matter which business specialization you start out in, is to work as a management analyst, perhaps in a consulting work arrangement. There are many aspects of management you might analyze, but remember that some of the best money is earned by those who know how to handle money—in other words, those with expertise in finance. The recent economic crisis demonstrates that this specialization can be insecure, but working in finance can also be extremely lucrative.

Moving On to Other Career Tracks

The Managerial track is a frequent route for advancement from this track. As part of your work in these occupations, you often provide vital information that managers use to make business decisions. After gaining some experience working with managers, you may be able to take on some managerial tasks and eventually a managerial job title. Another way to advance to the Managerial track is to take responsibility for supervising the specialized department (for example, accounting, finance, or public relations) where you work. You may start by supervising clerical workers and later advance to managing bachelor's-in-business workers. Getting a master's degree can help with either kind of advancement.

The Entrepreneurial track is an option for many of these business specializations. With work experience, skills for self-management, and a flair for self-promotion, you may be able to start up your own firm that markets your services to businesses—for example, a payroll-processing, market research, or public relations company. This work arrangement means facing more competition than working in an in-house department, but the financial rewards can be much greater. (Note that for many of the jobs listed in this chapter, one of the highest-paying industries is Professional, Scientific, and Technical Services.)

The Academic track is a possibility if you gain a master's or doctoral degree and have experience researching business problems. This career move may improve job security, but it usually does not improve earnings.

© JIST Works

Characteristics of Six-Figure Bachelor's-in-Business Jobs

Highest-Level Skills

Management of Financial Resources; Judgment and Decision Making; Systems Evaluation; Programming; Systems Analysis.

Highest-Level Work Activities

Analyzing Data or Processing Information; Processing Information; Provide Consultation and Advice to Others; Interacting with Computers; Evaluating Information to Determine Compliance with Standards.

Most Important Knowledges

Economics and Accounting; Clerical; Sales and Marketing; Personnel and Human Resources; Law and Government.

Most Important Work Contexts

Telephone; Face-to-Face Discussions; Electronic Mail; Indoors, Environmentally Controlled; Spend Time Sitting.

Most Important Work Needs

Working Conditions; Advancement; Compensation; Autonomy; Authority.

Most Important Work Styles

Integrity; Attention to Detail; Dependability; Analytical Thinking; Stress Tolerance.

© JIST Works

Facts About Six-Figure Bachelor's-in-Business Jobs

Six-Figure Occupations

(At least 25% of the workers earn more than $100,000.)

Personal Financial Advisors

Advise clients on financial plans, utilizing knowledge of tax and investment strategies, securities, insurance, pension plans, and real estate. Duties include assessing clients' assets, liabilities, cash flow, insurance coverage, tax status, and financial objectives to establish investment strategies. (Also included in the Enterprising career track.)

Personality Code: ECS

College Majors: Financial Planning and Services.

Median Annual Earnings: $67,660

Highly Paid Workforce: Out of a total salaried workforce of 132,460, 66,230 people (50%) earn more than $67,660 and 33,115 (25%) earn more than $115,750.

Annual Job Growth Through 2016: 41.0%

Average Annual Job Openings Through 2016: 17,114

Best-Paying Industries: Finance and Insurance; Professional, Scientific, and Technical Services.

Best-Paying Metro Areas: Boston-Cambridge-Quincy, MA-NH; Bridgeport-Stamford-Norwalk, CT; Chicago-Naperville-Joliet, IL-IN-WI; Cincinnati-Middletown, OH-KY-IN; Dallas–Fort Worth–Arlington, TX; Denver-Aurora, CO; Detroit-Warren-Livonia, MI; Hartford–West Hartford–East Hartford, CT; Houston–Sugar Land–Baytown, TX; Los Angeles–Long Beach–Santa Ana, CA; New York–Northern New Jersey–Long Island, NY-NJ-PA; Pittsburgh, PA; San Francisco–Oakland–Fremont, CA; Seattle-Tacoma-Bellevue, WA; St. Louis, MO-IL; Washington-Arlington-Alexandria, DC-VA-MD-WV.

© JIST Works

Six-Figure Niche-Industry Jobs

(At least 10% of workers in the best-paying industries earn more than $100,000.)

Accountants and Auditors

Examine, analyze, and interpret accounting records for the purpose of giving advice or preparing statements. Install or advise on systems of recording costs or other financial and budgetary data.

Personality Code: CEI

College Majors: Accounting; Accounting and Business/Management; Accounting and Computer Science; Accounting and Finance; Auditing; Taxation.

Median Annual Earnings: $57,060

Highly Paid Workforce: Out of a total salaried workforce of 1,115,010, 111,501 people (10%) earn more than $98,220.

Annual Job Growth Through 2016: 17.7%

Average Annual Job Openings Through 2016: 134,463

Best-Paying Industries: Professional, Scientific, and Technical Services.

Credit Analysts

Analyze current credit data and financial statements of individuals or firms to determine the degree of risk involved in extending credit or lending money. Prepare reports with this credit information for use in decision-making.

Personality Code: CE

College Majors: Accounting; Credit Management; Finance, General.

Median Annual Earnings: $54,580

Highly Paid Workforce: Out of a total salaried workforce of 70,890, 7,089 people (10%) earn more than $105,850.

Annual Job Growth Through 2016: 1.9%

Average Annual Job Openings Through 2016: 3,180

Best-Paying Industries: Finance and Insurance; Information; Professional, Scientific, and Technical Services; Retail Trade.

© JIST Works

Employment, Recruitment, and Placement Specialists

Recruit and place workers. (Also included in the Enterprising career track.)

Personality Code: ESC

College Majors: Human Resources Management/Personnel Administration, General; Labor and Industrial Relations.

Median Annual Earnings: $44,380

Highly Paid Workforce: Out of a total salaried workforce of 193,620, 19,362 people (10%) earn more than $85,410.

Annual Job Growth Through 2016: 18.4%

Average Annual Job Openings Through 2016: 33,588

Best-Paying Industries: Professional, Scientific, and Technical Services.

Financial Analysts

Conduct quantitative analyses of information affecting investment programs of public or private institutions.

Personality Code: CIE

College Majors: Accounting and Business/Management; Accounting and Finance; Finance, General.

Median Annual Earnings: $70,400

Highly Paid Workforce: Out of a total salaried workforce of 228,300, 57,075 people (25%) earn more than $95,580 and 22,830 (10%) earn more than $137,210.

Annual Job Growth Through 2016: 33.8%

Average Annual Job Openings Through 2016: 29,317

Best-Paying Industries: Administrative and Support and Waste Management and Remediation Services; Finance and Insurance; Information; Management of Companies and Enterprises; Manufacturing; Mining; Professional, Scientific, and Technical Services; Real Estate and Rental and Leasing; Utilities; Wholesale Trade.

Financial Examiners

Enforce or ensure compliance with laws and regulations governing financial and securities institutions and financial and real estate transactions. May examine, verify correctness of, or establish authenticity of records. (Also included in the Enterprising career track.)

Personality Code: EC

College Majors: Accounting; Taxation.

Median Annual Earnings: $66,670

Highly Paid Workforce: Out of a total salaried workforce of 25,510, 6,378 people (25%) earn more than $93,650 and 2,551 (10%) earn more than $122,050.

Annual Job Growth Through 2016: 10.7%

Average Annual Job Openings Through 2016: 2,449

Best-Paying Industries: Federal, State, and Local Government; Finance and Insurance; Management of Companies and Enterprises; Professional, Scientific, and Technical Services.

Loan Officers

Evaluate, authorize, or recommend approval of commercial, real estate, or credit loans. Advise borrowers on financial status and methods of payments. Includes mortgage loan officers and agents, collection analysts, loan servicing officers, and loan underwriters.

Personality Code: CES

College Majors: Credit Management; Finance, General.

Median Annual Earnings: $53,000

Highly Paid Workforce: Out of a total salaried workforce of 356,990, 35,699 people (10%) earn more than $106,130.

Annual Job Growth Through 2016: 11.5%

Average Annual Job Openings Through 2016: 54,237

Best-Paying Industries: Administrative and Support and Waste Management and Remediation Services; Finance and Insurance; Management of Companies and Enterprises; Professional, Scientific, and Technical Services; Real Estate and Rental and Leasing.

© JIST Works

Logisticians

Analyze and coordinate the logistical functions of a firm or organization. Responsible for the entire life cycle of a product, including acquisition, distribution, internal allocation, delivery, and final disposal of resources. (Also included in the Enterprising career track.)

Personality Code: EC

College Majors: Logistics and Materials Management; Operations Management and Supervision; Transportation/Transportation Management.

Median Annual Earnings: $64,250

Highly Paid Workforce: Out of a total salaried workforce of 90,340, 9,034 people (10%) earn more than $98,680.

Annual Job Growth Through 2016: 17.3%

Average Annual Job Openings Through 2016: 9,671

Best-Paying Industries: Federal, State, and Local Government; Information; Management of Companies and Enterprises; Professional, Scientific, and Technical Services; Wholesale Trade.

Management Analysts

Conduct organizational studies and evaluations, design systems and procedures, conduct work simplifications and measurement studies, and prepare operations and procedures manuals to assist management in operating more efficiently and effectively. Includes program analysts and management consultants. (Also included in the Enterprising career track.)

Personality Code: IEC

College Majors: Business Administration and Management, General; Business/Commerce, General.

Median Annual Earnings: $71,150

Highly Paid Workforce: Out of a total salaried workforce of 499,640, 124,910 people (25%) earn more than $96,400 and 49,964 (10%) earn more than $131,870.

Annual Job Growth Through 2016: 21.9%

Average Annual Job Openings Through 2016: 125,669

Best-Paying Industries: Administrative and Support and Waste Management and Remediation Services; Construction; Educational Services; Finance and Insurance; Information; Management of Companies and Enterprises; Manufacturing; Mining; Other Services (Except Public Administration); Professional, Scientific, and Technical Services; Real Estate and Rental and Leasing; Retail Trade; Transportation and Warehousing; Utilities; Wholesale Trade.

Market Research Analysts

Research market conditions in local, regional, or national areas to determine potential sales of a product or service. May gather information on competitors, prices, sales, and methods of marketing and distribution. May use survey results to create a marketing campaign based on regional preferences and buying habits. (Also included in the Enterprising career track.)

Personality Code: IEC

College Majors: Applied Economics; Business/Managerial Economics; Econometrics and Quantitative Economics; Economics, General; International Economics; Marketing Research.

Median Annual Earnings: $60,300

Highly Paid Workforce: Out of a total salaried workforce of 220,740, 55,185 people (25%) earn more than $85,760 and 22,074 (10%) earn more than $113,390.

Annual Job Growth Through 2016: 20.1%

Average Annual Job Openings Through 2016: 45,015

Best-Paying Industries: Administrative and Support and Waste Management and Remediation Services; Construction; Finance and Insurance; Information; Management of Companies and Enterprises; Manufacturing; Professional, Scientific, and Technical Services; Utilities; Wholesale Trade.

Public Relations Specialists

Engage in promoting or creating good will for individuals, groups, or organizations by writing or selecting favorable publicity material and releasing it through various communications media. May prepare and arrange displays and make speeches. (Also included in the Enterprising career track.)

Personality Code: EAS

© JIST Works

College Majors: Communication Studies/Speech Communication and Rhetoric; Family and Consumer Sciences/Human Sciences Communication; Health Communication; Political Communication; Public Relations/Image Management.

Median Annual Earnings: $49,800

Highly Paid Workforce: Out of a total salaried workforce of 225,880, 22,588 people (10%) earn more than $94,620.

Annual Job Growth Through 2016: 17.6%

Average Annual Job Openings Through 2016: 51,216

Best-Paying Industries: Manufacturing; Professional, Scientific, and Technical Services; Utilities; Wholesale Trade.

Six-Figure Niche-Location Jobs

None.

Chapter 7

The Distributive Career Track to a $100,000 Job

The Distributive career track leads to work in the fields of sales, purchasing, and advertising.

Every business needs customers or clients for its products or services, so there will always be a need for workers who can make these connections. Persistent and persuasive sales workers can earn six-figure commissions, especially if they sell big-ticket items. Salesworkers need to do more than just communicate with potential clients. They analyze sales statistics; prepare reports; and handle administrative duties, such as filing expense accounts, scheduling appointments, and making travel plans. They also read about new and existing products and monitor the sales, prices, and products of their competitors.

There usually are no formal educational requirements for working in sales, but sometimes the nature of what you sell requires licensure (for example, in insurance) or bachelor's-level education in a field such as engineering or finance. To succeed in sales, you also need to keep up to date with developments in your industry. Some employers organize and pay for seminars to train salesworkers, but you may have to take the initiative in researching the field.

Purchasing agents work the other side of the street, buying goods and services for their organization; they evaluate the quality of potential purchases and get the best price. Advertising is related to sales because it helps create customers for products and services.

Your Strategy for Getting on the Distributive Career Track

Realistic and Investigative

Of the 12 Distributive jobs included in this book, none is related to the Realistic or Investigative personality types except Sales Engineers, which has the personality code ERI. The usual entry route for this occupation is to get an engineering degree, followed by on-the-job sales training. It is possible to hold this job title with a background in another science, such as chemistry.

High school students aiming for this career goal should take college-prep science courses, plus math through at least pre-calculus. Summer jobs involving sales can be helpful.

College students with this goal usually major in engineering. Best earnings prospects are in high-demand specializations such as petroleum engineering. Business coursework and summer sales jobs also impart lucrative skills.

Experienced workers with technical skills in engineering or another scientific field may move from the Scientific career track into this occupation. Usually at least a bachelor's degree in your field is expected, but in some cases you may have acquired good technical skills with less formal preparation. Relevant leisure activities, such as selling tickets for a charity gala, may help both you and your employer gauge your aptitude for sales. Your employer may train you in selling by teaming you with an experienced sales engineer. It will be important for you to keep up to date with technology as you continue to work in this occupation, and specialized knowledge can lead to higher income. Opportunities for self-employment are very limited.

Artistic

In the Distributive career track, advertising is one field that appeals to the Artistic personality type and has potential for high earnings. Although the work tasks and environment are mostly commercial, the jobs offer opportunities to be involved in the creative process. Best preparation is to get a bachelor's degree in business or journalism and, through work experience, move into management. Only the most highly skilled Advertising Sales Agents in the biggest media markets earn six figures, so this job is best viewed as a stepping-stone for those who aspire to become Advertising and Promotions Managers.

© JIST Works

High school students can prepare by taking courses in art and in college-prep English. Work on the high school newspaper and in sales-related summer jobs is also helpful.

College students should take courses and perhaps major in journalism, advertising, or public relations. The college newspaper may offer opportunities for writing or for selling advertising. A summer job that involves sales, writing, or design is also a good idea. A master's degree in business with a specialization in advertising can help against the keen competition you may expect for a position in management.

Experienced workers who have sold other products or services may qualify for a job selling advertisements for newspapers, radio, or other media. Nonsales routes to management are from positions in copy writing, public relations, or purchasing, for which a bachelor's degree is the usual preparation. The best-paying positions are usually with large companies that specialize in advertising, as opposed to the advertising department of a company. Those who want to remain involved in the creative process usually earn less, unless they have truly unique skills, in which case they might be considered to be in the Technician/Artisan career track (for example, highly skilled Multi-Media Artists and Animators).

Social

Successful salesworkers usually have excellent people skills and like working with the public. This section covers First-Line Supervisors/Managers of Non-Retail Sales Workers. It also covers Agents and Business Managers of Artists, Performers, and Athletes.

High school students can prepare for these careers by taking courses such as math, accounting, and business computer applications that will prepare them to study business in college. Summer jobs involving sales or customer service are also useful experience. Those interested in being Agents and Business Managers of Artists, Performers, and Athletes may also want to take courses and participate in extracurricular activities relating to the arts or sports so they understand the industry they will be working in.

College students should take courses and perhaps major in finance, insurance, marketing, or business administration and should pursue summer jobs in sales or customer service. Those who want to work as agents for performers should continue to acquire experience in the arts or sports.

College graduates and *experienced workers* receive on-the-job training in the sales practices of the industry that hires them, usually by being teamed with

© JIST Works

an experienced salesworker. After some experience in sales, they may be able to compete for a job managing salesworkers, which usually requires additional training, perhaps in company-administered classes. Agents and Business Managers of Artists, Performers, and Athletes may get their start by working as an assistant in an agency, handling a variety of office tasks, including researching the market for the clients being represented. As they learn the business and make contacts, they may open their own agency.

Enterprising

All jobs in the Distributive track have Enterprising as a primary or secondary personality type. Look at the sections of this chapter that cover the other personality types to see what careers combine Enterprising with other types.

Conventional

Work in sales or purchasing offers several six-figure opportunities in jobs with Conventional as a primary or secondary type. This section covers Insurance Sales Agents; Purchasing Agents, Except Wholesale, Retail, and Farm Products; Real Estate Brokers; Real Estate Sales Agents; Sales Representatives, Wholesale and Manufacturing, Except Technical and Scientific Products; Sales Representatives, Wholesale and Manufacturing, Technical and Scientific Products; and Securities, Commodities, and Financial Services Sales Agents.

High school students should think about what industry interests them and gain some background knowledge and skills through coursework and extra-curricular activities. For example, students interested in technology may prepare for a career in technical sales by studying science and math and participating in a science club. This strategy leaves open the possibility of diverting to the Scientific career track. Similarly, those interested in fashion, agriculture, automobiles, sports, health care, or business in general may build their skills in these subjects with an eye toward a sales career while leaving open the possibility of working instead as a professional, a technician, a business specialist, a manager, or an academic. Summer jobs involving sales or customer service are valuable experience.

College students can continue to acquire knowledge and skills within a particular field by choosing an appropriate major. For example, a major in agriculture or agricultural business would be a good choice for someone who wants to sell agricultural equipment or supplies. It also leaves open the possibility of using the major for some other purpose, such as managing an agricultural operation or trading agricultural commodities. No matter what your major is, some courses in business subjects will be useful for understanding how the business world works and as preparation for possible career moves in the future. Summer jobs and internships in the targeted industry or in sales are also good to have on your resume.

Experienced workers can parlay their knowledge of an industry into a sales job if they are persuasive, goal-oriented, and have good people skills. Experience in volunteer sales roles, such as selling tickets for a charity event, can demonstrate these skills. A college degree is helpful for technical sales but often is not necessary. The company that hires you usually trains you through in-house classes and teaming up with an experienced salesworker. Real Estate Sales Agents come from a variety of backgrounds (including college majors in real estate), but all must study for and pass a licensing exam. Knowledge of the community is also very valuable. This field is highly competitive, and only a few very talented and persistent workers achieve high earnings or advance to become Real Estate Brokers, who are licensed to manage their own real estate business. College grads with a degree in finance may be hired as investment analysts to produce "pitchbooks"—information booklets used to sell investment products. Later they may be promoted to supervising entry-level workers. Those who want to be Insurance Sales Agents or Securities, Commodities, and Financial Services Sales Agents need to take specialized courses and pass state licensing exams. In the insurance and securities business, someone who represents one insurer or financial company is called an agent, whereas someone who helps clients choose between several companies is a broker. Many states require separate licensure for agents and brokers, and sometimes for different kinds of investment vehicles or insurance.

Achieving Six Figures in the Distributive Track

Many of the best-paid salesworkers are those who sell high-priced products and services, so one strategy to high earnings in this track is to get an engineering or science degree and sell technical products. Another strategy is to study business, get experience working with a business service (such as accounting or financial management), and then sell that business service or a related one.

Success in sales also depends on your selling skills: how to approach customers, how to listen to them, how to identify their needs. Some college

© JIST Works

courses in sales technique are available, and some training companies offer one- or two-day programs that teach these skills. Before you sign up for such a course or program, be sure to speak to people who have completed the training and find out whether or not they consider the experience helpful and worth the expense.

It also helps to start your sales career with a company that will give you excellent training. Some employers have a reputation for nurturing sales talent with both new hires and experienced sales staff. Talk to the human resources department of a company you're considering and ask about what sort of training they give to salesworkers. Also talk to experienced workers about their careers. A company that provides outstanding training not only helps you succeed while you work for them, but also adds luster to your resume.

Moving On to Other Career Tracks

For those who don't start off on the Managerial career track, experience in sales can be a good stepping-stone to a managerial position. Successful salesworkers with organizational ability may be promoted to supervising other salesworkers. With experience in this supervisory role, and perhaps with additional formal coursework or training, supervisors of salesworkers may be asked to take on other managerial roles. In some industries and companies it is common practice to start managers in sales roles so they will learn about the needs of the market and the psychology of customers.

In some fields it is possible to move from a sales role into the Entrepreneurial track by starting a business that exists entirely for the purpose of making sales. For example, successful Real Estate Sales Agents with an entrepreneurial flair can pass the licensing exam to become Real Estate Brokers and open their own real estate brokerage (often a franchise of a nationally known firm). Insurance Sales Agents, Advertising Sales Agents, and Securities, Commodities, and Financial Services Sales Agents with the right skills and ambitions may follow a similar path.

Characteristics of Six-Figure Distributive Jobs

Highest-Level Skills

Negotiation; Management of Financial Resources; Persuasion; Service Orientation; Time Management.

Highest-Level Work Activities

Selling or Influencing Others; Communicating with Persons Outside the Organization; Resolving Conflicts and Negotiating with Others; Establishing and Maintaining Interpersonal Relationships; Performing for or Working Directly with the Public.

Most Important Knowledges

Sales and Marketing; Economics and Accounting; Customer and Personal Service; Administration and Management; Mathematics.

Most Important Work Contexts

Telephone; Contact with Others; Face-to-Face Discussions; Structured versus Unstructured Work; Freedom to Make Decisions.

Most Important Work Needs

Autonomy; Recognition; Responsibility; Variety; Working Conditions.

Most Important Work Styles

Integrity; Dependability; Initiative; Attention to Detail; Persistence.

Facts About Six-Figure Distributive Jobs

Six-Figure Occupations

(At least 25% of the workers earn more than $100,000.)

Advertising and Promotions Managers

Plan and direct advertising policies and programs or produce collateral materials, such as posters, contests, coupons, or give-aways, to create extra interest in the purchase of a product or service for a department, an entire organization, or on an account basis. (Also included in the Managerial career track.)

Personality Code: EAC

College Majors: Advertising; Marketing/Marketing Management, General; Public Relations/Image Management.

© JIST Works

Median Annual Earnings: $78,250

Highly Paid Workforce: Out of a total salaried workforce of 36,300, 18,150 people (50%) earn more than $78,250 and 9,075 (25%) earn more than $115,910.

Annual Job Growth Through 2016: 6.2%

Average Annual Job Openings Through 2016: 2,955

Best-Paying Industries: Finance and Insurance; Information; Management of Companies and Enterprises; Manufacturing; Other Services (Except Public Administration); Professional, Scientific, and Technical Services; Wholesale Trade.

Best-Paying Metro Areas: Atlanta–Sandy Springs–Marietta, GA; Chicago-Naperville-Joliet, IL-IN-WI; Los Angeles–Long Beach–Santa Ana, CA; New York–Northern New Jersey–Long Island, NY-NJ-PA.

Agents and Business Managers of Artists, Performers, and Athletes

Represent and promote artists, performers, and athletes to prospective employers. May handle contract negotiation and other business matters for clients. (Also included in the Enterprising career track.)

Personality Code: ES

College Majors: Arts Management; Purchasing, Procurement/ Acquisitions and Contracts Management.

Median Annual Earnings: $66,440

Highly Paid Workforce: Out of a total salaried workforce of 11,680, 2,920 people (25%) earn more than $103,440.

Annual Job Growth Through 2016: 9.6%

Average Annual Job Openings Through 2016: 3,940

Best-Paying Industries: Arts, Entertainment, and Recreation.

Best-Paying Metro Areas: Los Angeles–Long Beach–Santa Ana, CA; New York–Northern New Jersey–Long Island, NY-NJ-PA.

Real Estate Brokers

Operate real estate office or work for commercial real estate firm, over-seeing real estate transactions. Other duties usually include selling real

© JIST Works

estate or renting properties and arranging loans. (Also included in the Enterprising career track.)

Personality Code: EC

College Majors: Real Estate.

Median Annual Earnings: $58,860

Highly Paid Workforce: Out of a total salaried workforce of 49,270, 12,318 people (25%) earn more than $100,570.

Annual Job Growth Through 2016: 11.1%

Average Annual Job Openings Through 2016: 18,689

Best-Paying Industries: Construction; Real Estate and Rental and Leasing.

Best-Paying Metro Areas: Los Angeles–Long Beach–Santa Ana, CA; Miami–Fort Lauderdale–Miami Beach, FL; New York–Northern New Jersey–Long Island, NY-NJ-PA; Phoenix-Mesa-Scottsdale, AZ; San Francisco–Oakland–Fremont, CA.

Sales Engineers

Sell business goods or services, the selling of which requires a technical background equivalent to a baccalaureate degree in engineering. (Also included in the Engineering career track.)

Personality Code: ERI

College Majors: Aerospace Engineering; Agricultural Engineering; Chemical Engineering; Computer Engineering; Construction Engineering; Electrical, Electronics and Communications Engineering; Environmental Engineering; Forest Engineering; Industrial Engineering; Manufacturing Engineering; Materials Engineering; Mechanical Engineering; Metallurgical Engineering; Mining and Mineral Engineering; Nuclear Engineering; Petroleum Engineering; Transportation and Highway Engineering; Water Resources Engineering; others.

Median Annual Earnings: $80,270

Highly Paid Workforce: Out of a total salaried workforce of 75,940, 18,985 people (25%) earn more than $104,240.

Annual Job Growth Through 2016: 8.5%

Average Annual Job Openings Through 2016: 7,371

© JIST Works

Best-Paying Industries: Information; Professional, Scientific, and Technical Services; Retail Trade.

Best-Paying Metro Areas: Boston-Cambridge-Quincy, MA-NH; Detroit-Warren-Livonia, MI; Houston–Sugar Land–Baytown, TX; Los Angeles–Long Beach–Santa Ana, CA; Minneapolis–St. Paul–Bloomington, MN-WI; New York–Northern New Jersey–Long Island, NY-NJ-PA; Portland-Vancouver-Beaverton, OR-WA; Sacramento–Arden-Arcade–Roseville, CA; San Diego–Carlsbad–San Marcos, CA; San Francisco–Oakland–Fremont, CA; San Jose–Sunnyvale–Santa Clara, CA; Washington-Arlington-Alexandria, DC-VA-MD-WV.

Securities, Commodities, and Financial Services Sales Agents

Buy and sell securities in investment and trading firms or call upon businesses and individuals to sell financial services. Provide financial services, such as loan, tax, and securities counseling. May advise securities customers about such things as stocks, bonds, and market conditions. (Also included in the Enterprising career track.)

Personality Code: EC

College Majors: Business and Personal/Financial Services Marketing Operations; Financial Planning and Services; Investments and Securities.

Median Annual Earnings: $68,430

Highly Paid Workforce: Out of a total salaried workforce of 268,480, 134,240 people (50%) earn more than $68,430 and 67,120 (25%) earn more than $122,260.

Annual Job Growth Through 2016: 24.8%

Average Annual Job Openings Through 2016: 47,750

Best-Paying Industries: Administrative and Support and Waste Management and Remediation Services; Finance and Insurance; Management of Companies and Enterprises.

Best-Paying Metro Areas: Austin–Round Rock, TX; Baltimore-Towson, MD; Boston-Cambridge-Quincy, MA-NH; Bridgeport-Stamford-Norwalk, CT; Buffalo–Niagara Falls, NY; Charlotte-Gastonia-Concord, NC-SC; Chicago-Naperville-Joliet, IL-IN-WI; Dallas–Fort Worth–Arlington, TX; Denver-Aurora, CO; Detroit-Warren-Livonia, MI; Houston–Sugar Land–Baytown, TX; Indianapolis-Carmel, IN; Jacksonville, FL; Kansas City,

MO-KS; Los Angeles–Long Beach–Santa Ana, CA; Louisville–Jefferson County, KY-IN; Memphis, TN-MS-AR; Miami–Fort Lauderdale–Miami Beach, FL; Minneapolis–St. Paul–Bloomington, MN-WI; New York–Northern New Jersey–Long Island, NY-NJ-PA; Philadelphia-Camden-Wilmington, PA-NJ-DE-MD; Pittsburgh, PA; Portland-Vancouver-Beaverton, OR-WA; Providence–Fall River–Warwick, RI-MA; Richmond, VA; Salt Lake City, UT; San Diego–Carlsbad–San Marcos, CA; San Francisco–Oakland–Fremont, CA; San Jose–Sunnyvale–Santa Clara, CA; Seattle-Tacoma-Bellevue, WA; Trenton-Ewing, NJ.

Six-Figure Niche-Industry Jobs

(At least 10% of workers in the best-paying industries earn more than $100,000.)

First-Line Supervisors/Managers of Non-Retail Sales Workers

Directly supervise and coordinate activities of sales workers other than retail sales workers. May perform duties such as budgeting, accounting, and personnel work in addition to supervisory duties. (Also included in the Managerial career track.)

Personality Code: ECS

College Majors: Business, Management, Marketing, and Related Support Services, Other; General Merchandising, Sales, and Related Marketing Operations, Other; Special Products Marketing Operations; Specialized Merchandising, Sales, and Related Marketing Operations, Other.

Median Annual Earnings: $67,020

Highly Paid Workforce: Out of a total salaried workforce of 280,770, 70,193 people (25%) earn more than $96,240.

Annual Job Growth Through 2016: 3.7%

Average Annual Job Openings Through 2016: 48,883

Best-Paying Industries: Accommodation and Food Service; Administrative and Support and Waste Management and Remediation Services; Arts, Entertainment, and Recreation; Construction; Finance and Insurance; Health Care and Social Assistance; Information; Management of Companies and Enterprises; Manufacturing; Other Services (Except Public Administration); Professional, Scientific, and Technical Services; Real Estate and Rental and Leasing; Retail Trade; Wholesale Trade.

© JIST Works

Real Estate Sales Agents

Rent, buy, or sell property for clients. Perform duties, such as study property listings, interview prospective clients, accompany clients to property site, discuss conditions of sale, and draw up real estate contracts. Include agents who represent buyer. (Also included in the Enterprising career track.)

Personality Code: EC

College Majors: Real Estate.

Median Annual Earnings: $40,600

Highly Paid Workforce: Out of a total salaried workforce of 172,030, 17,203 people (10%) earn more than $106,790.

Annual Job Growth Through 2016: 10.6%

Average Annual Job Openings Through 2016: 61,232

Best-Paying Industries: Administrative and Support and Waste Management and Remediation Services; Construction; Finance and Insurance; Management of Companies and Enterprises; Mining; Real Estate and Rental and Leasing.

Sales Representatives, Wholesale and Manufacturing, Except Technical and Scientific Products

Sell goods for wholesalers or manufacturers to businesses or groups of individuals. Work requires substantial knowledge of items sold.

Personality Code: CE

College Majors: Apparel and Accessories Marketing Operations; Business, Management, Marketing, and Related Support Services, Other; Fashion Merchandising; General Merchandising, Sales, and Related Marketing Operations, Other; Insurance; Sales, Distribution, and Marketing Operations, General; Special Products Marketing Operations; Specialized Merchandising, Sales, and Related Marketing Operations, Other.

Median Annual Earnings: $50,750

Highly Paid Workforce: Out of a total salaried workforce of 1,505,930, 150,593 people (10%) earn more than $103,910.

Annual Job Growth Through 2016: 8.4%

© JIST Works

Average Annual Job Openings Through 2016: 156,215

Best-Paying Industries: Construction; Finance and Insurance; Information; Management of Companies and Enterprises; Manufacturing; Professional, Scientific, and Technical Services; Utilities; Wholesale Trade.

Sales Representatives, Wholesale and Manufacturing, Technical and Scientific Products

Sell goods for wholesalers or manufacturers where technical or scientific knowledge is required in such areas as biology, engineering, chemistry, and electronics, normally obtained from at least two years of postsecondary education.

Personality Code: EC

College Majors: Business, Management, Marketing, and Related Support Services; Selling Skills and Sales Operations.

Median Annual Earnings: $68,270

Highly Paid Workforce: Out of a total salaried workforce of 403,320, 100,830 people (25%) earn more than $95,670.

Annual Job Growth Through 2016: 12.4%

Average Annual Job Openings Through 2016: 43,469

Best-Paying Industries: Administrative and Support and Waste Management and Remediation Services; Construction; Finance and Insurance; Health Care and Social Assistance; Information; Management of Companies and Enterprises; Manufacturing; Mining; Other Services (except Public Administration); Professional, Scientific, and Technical Services; Real Estate and Rental and Leasing; Retail Trade; Wholesale Trade.

Six-Figure Niche-Location Jobs

(At least 10% of workers in the best-paying metro areas earn more than $100,000.)

Advertising Sales Agents

Sell or solicit advertising, including graphic art, advertising space in publications, custom-made signs, or TV and radio advertising time. May obtain leases for outdoor advertising sites or persuade retailer to use sales promotion display items.

© JIST Works

Personality Code: ECA

College Majors: Advertising.

Median Annual Earnings: $42,820

Highly Paid Workforce: Out of a total salaried workforce of 161,440, 16,144 people (10%) earn more than $92,800.

Annual Job Growth Through 2016: 20.3%

Average Annual Job Openings Through 2016: 29,233

Best-Paying Metro Areas: Atlanta–Sandy Springs–Marietta, GA; Boston-Cambridge-Quincy, MA-NH; Charlotte-Gastonia-Concord, NC-SC; Detroit-Warren-Livonia, MI; Kansas City, MO-KS; Los Angeles–Long Beach–Santa Ana, CA; New York–Northern New Jersey–Long Island, NY-NJ-PA; Philadelphia-Camden-Wilmington, PA-NJ-DE-MD; Portland-Vancouver-Beaverton, OR-WA; Sacramento–Arden-Arcade–Roseville, CA; San Francisco–Oakland–Fremont, CA; Seattle-Tacoma-Bellevue, WA; Washington-Arlington-Alexandria, DC-VA-MD-WV.

Insurance Sales Agents

Sell life, property, casualty, health, automotive, or other types of insurance. May refer clients to independent brokers, work as independent broker, or be employed by an insurance company. (Also included in the Enterprising career track.)

Personality Code: ECS

College Majors: Insurance.

Median Annual Earnings: $44,110

Highly Paid Workforce: Out of a total salaried workforce of 321,920, 80,480 people (25%) earn more than $67,510 and 32,192 (10%) earn more than $113,190.

Annual Job Growth Through 2016: 12.9%

Average Annual Job Openings Through 2016: 64,162

Best-Paying Metro Areas: Albany-Schenectady-Troy, NY; Atlanta–Sandy Springs–Marietta, GA; Baltimore-Towson, MD; Birmingham-Hoover, AL; Boston-Cambridge-Quincy, MA-NH; Bridgeport-Stamford-Norwalk, CT; Charlotte-Gastonia-Concord, NC-SC; Chicago-Naperville-Joliet, IL-IN-WI; Cincinnati-Middletown, OH-KY-IN; Cleveland-Elyria-Mentor, OH;

© JIST Works

Dallas–Fort Worth–Arlington, TX; Denver-Aurora, CO; Detroit-Warren-Livonia, MI; Grand Rapids–Wyoming, MI; Hartford–West Hartford–East Hartford, CT; Indianapolis-Carmel, IN; Kansas City, MO-KS; Las Vegas–Paradise, NV; Los Angeles–Long Beach–Santa Ana, CA; Louisville–Jefferson County, KY-IN; Memphis, TN-MS-AR; Milwaukee–Waukesha–West Allis, WI; Minneapolis–St. Paul–Bloomington, MN-WI; New York–Northern New Jersey–Long Island, NY-NJ-PA; Orlando-Kissimmee, FL; Philadelphia-Camden-Wilmington, PA-NJ-DE-MD; Phoenix-Mesa-Scottsdale, AZ; Pittsburgh, PA; Portland-Vancouver-Beaverton, OR-WA; Riverside–San Bernardino–Ontario, CA; Sacramento–Arden-Arcade–Roseville, CA; Salt Lake City, UT; San Diego–Carlsbad–San Marcos, CA; San Francisco–Oakland–Fremont, CA; San Jose–Sunnyvale–Santa Clara, CA; Seattle-Tacoma-Bellevue, WA; St. Louis, MO-IL; Tampa–St. Petersburg–Clearwater, FL; Tulsa, OK; Virginia Beach–Norfolk–Newport News, VA-NC; Washington-Arlington-Alexandria, DC-VA-MD-WV.

Purchasing Agents, Except Wholesale, Retail, and Farm Products

Purchase machinery, equipment, tools, parts, supplies, or services necessary for the operation of an establishment. Purchase raw or semi-finished materials for manufacturing. Include contract specialists, field contractors, purchasers, price analysts, tooling coordinators, and media buyers.

Personality Code: CE

College Majors: Merchandising and Buying Operations; Sales, Distribution, and Marketing Operations, General.

Median Annual Earnings: $52,460

Highly Paid Workforce: Out of a total salaried workforce of 281,950, 28,195 people (10%) earn more than $86,860.

Annual Job Growth Through 2016: 0.1%

Average Annual Job Openings Through 2016: 22,349

Best-Paying Metro Areas: Detroit-Warren-Livonia, MI; Washington-Arlington-Alexandria, DC-VA-MD-WV.

© JIST Works

Chapter 8

The Engineering Career Track to a $100,000 Job

E ngineers apply the principles of science and mathematics to develop economical solutions to technical problems. Their work is the link between scientific discoveries and the commercial applications that meet the needs of society and consumers. Much of our economy depends on the work of engineers, yet the volume of graduates in this career track has not kept pace with the increasing need for workers. Therefore, the Engineering track has great potential for those who are willing and able to master the challenging curriculum.

Your Strategy for Getting on the Engineering Career Track

Realistic and Investigative

Of the 16 Engineering jobs included in this book, all but two combine the Realistic and Investigative personality types. One that does not, Industrial Engineers, does have Investigative as its primary type. Only Cost Estimators is linked to neither the R nor I type (see the **Conventional** section of this chapter).

High school students should take as much math and science as possible, including computer science. Independent research projects are useful experience.

College students should major in an engineering field, although some graduates of science majors find work as engineers. A bachelor's degree is required for almost all entry-level engineering jobs. Most engineering programs involve a concentration of study in an engineering specialty, along with courses in both mathematics and the physical and life sciences. Many programs also include courses in general engineering. A design course, sometimes accompanied by a computer or laboratory class or both, is part of the curriculum of most programs. Check to ensure that your college's program is accredited by the Accreditation Board for Engineering and Technology (ABET) and that its mix of theory and industrial practices matches your career interests. Many engineering bachelor's programs require five years to complete. In some cases, the extra year is needed because the program includes cooperative work experience that can teach you valuable practical skills, create contacts with employers, and help finance your education. Graduate training is essential for engineering faculty positions and many research and development programs, but is not required for the majority of entry-level engineering jobs.

Beginning *college graduates* usually work under the supervision of experienced engineers and, in large companies, also may receive formal classroom or seminar-type training. As new engineers gain knowledge and experience, they are assigned more difficult projects with greater independence to develop designs, solve problems, and make decisions. *Experienced workers* trained in one engineering field sometimes may work in another field, especially one that is closely related. Engineers who offer their services directly to the public (most typically civil, electrical, mechanical, and chemical engineers) need to be licensed and then are called professional engineers (PE). This licensure generally requires a degree from an ABET-accredited engineering program, four years of relevant work experience, and successful completion of a state examination. Some engineers take the exam in two stages—one part during the last year of college or immediately after graduation and the remaining part after acquiring suitable work experience. Several states have imposed mandatory continuing education requirements for relicensure, and it is vitally important for all engineers to keep abreast of current developments in their field. Various certification programs are offered by professional organizations to allow engineers to demonstrate competency in their specific fields.

Artistic

None of the Engineering jobs has Artistic as a primary or secondary personality type. If you have an interest in combining art and technology, you may want to consider Multi-Media Artists and Animators, in the Technician/Artisan or Information Technology career track (chapter 10 or 14).

© JIST Works

Social

None of the Engineering jobs has Social as a primary or secondary personality type. However, it is a secondary type for Engineering Teachers, Postsecondary, an occupation in the Academic career track (see chapter 5). To prepare for this career goal, you should follow the suggestions in the **Realistic and Investigative** section of this chapter and continue your education through a master's and, even better, a doctorate.

Enterprising

Sales Engineers is the only Engineering job that has Enterprising as its primary personality type. These workers solve engineering problems so that buyers are able to use the products or services being sold. Details about preparing for this occupation may be found in chapter 7, which is on the Distributive career track.

Three other jobs have Enterprising as a secondary type. Of these, Cost Estimators is discussed in the **Conventional** section of this chapter; the other two (Industrial Engineers and Materials Engineers) are covered by the **Realistic and Investigative** section.

Conventional

Of the 16 Engineering jobs, only Cost Estimators has Conventional as its primary personality type. Many people enter this job through the Technician/Artisan career track, but the Engineering track can lead to an especially good-paying position, usually in manufacturing. Another nine Engineering jobs have Conventional as a secondary type, largely because of the importance of cost estimating as an engineering task. If you identify with this personality type, you may want to emphasize this aspect of engineering work while following the engineering preparation outlined in the **Realistic and Investigative** section of this chapter.

High school students should get the standard pre-engineering preparation.

College students should be sure to include one or more courses in cost estimation in their curriculum. (In some programs it is a requirement.) Civil, manufacturing, and industrial engineering may be the most appropriate specializations, but all branches of engineering require cost estimating.

Experienced workers in engineering may take college courses to improve their cost estimation skills or may enroll in an educational program offered by one of the relevant professional associations, such as the Association for the Advancement of Cost Engineering (AACE International) or the Society of Cost Estimating and Analysis (SCEA).

Achieving Six Figures in the Engineering Track

The most obvious way to earn the big bucks in the Engineering track is to choose a high-demand specialization, such as petroleum engineering. Studies also show that engineers who achieve licensure earn higher incomes. Engineers who have worked for several decades sometimes have trouble competing with recent graduates of engineering school, who are cheaper to hire and have cutting-edge technical skills. The experienced engineers often find they can advance only by taking on managerial duties and, eventually, a managerial job title. The transition need not be abrupt because engineers tend to work in teams and can take on supervisory tasks for the team gradually, as they gain experience.

Moving On to Other Career Tracks

The Managerial track is a popular route for engineers. A master's degree in business (MBA) can help, and some professional associations offer certification programs that teach managerial skills. Industrial Engineers are particularly well positioned to move into management because they focus on productivity and work closely with managers. Engineering Managers are covered by the Managerial track in chapter 11.

The occupation Sales Engineers can be considered to be in both the Distributive track and the Engineering track. Trained engineers may move into this occupation at any time in their careers.

Engineers with a flair for self-management and self-promotion may be able to succeed in the Entrepreneurial track by forming their own company. Some start-up companies develop a product; this is especially feasible for products, such as software, that do not require a large manufacturing facility. Other start-ups are consulting businesses offering engineering expertise on a temporary basis.

With a master's or doctoral degree, an engineer may move into the Academic track, teaching the subject and doing research in a college or university. A trail of published research articles is helpful, but it may not be necessary for those with expertise in a hot field that students are eager to study. Engineering teachers are among the best-paid in the Academic track.

© JIST Works

Characteristics of Six-Figure Engineering Jobs

Highest-Level Skills

Programming; Systems Analysis; Technology Design; Science; Operations Analysis.

Highest-Level Work Activities

Interacting with Computers; Drafting, Laying Out, and Specifying Technical Devices, Parts, and Equipment; Analyzing Data or Information; Thinking Creatively; Processing Information.

Most Important Knowledges

Engineering and Technology; Design; Computers and Electronics; Physics; Mathematics.

Most Important Work Contexts

Face-to-Face Discussions; Electronic Mail; Indoors, Environmentally Controlled; Importance of Being Exact or Accurate; Work with Work Group or Team.

Most Important Work Needs

Creativity; Ability Utilization; Social Status; Responsibility; Authority.

Most Important Work Styles

Analytical Thinking; Attention to Detail; Dependability; Cooperation; Integrity.

Facts About Six-Figure Engineering Jobs

Six-Figure Occupations

(At least 25% of the workers earn more than $100,000.)

Aerospace Engineers

Perform a variety of engineering work in designing, constructing, and testing aircraft, missiles, and spacecraft. May conduct basic and applied research to evaluate adaptability of materials and equipment to aircraft design and manufacture. May recommend improvements in testing equipment and techniques.

Personality Code: IR

College Majors: Aerospace, Aeronautical, and Astronautical Engineering.

Median Annual Earnings: $90,930

Highly Paid Workforce: Out of a total salaried workforce of 85,510, 42,755 people (50%) earn more than $90,930 and 21,378 (25%) earn more than $110,990.

Annual Job Growth Through 2016: 10.2%

Average Annual Job Openings Through 2016: 6,498

Best-Paying Industries: Administrative and Support and Waste Management and Remediation Services; Federal, State, and Local Government; Manufacturing; Professional, Scientific, and Technical Services.

Best-Paying Metro Areas: Dallas–Fort Worth–Arlington, TX; Denver-Aurora, CO; Houston–Sugar Land–Baytown, TX; Huntsville, AL; Palm Bay–Melbourne–Titusville, FL; Philadelphia-Camden-Wilmington, PA-NJ-DE-MD; Phoenix-Mesa-Scottsdale, AZ; San Diego–Carlsbad–San Marcos, CA; San Francisco–Oakland–Fremont, CA; San Jose–Sunnyvale–Santa Clara, CA; Seattle-Tacoma-Bellevue, WA; Virginia Beach–Norfolk–Newport News, VA-NC.

Chemical Engineers

Design chemical plant equipment and devise processes for manufacturing chemicals and products, such as gasoline, synthetic rubber, plastics, detergents, cement, paper, and pulp, by applying principles and technology of chemistry, physics, and engineering.

Personality Code: IR

College Majors: Chemical Engineering.

Median Annual Earnings: $81,500

Highly Paid Workforce: Out of a total salaried workforce of 28,780, 7,195 people (25%) earn more than $100,980.

Annual Job Growth Through 2016: 7.9%

© JIST Works

Average Annual Job Openings Through 2016: 2,111

Best-Paying Industries: Federal, State, and Local Government; Professional, Scientific, and Technical Services.

Best-Paying Metro Areas: Boston-Cambridge-Quincy, MA-NH; Houston–Sugar Land–Baytown, TX; New York–Northern New Jersey–Long Island, NY-NJ-PA; Philadelphia-Camden-Wilmington, PA-NJ-DE-MD.

Computer Hardware Engineers

Research, design, develop, and test computer or computer-related equipment for commercial, industrial, military, or scientific use. May supervise the manufacturing and installation of computer or computer-related equipment and components.

Personality Code: IRC

College Majors: Computer Engineering, General; Computer Hardware Engineering.

Median Annual Earnings: $91,860

Highly Paid Workforce: Out of a total salaried workforce of 79,330, 39,665 people (50%) earn more than $91,860 and 19,833 (25%) earn more than $115,140.

Annual Job Growth Through 2016: 4.6%

Average Annual Job Openings Through 2016: 3,572

Best-Paying Industries: Administrative and Support and Waste Management and Remediation Services; Federal, State, and Local Government; Information; Management of Companies and Enterprises; Manufacturing; Professional, Scientific, and Technical Services; Wholesale Trade.

Best-Paying Metro Areas: Atlanta–Sandy Springs–Marietta, GA; Austin–Round Rock, TX; Boston-Cambridge-Quincy, MA-NH; Boulder, CO; Chicago-Naperville-Joliet, IL-IN-WI; Dallas–Fort Worth–Arlington, TX; Houston–Sugar Land–Baytown, TX; Los Angeles–Long Beach–Santa Ana, CA; Minneapolis–St. Paul–Bloomington, MN-WI; New York–Northern New Jersey–Long Island, NY-NJ-PA; Sacramento–Arden-Arcade–Roseville, CA; San Diego–Carlsbad–San Marcos, CA; San Francisco–Oakland–Fremont, CA; San Jose–Sunnyvale–Santa Clara, CA; Washington-Arlington-Alexandria, DC-VA-MD-WV.

© JIST Works

Computer Software Engineers, Applications

Develop, create, and modify general computer applications software or specialized utility programs. Analyze user needs and develop software solutions. Design software or customize software for client use with the aim of optimizing operational efficiency. May analyze and design databases within an application area, working individually or coordinating database development as part of a team. (Also included in the Information Technology career track.)

Personality Code: IRC

College Majors: Artificial Intelligence and Robotics; Bioinformatics; Computer Engineering Technologies/Technician Training, Other; Computer Engineering, General; Computer Science; Computer Software Engineering; Information Technology; Medical Illustration and Informatics, Other; Medical Informatics.

Median Annual Earnings: $83,130

Highly Paid Workforce: Out of a total salaried workforce of 495,810, 123,953 people (25%) earn more than $102,710.

Annual Job Growth Through 2016: 44.6%

Average Annual Job Openings Through 2016: 58,690

Best-Paying Industries: Finance and Insurance; Information; Management of Companies and Enterprises; Manufacturing; Other Services (Except Public Administration); Professional, Scientific, and Technical Services; Real Estate and Rental and Leasing; Transportation and Warehousing; Wholesale Trade.

Best-Paying Metro Areas: Austin–Round Rock, TX; Baltimore-Towson, MD; Boston-Cambridge-Quincy, MA-NH; Boulder, CO; Bridgeport-Stamford-Norwalk, CT; Charlotte-Gastonia-Concord, NC-SC; Chicago-Naperville-Joliet, IL-IN-WI; Dallas–Fort Worth–Arlington, TX; Denver-Aurora, CO; Durham, NC; Houston–Sugar Land–Baytown, TX; Jacksonville, FL; Los Angeles–Long Beach–Santa Ana, CA; New York–Northern New Jersey–Long Island, NY-NJ-PA; Oxnard–Thousand Oaks–Ventura, CA; Philadelphia-Camden-Wilmington, PA-NJ-DE-MD; Portland-Vancouver-Beaverton, OR-WA; Raleigh-Cary, NC; Riverside–San Bernardino–Ontario, CA; San Diego–Carlsbad–San Marcos, CA; San Francisco–Oakland–Fremont, CA; San Jose–Sunnyvale–Santa Clara, CA; Seattle-Tacoma-Bellevue, WA; Trenton-Ewing, NJ; Tucson, AZ; Washington-Arlington-Alexandria, DC-VA-MD-WV; Worcester, MA-CT.

© JIST Works

Computer Software Engineers, Systems Software

Research, design, develop, and test operating systems–level software, compilers, and network distribution software for medical, industrial, military, communications, aerospace, business, scientific, and general computing applications. Set operational specifications and formulate and analyze software requirements. Apply principles and techniques of computer science, engineering, and mathematical analysis. (Also included in the Information Technology career track.)

Personality Code: ICR

College Majors: Artificial Intelligence and Robotics; Computer Engineering Technologies/Technician Training, Other; Computer Engineering, General; Computer Science; Information Science/Studies; Information Technology; System, Networking, and LAN/WAN Management/Manager Training.

Median Annual Earnings: $89,070

Highly Paid Workforce: Out of a total salaried workforce of 349,140, 87,285 people (25%) earn more than $109,320.

Annual Job Growth Through 2016: 28.2%

Average Annual Job Openings Through 2016: 33,139

Best-Paying Industries: Administrative and Support and Waste Management and Remediation Services; Finance and Insurance; Information; Management of Companies and Enterprises; Manufacturing; Professional, Scientific, and Technical Services; Retail Trade; Wholesale Trade.

Best-Paying Metro Areas: Albuquerque, NM; Austin–Round Rock, TX; Baltimore-Towson, MD; Boise City–Nampa, ID; Boston-Cambridge-Quincy, MA-NH; Boulder, CO; Bridgeport-Stamford-Norwalk, CT; Charlotte-Gastonia-Concord, NC-SC; Chicago-Naperville-Joliet, IL-IN-WI; Dallas–Fort Worth–Arlington, TX; Dayton, OH; Denver-Aurora, CO; Durham, NC; Hartford–West Hartford–East Hartford, CT; Houston–Sugar Land–Baytown, TX; Huntsville, AL; Los Angeles–Long Beach–Santa Ana, CA; Minneapolis–St. Paul–Bloomington, MN-WI; New York–Northern New Jersey–Long Island, NY-NJ-PA; Orlando-Kissimmee, FL; Palm Bay–Melbourne–Titusville, FL; Philadelphia-Camden-Wilmington, PA-NJ-DE-MD; Portland-Vancouver-Beaverton, OR-WA; Providence–Fall River–Warwick, RI-MA; Raleigh-Cary, NC; Richmond, VA; San

Diego–Carlsbad–San Marcos, CA; San Francisco–Oakland–Fremont, CA; San Jose–Sunnyvale–Santa Clara, CA; Seattle-Tacoma-Bellevue, WA; Washington-Arlington-Alexandria, DC-VA-MD-WV.

Electronics Engineers, Except Computer

Research, design, develop, and test electronic components and systems for commercial, industrial, military, or scientific use, utilizing knowledge of electronic theory and materials properties. Design electronic circuits and components for use in fields such as telecommunications, aerospace guidance and propulsion control, acoustics, or instruments and controls.

Personality Code: IR

College Majors: Electrical, Electronics and Communications Engineering.

Median Annual Earnings: $83,340

Highly Paid Workforce: Out of a total salaried workforce of 133,870, 33,468 people (25%) earn more than $102,820.

Annual Job Growth Through 2016: 3.7%

Average Annual Job Openings Through 2016: 5,699

Best-Paying Industries: Federal, State, and Local Government; Management of Companies and Enterprises; Manufacturing; Professional, Scientific, and Technical Services.

Best-Paying Metro Areas: Albuquerque, NM; Boston-Cambridge-Quincy, MA-NH; Colorado Springs, CO; Dallas–Fort Worth–Arlington, TX; Dayton, OH; Denver-Aurora, CO; Houston–Sugar Land–Baytown, TX; Huntsville, AL; Los Angeles–Long Beach–Santa Ana, CA; Minneapolis–St. Paul–Bloomington, MN-WI; New York–Northern New Jersey–Long Island, NY-NJ-PA; Oxnard–Thousand Oaks–Ventura, CA; Philadelphia-Camden-Wilmington, PA-NJ-DE-MD; Portland-Vancouver-Beaverton, OR-WA; Providence–Fall River–Warwick, RI-MA; San Diego–Carlsbad–San Marcos, CA; San Francisco–Oakland–Fremont, CA; San Jose–Sunnyvale–Santa Clara, CA; Washington-Arlington-Alexandria, DC-VA-MD-WV.

Nuclear Engineers

Conduct research on nuclear engineering problems or apply principles and theory of nuclear science to problems concerned with release, control, and utilization of nuclear energy and nuclear waste disposal.

© JIST Works

Personality Code: IRC

College Majors: Nuclear Engineering.

Median Annual Earnings: $94,420

Highly Paid Workforce: Out of a total salaried workforce of 14,300, 7,150 people (50%) earn more than $94,420 and 3,575 (25%) earn more than $111,900.

Annual Job Growth Through 2016: 7.2%

Average Annual Job Openings Through 2016: 1,046

Best-Paying Industries: Professional, Scientific, and Technical Services; Utilities.

Best-Paying Metro Areas: No metro area has a large number of six-figure workers.

Petroleum Engineers

Devise methods to improve oil and gas well production and determine the need for new or modified tool designs. Oversee drilling and offer technical advice to achieve economical and satisfactory progress.

Personality Code: IRC

College Majors: Petroleum Engineering.

Median Annual Earnings: $103,960

Highly Paid Workforce: Out of a total salaried workforce of 16,060, 8,030 people (50%) earn more than $103,960.

Annual Job Growth Through 2016: 5.2%

Average Annual Job Openings Through 2016: 1,016

Best-Paying Industries: Management of Companies and Enterprises; Manufacturing; Mining; Professional, Scientific, and Technical Services.

Best-Paying Metro Areas: Dallas–Fort Worth–Arlington, TX; Houston–Sugar Land–Baytown, TX.

Sales Engineers

Sell business goods or services, the selling of which requires a technical background equivalent to a baccalaureate degree in engineering. (Also included in the Distributive career track.)

© JIST Works

Personality Code: ERI

College Majors: Aerospace Engineering; Agricultural Engineering; Chemical Engineering; Computer Engineering; Construction Engineering; Electrical, Electronics and Communications Engineering; Environmental Engineering; Forest Engineering; Industrial Engineering; Manufacturing Engineering; Materials Engineering; Mechanical Engineering; Metallurgical Engineering; Mining and Mineral Engineering; Nuclear Engineering; Petroleum Engineering; Transportation and Highway Engineering; Water Resources Engineering; others.

Median Annual Earnings: $80,270

Highly Paid Workforce: Out of a total salaried workforce of 75,940, 18,985 people (25%) earn more than $104,240.

Annual Job Growth Through 2016: 8.5%

Average Annual Job Openings Through 2016: 7,371

Best-Paying Industries: Information; Professional, Scientific, and Technical Services; Retail Trade.

Best-Paying Metro Areas: Boston-Cambridge-Quincy, MA-NH; Detroit-Warren-Livonia, MI; Houston–Sugar Land–Baytown, TX; Los Angeles–Long Beach–Santa Ana, CA; Minneapolis–St. Paul–Bloomington, MN-WI; New York–Northern New Jersey–Long Island, NY-NJ-PA; Portland-Vancouver-Beaverton, OR-WA; Sacramento–Arden-Arcade–Roseville, CA; San Diego–Carlsbad–San Marcos, CA; San Francisco–Oakland–Fremont, CA; San Jose–Sunnyvale–Santa Clara, CA; Washington-Arlington-Alexandria, DC-VA-MD-WV.

Six-Figure Niche-Industry Jobs

(At least 10% of workers in the best-paying industries earn more than $100,000.)

Civil Engineers

Perform engineering duties in planning, designing, and overseeing construction and maintenance of building structures and facilities, such as roads, railroads, airports, bridges, harbors, channels, dams, irrigation projects, pipelines, power plants, water and sewage systems, and waste disposal units. Includes architectural, structural, traffic, ocean, and geo-technical engineers.

© JIST Works

Personality Code: RIC

College Majors: Civil Engineering, General; Civil Engineering, Other; Transportation and Highway Engineering; Water Resources Engineering.

Median Annual Earnings: $71,710

Highly Paid Workforce: Out of a total salaried workforce of 247,370, 24,737 people (10%) earn more than $109,100.

Annual Job Growth Through 2016: 18.0%

Average Annual Job Openings Through 2016: 15,979

Best-Paying Industries: Administrative and Support and Waste Management and Remediation Services; Construction; Management of Companies and Enterprises; Manufacturing; Professional, Scientific, and Technical Services; Real Estate and Rental and Leasing; Utilities.

Electrical Engineers

Design, develop, test, or supervise the manufacturing and installation of electrical equipment, components, or systems for commercial, industrial, military, or scientific use.

Personality Code: IR

College Majors: Electrical, Electronics, and Communications Engineering.

Median Annual Earnings: $79,240

Highly Paid Workforce: Out of a total salaried workforce of 148,800, 37,200 people (25%) earn more than $98,530.

Annual Job Growth Through 2016: 6.3%

Average Annual Job Openings Through 2016: 6,806

Best-Paying Industries: Administrative and Support and Waste Management and Remediation Services; Construction; Educational Services; Federal, State, and Local Government; Information; Management of Companies and Enterprises; Manufacturing; Professional, Scientific, and Technical Services; Utilities; Wholesale Trade.

Environmental Engineers

Design, plan, or perform engineering duties in the prevention, control, and remediation of environmental health hazards, utilizing various engineering disciplines. Work may include waste treatment, site remediation, or pollution control technology.

Personality Code: IRC

College Majors: Environmental/Environmental Health Engineering.

Median Annual Earnings: $72,350

Highly Paid Workforce: Out of a total salaried workforce of 51,210, 5,121 people (10%) earn more than $108,670.

Annual Job Growth Through 2016: 25.4%

Average Annual Job Openings Through 2016: 5,003

Best-Paying Industries: Administrative and Support and Waste Management and Remediation Services; Federal, State, and Local Government; Manufacturing; Professional, Scientific, and Technical Services.

Industrial Engineers

Design, develop, test, and evaluate integrated systems for managing industrial production processes, including human work factors, quality control, inventory control, logistics and material flow, cost analysis, and production coordination.

Personality Code: ICE

College Majors: Industrial Engineering.

Median Annual Earnings: $71,430

Highly Paid Workforce: Out of a total salaried workforce of 204,210, 20,421 people (10%) earn more than $104,490.

Annual Job Growth Through 2016: 20.3%

Average Annual Job Openings Through 2016: 11,272

Best-Paying Industries: Administrative and Support and Waste Management and Remediation Services; Construction; Federal, State, and Local Government; Information; Management of Companies and Enterprises; Manufacturing; Mining; Professional, Scientific, and Technical Services; Utilities; Wholesale Trade.

Materials Engineers

Evaluate materials and develop machinery and processes to manufacture materials for use in products that must meet specialized design and performance specifications. Develop new uses for known materials. Includes

© JIST Works

those working with composite materials or specializing in one type of material, such as graphite, metal and metal alloys, ceramics and glass, plastics and polymers, and naturally occurring materials.

Personality Code: IRE

College Majors: Ceramic Sciences and Engineering; Materials Engineering; Metallurgical Engineering.

Median Annual Earnings: $77,170

Highly Paid Workforce: Out of a total salaried workforce of 21,910, 5,478 people (25%) earn more than $95,940.

Annual Job Growth Through 2016: 4.0%

Average Annual Job Openings Through 2016: 1,390

Best-Paying Industries: Federal, State, and Local Government; Manufacturing; Professional, Scientific, and Technical Services; Wholesale Trade.

Mechanical Engineers

Perform engineering duties in planning and designing tools, engines, machines, and other mechanically functioning equipment. Oversee installation, operation, maintenance, and repair of such equipment as centralized heat, gas, water, and steam systems.

Personality Code: IRC

College Majors: Mechanical Engineering.

Median Annual Earnings: $72,300

Highly Paid Workforce: Out of a total salaried workforce of 222,330, 22,233 people (10%) earn more than $108,740.

Annual Job Growth Through 2016: 4.2%

Average Annual Job Openings Through 2016: 12,394

Best-Paying Industries: Administrative and Support and Waste Management and Remediation Services; Construction; Federal, State, and Local Government; Management of Companies and Enterprises; Manufacturing; Mining; Professional, Scientific, and Technical Services; Real Estate and Rental and Leasing; Utilities; Wholesale Trade.

© JIST Works

Six-Figure Niche-Location Jobs

(At least 10% of workers in the best-paying metro areas earn more than $100,000.)

Cost Estimators

Prepare cost estimates for product manufacturing, construction projects, or services to aid management in bidding on or determining price of product or service. May specialize according to particular service performed or type of product manufactured. (Also included in the Technician/Artisan career track.)

Personality Code: CE

College Majors: Business Administration and Management, General; Business/Commerce, General; Construction Engineering; Construction Engineering Technology/Technician Training; Manufacturing Engineering; Materials Engineering; Mechanical Engineering.

Median Annual Earnings: $54,920

Highly Paid Workforce: Out of a total salaried workforce of 219,070, 21,907 people (10%) earn more than $91,350.

Annual Job Growth Through 2016: 18.5%

Average Annual Job Openings Through 2016: 38,379

Best-Paying Metro Areas: Boston-Cambridge-Quincy, MA-NH; Chicago-Naperville-Joliet, IL-IN-WI; Detroit-Warren-Livonia, MI; Houston–Sugar Land–Baytown, TX; New York–Northern New Jersey–Long Island, NY-NJ-PA; San Francisco–Oakland–Fremont, CA; San Jose–Sunnyvale–Santa Clara, CA.

© JIST Works

Chapter 9

The Entrepreneurial Career Track to a $100,000 Job

E ntrepreneurs start up businesses and take on most of the responsibilities of running them. Compared to working for somebody else, this work arrangement means assuming more of the risks but also being able to claim more of the rewards. Normally the term is not used for people who hire out their own labor or expertise, such as a plumber or management consultant, but the term would be accurate for someone who starts a business that hires several plumbers or consultants, markets their services, schedules and bills for their work, and pays them. It would also apply to a plumber who has a sideline of selling plumbing supplies or a management consultant who also sells clients customized inventory-management software. Of course, you would not expect a plumber to start a management consulting business or a management consultant to start a plumbing service. Just as aspiring authors are told to write about what they know, entrepreneurs are usually most successful in a field where they have a lot of background.

Starting a business is complicated and requires a great amount of dedication. Most businesses require some level of investment to get started, and unless you personally have the necessary funds, you'll need to convince a banker or other investors to finance your startup. That requires a business plan, in which you spell out what product or service you intend to offer and how you will produce it, find a market for it, and distribute it. Guy Kawasaki, who has written several books about entrepreneurship, emphasizes that you need to be able to explain in 30 seconds what your company does. Usually you need to be able to fill a niche in the market that nobody else is filling.

You may need an office or production facilities and workers with appropriate skills. Sometimes a license, permit, or insurance is necessary. You may want to plan for how you will scale up the business if it is successful. These considerations are just a brief overview of the concerns that entrepreneurs have to address.

Success in entrepreneurship requires certain personal traits, such as believing in yourself and having the willingness to take risks. It's no coincidence that almost all of the 28 Entrepreneurial jobs in this book have Enterprising as their dominant personality type, and the few others have it as a secondary type. Guy Kawasaki observes that you may stretch the truth when promoting your business, even to the point of deceiving yourself about its likelihood of success, and therefore one of the greatest challenges is changing your mindset after the product ships and listening to what your customers tell you rather than hearing what you want to believe.

Strictly speaking, entrepreneurs are managers, but they have a unique work arrangement that differs from that of managers who are employed by somebody else's company, and they may have arrived in the Entrepreneurial career track from any of the other tracks.

This chapter focuses on 28 occupations for which the transition to the Entrepreneurial track is particularly suitable. Some other six-figure jobs not included in this chapter might also permit such a transition for workers who have a flair for self-motivation and self-promotion.

Your Strategy for Getting on the Entrepreneurial Career Track

Realistic

Of the 28 Entrepreneurial jobs included in this book, two have Realistic as a secondary personality type: Construction Managers and Engineering Managers. The usual route into both of these jobs is through the Managerial career track, which is covered in detail in chapter 11.

Those Construction Managers who transition to the Entrepreneurial track usually start up a business that supplies managerial services for construction projects or that contracts to do construction. The latter may do subcontracting for a specialization such as roofing, plumbing, electrical wiring, or paving. Starting a contracting business usually requires investments in tools, equipment, and building supplies, which can be substantial for heavy-duty tasks.

Some Engineering Managers with Entrepreneurial goals start up a firm that offers engineering consulting services to other businesses. Others launch

© JIST Works

a research and development business that invents new products or services. As in the construction business, this can require heavy investments, depending on the nature of the R&D and the scale of the marketing that is needed to reach buyers.

Investigative

Six of the 28 Entrepreneurial jobs have Investigative as a primary or secondary personality type. One of these, Engineering Managers, is covered in the **Realistic** section of this chapter. Another, Accountants and Auditors, is covered in the **Conventional** section. The remaining five jobs are Economists, Management Analysts, Market Research Analysts, and Operations Research Analysts. As the jobs' titles indicate, they appeal to people with an analytical mindset.

Economists and Operations Research Analysts are discussed in detail in chapter 13, which covers the Scientific track. They usually need to get graduate degrees and work experience before they can establish an Entrepreneurial career, most likely by starting up a consulting firm or by publishing research reports on the economy.

Management Analysts and Market Research Analysts are covered by chapter 6, which discusses the Bachelor's-in-Business track. Their usual route to entrepreneurship is to launch a consulting company. Some market researchers publish research reports on consumer attitudes and other marketing issues.

Artistic

The only Entrepreneurial job that has Artistic as a secondary personality type is Public Relations Managers, which is covered by chapter 11, about the Managerial career track. Those with managerial experience and a good network of business contacts may start up their own PR firm. Some specializations are crisis management, marketing, and media relations.

Social

Eight of the Entrepreneurial jobs have Social as a secondary personality type.

Four of these jobs are covered by chapter 11, about the Managerial career track: Compensation and Benefits Managers, General and Operations Managers, Medical and Health Services Managers, and Training and Development Managers. These workers generally shift to the

Entrepreneurial track by launching a business that offers management services in their specialization. For example, a training manager might start up a business to teach office-automation skills to clerical workers in companies that contract for these services. Similarly, someone with experience in health-care management might start up a business to provide visiting nurse services to home-bound people. General and Operations Managers work in all kinds of industries and find diverse entrepreneurial opportunities.

Two of these jobs are covered by chapter 7, about the Distributive track: Agents and Business Managers of Artists, Performers, and Athletes, and Insurance Sales Agents. These workers often gain experience working in an agency and then parlay their experience and contacts into an agency of their own. Insurance licensure requirements are discussed in chapter 7.

Chapter 6, about the Bachelor's-in-Business track, covers the remaining two jobs: Employment, Recruitment, and Placement Specialists, and Personal Financial Advisors. Experienced personnel recruiters can move into the Entrepreneurial track by setting up an agency. Companies in search of managers pay "head-hunting" agencies substantial fees for identifying and recruiting job candidates with the right mix of talents and experience. Other agencies specialize in workers with unusual technical skills. Personal Financial Advisors with entrepreneurial talent may set up a company to market financial-planning services to the public. Sometimes they combine these services with others, such as tax preparation. Usually they are not allowed to take their clients with them after they leave a firm, so they must start by finding new customers. Those who are reluctant to run the risks associated with an independent business may open a branch office of a large securities firm. Licensure requirements are discussed in chapter 6.

Enterprising

Twelve of the Entrepreneurial jobs are coded EC.

Many of these workers make various aspects of a business, or the organization as a whole, run with maximum efficiency and profitability. Logisticians (covered in chapter 6, about the Bachelor's-in-Business track) sometimes create consulting firms to help other businesses coordinate all the functions that make up the life cycle of a product.

Chapter 7, about the Distributive track, covers Real Estate Brokers; Real Estate Sales Agents; and Securities, Commodities, and Financial Services Sales Agents. With experience, a knack for running one's own business,

© JIST Works

and the appropriate licensure, these workers can open a brokerage to sell real estate, stocks, bonds, or other investment instruments.

Another set of workers (covered in chapter 11, about the Managerial track) supervise larger business functions. Administrative Services Managers; Financial Managers; Industrial Production Managers; Purchasing Managers; and Transportation, Storage, and Distribution Managers can all start up consulting businesses to market their own expertise and the services of appropriate technicians and clerical workers. Property, Real Estate, and Community Association Managers often advance from on-site management of one property to off-site management of a portfolio of properties. With experience, some may be able to launch a property management company.

Chief Executives, also part of the Managerial track, are by definition the heads of their firms and therefore are entrepreneurial to the extent that they assume the risks and profit from the rewards of the business. Some gain experience by managing large corporations owned by stockholders or wealthy private investors and later create their own smaller business in which they have a large personal stake. As that business grows and attracts investment from outside, they may cash in their now-valuable holdings in the company and move on to another start-up enterprise.

Conventional

Accountants and Auditors is the only Entrepreneurial job that has Conventional as its primary personality type. Financial Examiners has Conventional as its secondary type. Both of these jobs are covered in detail by the Bachelor's-in-Business track in chapter 6. The usual route by which these workers become entrepreneurial is to launch an independent firm to do accounting, auditing, or both for other businesses or for households. (Another 12 jobs coded EC may be found in the **Enterprising** section of this chapter.)

Achieving Six Figures in the Entrepreneurial Track

One of the key factors for success in this track is reaching a large market. The plumbing service example at the beginning of this chapter is worth reconsidering here. For such a business to reach a large number of buyers, it would have to employ a large workforce of plumbers; however, most of these workers could easily set up a competing one-plumber business and would probably prefer to be self-employed, so a plumbing service does

© JIST Works

not seem to be a promising opportunity for large-scale entrepreneurship. On the other hand, someone who understands how to roast coffee beans could open a coffee shop that sells a gourmet-quality brew and employs workers who would be less able to set up their own competing businesses. It would be possible to open several such coffee shops in a major city and thus reach a large market, and if the brand gains a good reputation, the owner eventually could franchise it to far-flung cities and towns in order to reach a market of millions. This is how a business such as Starbucks might succeed for an entrepreneur.

Franchising is especially well suited to service businesses; other kinds of businesses may grow in other ways. But almost any enterprise needs capital to grow and reach a larger market, so another key factor is attracting investment. As noted earlier in this chapter, a good business plan is necessary to persuade people to invest in your idea. On the basis of the business plan, a bank may lend you the necessary funds, to be paid back with interest. Another source of investment is a venture capital fund, which may offer perhaps $1 million to $15 million in exchange for an ownership stake in the company, usually 20 to 40 percent. If the expanded business then shows signs that it can be successful at a very large scale, the business may be able to sell shares to the public in what is known as an initial public offering (IPO). If the shares sell well, the entrepreneur's stake in the business (along with the venture capitalists') becomes extremely valuable. Many entrepreneurs sell off their stake at this point, but others continue to manage the business.

This chapter does not have enough room for discussion of all the other factors that contribute to the success of an entrepreneurial business. For more on the subject, read *Self-Employment: From Dream to Reality! An Interactive Workbook for Starting Your Small Business,* by Linda Gilkerson and Theresia Paauwe (JIST). The Small Business Administration also has many useful suggestions at its Web site, www.sba.gov/smallbusinessplanner/.

Moving On to Other Career Tracks

Most small businesses fail, and they are especially sensitive to downturns in the economy. When entrepreneurs decide to shut down their businesses and seek employed work, they often return to the track where they have previous experience.

In some cases they may try to enter still another track that is new to them. For example, an engineer who becomes discouraged by an attempt to start

© JIST Works

up a research and development firm may decide to go into the Distributive track as a salesworker. Other former entrepreneurs work in the Managerial track, supervising some aspect of someone else's business.

An entrepreneur with a master's or doctoral degree may move into the Academic track. Some universities offer programs in entrepreneurial studies and hire former entrepreneurs to teach some of the classes.

Characteristics of Six-Figure Entrepreneurial Jobs

Highest-Level Skills

Management of Financial Resources; Negotiation; Management of Personnel Resources; Systems Analysis; Systems Evaluation.

Highest-Level Work Activities

Resolving Conflicts and Negotiating with Others; Monitoring and Controlling Resources; Analyzing Data or Information; Communicating with Persons Outside the Organization; Providing Consultation and Advice to Others.

Most Important Knowledges

Economics and Accounting; Sales and Marketing; Personnel and Human Resources; Administration and Management; Clerical.

Most Important Work Contexts

Telephone; Face-to-Face Discussions; Electronic Mail; Contact with Others; Structured versus Unstructured Work.

Most Important Work Needs

Authority; Working Conditions; Autonomy; Responsibility; Compensation.

Most Important Work Styles

Integrity; Dependability; Attention to Detail; Initiative; Stress Tolerance.

© JIST Works

Facts About Six-Figure Entrepreneurial Jobs

Six-Figure Occupations

(At least 25% of the workers earn more than $100,000.)

Agents and Business Managers of Artists, Performers, and Athletes

Represent and promote artists, performers, and athletes to prospective employers. May handle contract negotiation and other business matters for clients. (Also included in the Distributive career track.)

Personality Code: ES

College Majors: Arts Management; Purchasing, Procurement/ Acquisitions and Contracts Management.

Median Annual Earnings: $66,440

Highly Paid Workforce: Out of a total salaried workforce of 11,680, 2,920 people (25%) earn more than $103,440.

Annual Job Growth Through 2016: 9.6%

Average Annual Job Openings Through 2016: 3,940

Best-Paying Industries: Arts, Entertainment, and Recreation.

Best-Paying Metro Areas: Los Angeles–Long Beach–Santa Ana, CA; New York–Northern New Jersey–Long Island, NY-NJ-PA.

Chief Executives

Determine and formulate policies and provide the overall direction of companies or private and public sector organizations within the guidelines set up by a board of directors or similar governing body. Plan, direct, or coordinate operational activities at the highest level of management with the help of subordinate executives and staff managers. (Also included in the Managerial career track.)

Personality Code: EC

College Majors: Business Administration/Management; Business/ Commerce, General; Entrepreneurship/Entrepreneurial Studies; International Business/Trade/Commerce; International Relations and

© JIST Works

Affairs; Public Administration; Public Administration and Services, Other; Public Policy Analysis; Transportation/Transportation Management.

Median Annual Earnings: More than $145,600

Highly Paid Workforce: Out of a total salaried workforce of 299,160, 224,370 people (75%) earn more than $97,960.

Annual Job Growth Through 2016: 2.0%

Average Annual Job Openings Through 2016: 21,209

Best-Paying Industries: Accommodation and Food Service; Administrative Support and Waste Management and Remediation Services; Arts, Entertainment, and Recreation; Construction; Educational Services; Federal, State, and Local Government; Finance and Insurance; Health Care and Social Assistance; Information; Management of Companies and Enterprises; Manufacturing; Mining; Other Services (Except Public Administration); Professional, Scientific, and Technical Services; Real Estate and Rental and Leasing; Retail Trade; Transportation and Warehousing; Utilities; Wholesale Trade.

Best-Paying Metro Areas: Albany-Schenectady-Troy, NY; Atlanta–Sandy Springs–Marietta, GA; Austin–Round Rock, TX; Baltimore-Towson, MD; Birmingham-Hoover, AL; Boise City–Nampa, ID; Boston-Cambridge-Quincy, MA-NH; Charleston–North Charleston, SC; Charlotte-Gastonia-Concord, NC-SC; Chicago-Naperville-Joliet, IL-IN-WI; Cincinnati-Middletown, OH-KY-IN; Cleveland-Elyria-Mentor, OH; Columbia, SC; Columbus, OH; Dallas–Fort Worth–Arlington, TX; Denver-Aurora, CO; Detroit-Warren-Livonia, MI; Grand Rapids–Wyoming, MI; Greenville, SC; Hartford–West Hartford–East Hartford, CT; Honolulu, HI; Houston–Sugar Land–Baytown, TX; Indianapolis-Carmel, IN; Jackson, MS; Jacksonville, FL; Kansas City, MO-KS; Knoxville, TN; Los Angeles–Long Beach–Santa Ana, CA; Louisville–Jefferson County, KY-IN; Memphis, TN-MS-AR; Miami–Fort Lauderdale–Miami Beach, FL; Milwaukee–Waukesha–West Allis, WI; Minneapolis–St. Paul–Bloomington, MN-WI; Nashville-Davidson-Murfreesboro, TN; New York–Northern New Jersey–Long Island, NY-NJ-PA; Oklahoma City, OK; Orlando-Kissimmee, FL; Philadelphia-Camden-Wilmington, PA-NJ-DE-MD; Phoenix-Mesa-Scottsdale, AZ; Pittsburgh, PA; Portland-Vancouver-Beaverton, OR-WA; Providence–Fall River–Warwick, RI-MA; Riverside–San Bernardino–Ontario, CA; Sacramento–Arden-Arcade–Roseville, CA; Salt Lake City, UT; San Diego–Carlsbad–San Marcos, CA; San Francisco–Oakland–Fremont, CA; San Jose–Sunnyvale–Santa Clara,

CA; San Juan–Caguas–Guaynabo, PR; Seattle-Tacoma-Bellevue, WA; Springfield, MA-CT; St. Louis, MO-IL; Tampa–St. Petersburg–Clearwater, FL; Tulsa, OK; Washington-Arlington-Alexandria, DC-VA-MD-WV; Wichita, KS; Worcester, MA-CT.

Compensation and Benefits Managers

Plan, direct, or coordinate compensation and benefits activities and staff of an organization. (Also included in the Managerial career track.)

Personality Code: ECS

College Majors: Labor and Industrial Relations.

Median Annual Earnings: $81,410

Highly Paid Workforce: Out of a total salaried workforce of 41,780, 10,445 people (25%) earn more than $107,370.

Annual Job Growth Through 2016: 12.0%

Average Annual Job Openings Through 2016: 6,121

Best-Paying Industries: Administrative Support and Waste Management and Remediation Services; Educational Services; Finance and Insurance; Information; Management of Companies and Enterprises; Manufacturing; Professional, Scientific, and Technical Services; Wholesale Trade.

Best-Paying Metro Areas: Boston-Cambridge-Quincy, MA-NH; Dallas–Fort Worth–Arlington, TX; Los Angeles–Long Beach–Santa Ana, CA; New York–Northern New Jersey–Long Island, NY-NJ-PA; Philadelphia-Camden-Wilmington, PA-NJ-DE-MD; Washington-Arlington-Alexandria, DC-VA-MD-WV.

Construction Managers

Plan, direct, coordinate, or budget, usually through subordinate supervisory personnel, activities concerned with the construction and maintenance of structures, facilities, and systems. Participate in the conceptual development of a construction project and oversee its organization, scheduling, and implementation. (Also included in the Managerial career track.)

Personality Code: ERC

College Majors: Business Administration and Management, General; Business/Commerce, General; Construction Engineering Technology/ Technician Training; Construction Management; Operations Management and Supervision.

© JIST Works

Median Annual Earnings: $76,230

Highly Paid Workforce: Out of a total salaried workforce of 216,120, 54,030 people (25%) earn more than $102,190.

Annual Job Growth Through 2016: 15.7%

Average Annual Job Openings Through 2016: 44,158

Best-Paying Industries: Administrative Support and Waste Management and Remediation Services; Construction; Management of Companies and Enterprises; Manufacturing; Professional, Scientific, and Technical Services; Real Estate and Rental and Leasing.

Best-Paying Metro Areas: Baltimore-Towson, MD; Boston-Cambridge-Quincy, MA-NH; Chicago-Naperville-Joliet, IL-IN-WI; Cincinnati-Middletown, OH-KY-IN; Columbus, OH; Detroit-Warren-Livonia, MI; Las Vegas–Paradise, NV; Los Angeles–Long Beach–Santa Ana, CA; Miami–Fort Lauderdale–Miami Beach, FL; Minneapolis–St. Paul–Bloomington, MN-WI; New York–Northern New Jersey–Long Island, NY-NJ-PA; Philadelphia-Camden-Wilmington, PA-NJ-DE-MD; Phoenix-Mesa-Scottsdale, AZ; Riverside–San Bernardino–Ontario, CA; Sacramento–Arden-Arcade–Roseville, CA; San Diego–Carlsbad–San Marcos, CA; San Francisco–Oakland–Fremont, CA; Seattle-Tacoma-Bellevue, WA; Virginia Beach–Norfolk–Newport News, VA-NC; Washington-Arlington-Alexandria, DC-VA-MD-WV.

Economists

Conduct research, prepare reports, or formulate plans to aid in solution of economic problems arising from production and distribution of goods and services. May collect and process economic and statistical data, using econometric and sampling techniques. (Also included in the Scientific career track.)

Personality Code: ICE

College Majors: Agricultural Economics; Applied Economics; Business/Managerial Economics; Development Economics and International Development; Econometrics and Quantitative Economics; Economics, General; Economics, Other; International Economics.

Median Annual Earnings: $80,220

Highly Paid Workforce: Out of a total salaried workforce of 12,740, 3,185 people (25%) earn more than $106,200.

© JIST Works

Annual Job Growth Through 2016: 7.5%

Average Annual Job Openings Through 2016: 1,555

Best-Paying Industries: Federal, State, and Local Government; Professional, Scientific, and Technical Services.

Best-Paying Metro Areas: Washington-Arlington-Alexandria, DC-VA-MD-WV.

Engineering Managers

Plan, direct, or coordinate activities in such fields as architecture and engineering or research and development in these fields. (Also included in the Managerial career track.)

Personality Code: ERI

College Majors: Aerospace Engineering; Agricultural/Biological Engineering; Architectural Engineering; Biomedical Engineering; Ceramic Sciences and Engineering; City/Urban, Community and Regional Planning; Civil Engineering, General; Computer Engineering, General; Electrical, Electronics and Communications Engineering; Engineering, General; Industrial Engineering; Materials Engineering; Mechanical Engineering; Metallurgical Engineering; Nuclear Engineering; Ocean Engineering; Petroleum Engineering; others.

Median Annual Earnings: $111,020

Highly Paid Workforce: Out of a total salaried workforce of 184,410, 138,308 people (75%) earn more than $88,350 and 92,205 (50%) earn more than $111,020.

Annual Job Growth Through 2016: 7.3%

Average Annual Job Openings Through 2016: 7,404

Best-Paying Industries: Administrative Support and Waste Management and Remediation Services; Construction; Federal, State, and Local Government; Information; Management of Companies and Enterprises; Manufacturing; Mining; Professional, Scientific, and Technical Services; Transportation and Warehousing; Utilities; Wholesale Trade.

Best-Paying Metro Areas: Atlanta–Sandy Springs–Marietta, GA; Austin–Round Rock, TX; Baltimore-Towson, MD; Boston-Cambridge-Quincy, MA-NH; Charlotte-Gastonia-Concord, NC-SC; Chicago-Naperville-

© JIST Works

Joliet, IL-IN-WI; Cincinnati-Middletown, OH-KY-IN; Cleveland-Elyria-Mentor, OH; Dallas–Fort Worth–Arlington, TX; Denver-Aurora, CO; Detroit-Warren-Livonia, MI; Hartford–West Hartford–East Hartford, CT; Houston–Sugar Land–Baytown, TX; Huntsville, AL; Indianapolis-Carmel, IN; Kansas City, MO-KS; Los Angeles–Long Beach–Santa Ana, CA; Miami–Fort Lauderdale–Miami Beach, FL; Milwaukee–Waukesha–West Allis, WI; Minneapolis–St. Paul–Bloomington, MN-WI; New York–Northern New Jersey–Long Island, NY-NJ-PA; Philadelphia-Camden-Wilmington, PA-NJ-DE-MD; Phoenix-Mesa-Scottsdale, AZ; Pittsburgh, PA; Raleigh-Cary, NC; Riverside–San Bernardino–Ontario, CA; Rochester, NY; Sacramento–Arden-Arcade–Roseville, CA; San Diego–Carlsbad–San Marcos, CA; San Francisco–Oakland–Fremont, CA; San Jose–Sunnyvale–Santa Clara, CA; St. Louis, MO-IL; Washington-Arlington-Alexandria, DC-VA-MD-WV.

Financial Managers

Plan, direct, and coordinate accounting, investing, banking, insurance, securities, and other financial activities of a branch, office, or department of an establishment. (Also included in the Managerial career track.)

Personality Code: EC

College Majors: Accounting and Business/Management; Accounting and Finance; Credit Management; Finance and Financial Management Services, Other; Finance, General; International Finance; Public Finance.

Median Annual Earnings: $95,310

Highly Paid Workforce: Out of a total salaried workforce of 484,390, 242,195 people (50%) earn more than $95,310 and 121,097 (25%) earn more than $130,860.

Annual Job Growth Through 2016: 12.6%

Average Annual Job Openings Through 2016: 57,589

Best-Paying Industries: Accommodation and Food Service; Administrative Support and Waste Management and Remediation Services; Arts, Entertainment, and Recreation; Construction; Educational Services; Federal, State, and Local Government; Finance and Insurance; Health Care and Social Assistance; Information; Management of Companies and Enterprises; Manufacturing; Mining; Other Services (Except Public Administration); Professional, Scientific, and Technical Services;

Real Estate and Rental and Leasing; Retail Trade; Transportation and Warehousing; Utilities; Wholesale Trade.

Best-Paying Metro Areas: Albany-Schenectady-Troy, NY; Atlanta–Sandy Springs–Marietta, GA; Austin–Round Rock, TX; Baltimore-Towson, MD; Birmingham-Hoover, AL; Boston-Cambridge-Quincy, MA-NH; Bridgeport-Stamford-Norwalk, CT; Buffalo–Niagara Falls, NY; Charlotte-Gastonia-Concord, NC-SC; Chattanooga, TN-GA; Chicago-Naperville-Joliet, IL-IN-WI; Cincinnati-Middletown, OH-KY-IN; Cleveland-Elyria-Mentor, OH; Columbia, SC; Columbus, OH; Dallas–Fort Worth–Arlington, TX; Dayton, OH; Denver-Aurora, CO; Des Moines–West Des Moines, IA; Detroit-Warren-Livonia, MI; Durham, NC; Greensboro–High Point, NC; Hartford–West Hartford–East Hartford, CT; Honolulu, HI; Houston–Sugar Land–Baytown, TX; Indianapolis-Carmel, IN; Jacksonville, FL; Kansas City, MO-KS; Las Vegas–Paradise, NV; Lexington-Fayette, KY; Los Angeles–Long Beach–Santa Ana, CA; Louisville–Jefferson County, KY-IN; Madison, WI; Memphis, TN-MS-AR; Miami–Fort Lauderdale–Miami Beach, FL; Milwaukee–Waukesha–West Allis, WI; Minneapolis–St. Paul–Bloomington, MN-WI; New Haven, CT; New Orleans–Metairie–Kenner, LA; New York–Northern New Jersey–Long Island, NY-NJ-PA; Omaha–Council Bluffs, NE-IA; Orlando-Kissimmee, FL; Oxnard–Thousand Oaks–Ventura, CA; Philadelphia-Camden-Wilmington, PA-NJ-DE-MD; Phoenix-Mesa-Scottsdale, AZ; Pittsburgh, PA; Portland-Vancouver-Beaverton, OR-WA; Providence–Fall River–Warwick, RI-MA; Raleigh-Cary, NC; Richmond, VA; Riverside–San Bernardino–Ontario, CA; Rochester, NY; Sacramento–Arden-Arcade–Roseville, CA; Salt Lake City, UT; San Antonio, TX; San Diego–Carlsbad–San Marcos, CA; San Francisco–Oakland–Fremont, CA; San Jose–Sunnyvale–Santa Clara, CA; Seattle-Tacoma-Bellevue, WA; Springfield, MA-CT; St. Louis, MO-IL; Syracuse, NY; Tampa–St. Petersburg–Clearwater, FL; Trenton-Ewing, NJ; Virginia Beach–Norfolk–Newport News, VA-NC; Washington-Arlington-Alexandria, DC-VA-MD-WV; Winston-Salem, NC; Worcester, MA-CT.

General and Operations Managers

Plan, direct, or coordinate the operations of companies or public and private sector organizations. Duties and responsibilities include formulating policies, managing daily operations, and planning the use of materials and human resources, but are too diverse and general in nature to be classified in any one functional area of management or administration, such as personnel, purchasing, or administrative services. Includes owners and

© JIST Works

managers who head small business establishments whose duties are primarily managerial. (Also included in the Managerial career track.)

Personality Code: ECS

College Majors: Business Administration and Management, General; Business/Commerce, General; Entrepreneurship/Entrepreneurial Studies; International Business/Trade/Commerce; Public Administration.

Median Annual Earnings: $88,700

Highly Paid Workforce: Out of a total salaried workforce of 1,655,410, 827,705 people (50%) earn more than $88,700 and 413,853 (25%) earn more than $133,570.

Annual Job Growth Through 2016: 1.5%

Average Annual Job Openings Through 2016: 112,072

Best-Paying Industries: Administrative Support and Waste Management and Remediation Services; Agriculture, Forestry, Fishing, and Hunting; Arts, Entertainment, and Recreation; Construction; Educational Services; Federal, State, and Local Government; Finance and Insurance; Health Care and Social Assistance; Information; Management of Companies and Enterprises; Manufacturing; Mining; Other Services (Except Public Administration); Professional, Scientific, and Technical Services; Real Estate and Rental and Leasing; Retail Trade; Transportation and Warehousing; Utilities; Wholesale Trade.

Best-Paying Metro Areas: Akron, OH; Albany-Schenectady-Troy, NY; Albuquerque, NM; Alexandria, LA; Allentown-Bethlehem-Easton, PA-NJ; Amarillo, TX; Ann Arbor, MI; Appleton, WI; Asheville, NC; Atlanta–Sandy Springs–Marietta, GA; Augusta–Richmond County, GA-SC; Austin–Round Rock, TX; Bakersfield, CA; Baltimore-Towson, MD; Barnstable Town, MA; Baton Rouge, LA; Beaumont–Port Arthur, TX; Binghamton, NY; Birmingham-Hoover, AL; Boston-Cambridge-Quincy, MA-NH; Boulder, CO; Bridgeport-Stamford-Norwalk, CT; Buffalo–Niagara Falls, NY; Canton-Massillon, OH; Cape Coral–Fort Myers, FL; Charleston–North Charleston, SC; Charlotte-Gastonia-Concord, NC-SC; Chattanooga, TN-GA; Chicago-Naperville-Joliet, IL-IN-WI; Cincinnati-Middletown, OH-KY-IN; Cleveland-Elyria-Mentor, OH; College Station–Bryan, TX; Colorado Springs, CO; Columbia, SC; Columbus, OH; Corpus Christi, TX; Dallas–Fort Worth–Arlington, TX; Dalton, GA; Danbury, CT; Davenport–Moline–Rock Island, IA-IL; Dayton, OH; Denver-Aurora, CO; Des Moines–West Des Moines, IA; Detroit-Warren-Livonia,

MI; Duluth, MN-WI; Durham, NC; El Paso, TX; Elkhart-Goshen, IN; Eugene-Springfield, OR; Evansville, IN-KY; Fargo, ND-MN; Fayetteville, NC; Fayetteville-Springdale-Rogers, AR-MO; Florence, SC; Fort Collins–Loveland, CO; Fort Wayne, IN; Fresno, CA; Grand Rapids–Wyoming, MI; Greeley, CO; Green Bay, WI; Greensboro–High Point, NC; Greenville, SC; Gulfport-Biloxi, MS; Hagerstown-Martinsburg, MD-WV; Harrisburg-Carlisle, PA; Hartford–West Hartford–East Hartford, CT; Hickory-Lenior-Morganton, NC; Honolulu, HI; Houma–Bayou Cane–Thibodaux, LA; Houston–Sugar Land–Baytown, TX; Huntsville, AL; Indianapolis-Carmel, IN; Jackson, MS; Jacksonville, FL; Kalamazoo-Portage, MI; Kansas City, MO-KS; Knoxville, TN; Lafayette, LA; Lake Charles, LA; Lakeland, FL; Lancaster, PA; Lansing–East Lansing, MI; Laredo, TX; Las Vegas–Paradise, NV; Lexington-Fayette, KY; Lincoln, NE; Little Rock–North Little Rock, AR; Longview, TX; Los Angeles–Long Beach–Santa Ana, CA; Louisville–Jefferson County, KY-IN; Lubbock, TX; Madison, WI; Manchester, NH; Memphis, TN-MS-AR; Miami–Fort Lauderdale–Miami Beach, FL; Midland, TX; Milwaukee–Waukesha–West Allis, WI; Minneapolis–St. Paul–Bloomington, MN-WI; Mobile, AL; Modesto, CA; Montgomery, AL; Napa, CA; Naples–Marco Island, FL; Nashville-Davidson-Murfreesboro, TN; New Haven, CT; New Orleans–Metairie–Kenner, LA; New York–Northern New Jersey–Long Island, NY-NJ-PA; Norwich–New London, CT-RI; Odessa, TX; Omaha–Council Bluffs, NE-IA; Orlando-Kissimmee, FL; Oxnard–Thousand Oaks–Ventura, CA; Palm Bay–Melbourne–Titusville, FL; Pensacola–Ferry Pass–Brent, FL; Peoria, IL; Philadelphia-Camden-Wilmington, PA-NJ-DE-MD; Phoenix-Mesa-Scottsdale, AZ; Pittsburgh, PA; Portland–South Portland–Biddeford, ME; Portland-Vancouver-Beaverton, OR-WA; Poughkeepsie-Newburgh-Middletown, NY; Providence–Fall River–Warwick, RI-MA; Provo-Orem, UT; Raleigh-Cary, NC; Reading, PA; Redding, CA; Reno-Sparks, NV; Richmond, VA; Riverside–San Bernardino–Ontario, CA; Roanoke, VA; Rochester, NY; Rockford, IL; Sacramento–Arden-Arcade–Roseville, CA; Salem, OR; Salinas, CA; Salt Lake City, UT; San Antonio, TX; San Diego–Carlsbad–San Marcos, CA; San Francisco–Oakland–Fremont, CA; San Jose–Sunnyvale–Santa Clara, CA; San Juan–Caguas–Guaynabo, PR; San Luis Obispo–Paso Robles, CA; Santa Barbara–Santa Maria, CA; Santa Cruz–Watsonville, CA; Santa Rosa–Petaluma, CA; Sarasota-Bradenton-Venice, FL; Scranton–Wilkes-Barre, PA; Seattle-Tacoma-Bellevue, WA; Shreveport–Bossier City, LA; Sioux Falls, SD; South Bend–Mishawaka, IN-MI; Spartanburg, SC; Spokane, WA; Springfield, MA-CT; Springfield, MO; St. Cloud, MN; St. Louis, MO-IL; Stockton, CA; Syracuse, NY;

© JIST Works

Tallahassee, FL; Tampa–St. Petersburg–Clearwater, FL; Toledo, OH; Trenton-Ewing, NJ; Tucson, AZ; Tuscaloosa, AL; Tyler, TX; Utica-Rome, NY; Vallejo-Fairfield, CA; Virginia Beach–Norfolk–Newport News, VA-NC; Visalia-Porterville, CA; Waco, TX; Washington-Arlington-Alexandria, DC-VA-MD-WV; Waterbury, CT; Wilmington, NC; Winston-Salem, NC; Worcester, MA-CT; York-Hanover, PA; Youngstown-Warren-Boardman, OH-PA.

Industrial Production Managers

Plan, direct, or coordinate the work activities and resources necessary for manufacturing products in accordance with cost, quality, and quantity specifications. (Also included in the Managerial career track.)

Personality Code: EC

College Majors: Business Administration and Management, General; Business/Commerce, General; Operations Management and Supervision.

Median Annual Earnings: $80,560

Highly Paid Workforce: Out of a total salaried workforce of 152,870, 38,218 people (25%) earn more than $104,860.

Annual Job Growth Through 2016: –5.9%

Average Annual Job Openings Through 2016: 14,889

Best-Paying Industries: Administrative Support and Waste Management and Remediation Services; Information; Management of Companies and Enterprises; Manufacturing; Mining; Professional, Scientific, and Technical Services; Utilities; Wholesale Trade.

Best-Paying Metro Areas: Baltimore-Towson, MD; Boston-Cambridge-Quincy, MA-NH; Chicago-Naperville-Joliet, IL-IN-WI; Cincinnati-Middletown, OH-KY-IN; Cleveland-Elyria-Mentor, OH; Dallas–Fort Worth–Arlington, TX; Detroit-Warren-Livonia, MI; Hartford–West Hartford–East Hartford, CT; Houston–Sugar Land–Baytown, TX; Los Angeles–Long Beach–Santa Ana, CA; Minneapolis–St. Paul–Bloomington, MN-WI; New York–Northern New Jersey–Long Island, NY-NJ-PA; Philadelphia-Camden-Wilmington, PA-NJ-DE-MD; Phoenix-Mesa-Scottsdale, AZ; Portland-Vancouver-Beaverton, OR-WA; San Diego–Carlsbad–San Marcos, CA; San Francisco–Oakland–Fremont, CA; San Jose–Sunnyvale–Santa Clara, CA; Seattle-Tacoma-Bellevue, WA; St. Louis, MO-IL.

Personal Financial Advisors

Advise clients on financial plans, utilizing knowledge of tax and investment strategies, securities, insurance, pension plans, and real estate. Duties include assessing clients' assets, liabilities, cash flow, insurance coverage, tax status, and financial objectives to establish investment strategies. (Also included in the Entrepreneurial career track.)

Personality Code: ECS

College Majors: Financial Planning and Services.

Median Annual Earnings: $67,660

Highly Paid Workforce: Out of a total salaried workforce of 132,460, 66,230 people (50%) earn more than $67,660 and 33,115 (25%) earn more than $115,750.

Annual Job Growth Through 2016: 41.0%

Average Annual Job Openings Through 2016: 17,114

Best-Paying Industries: Finance and Insurance; Professional, Scientific, and Technical Services.

Best-Paying Metro Areas: Boston-Cambridge-Quincy, MA-NH; Bridgeport-Stamford-Norwalk, CT; Chicago-Naperville-Joliet, IL-IN-WI; Cincinnati-Middletown, OH-KY-IN; Dallas–Fort Worth–Arlington, TX; Denver-Aurora, CO; Detroit-Warren-Livonia, MI; Hartford–West Hartford–East Hartford, CT; Houston–Sugar Land–Baytown, TX; Los Angeles–Long Beach–Santa Ana, CA; New York–Northern New Jersey–Long Island, NY-NJ-PA; Pittsburgh, PA; San Francisco–Oakland–Fremont, CA; Seattle-Tacoma-Bellevue, WA; St. Louis, MO-IL; Washington-Arlington-Alexandria, DC-VA-MD-WV.

Public Relations Managers

Plan and direct public relations programs designed to create and maintain a favorable public image for employer or client or, if engaged in fundraising, plan and direct activities to solicit and maintain funds for special projects and nonprofit organizations. (Also included in the Managerial career track.)

Personality Code: EA

College Majors: Public Relations/Image Management.

Median Annual Earnings: $86,470

© JIST Works

Highly Paid Workforce: Out of a total salaried workforce of 47,210, 23,605 people (50%) earn more than $86,470 and 11,803 (25%) earn more than $121,500.

Annual Job Growth Through 2016: 16.9%

Average Annual Job Openings Through 2016: 5,781

Best-Paying Industries: Arts, Entertainment, and Recreation; Educational Services; Federal, State, and Local Government; Finance and Insurance; Information; Management of Companies and Enterprises; Manufacturing; Other Services (except Public Administration); Professional, Scientific, and Technical Services.

Best-Paying Metro Areas: Boston-Cambridge-Quincy, MA-NH; Chicago-Naperville-Joliet, IL-IN-WI; Los Angeles–Long Beach–Santa Ana, CA; New York–Northern New Jersey–Long Island, NY-NJ-PA; Philadelphia-Camden-Wilmington, PA-NJ-DE-MD; San Francisco–Oakland–Fremont, CA; Washington-Arlington-Alexandria, DC-VA-MD-WV.

Purchasing Managers

Plan, direct, or coordinate the activities of buyers, purchasing officers, and related workers involved in purchasing materials, products, and services. (Also included in the Managerial career track.)

Personality Code: EC

College Majors: Purchasing, Procurement/Acquisitions and Contracts Management.

Median Annual Earnings: $85,440

Highly Paid Workforce: Out of a total salaried workforce of 65,600, 32,800 people (50%) earn more than $85,440 and 16,400 (25%) earn more than $111,240.

Annual Job Growth Through 2016: 3.4%

Average Annual Job Openings Through 2016: 7,243

Best-Paying Industries: Administrative Support and Waste Management and Remediation Services; Construction; Educational Services; Federal, State, and Local Government; Health Care and Social Assistance; Management of Companies and Enterprises; Manufacturing; Professional, Scientific, and Technical Services; Wholesale Trade.

Best-Paying Metro Areas: Atlanta–Sandy Springs–Marietta, GA; Boston-Cambridge-Quincy, MA-NH; Chicago-Naperville-Joliet, IL-IN-WI; Dallas–Fort Worth–Arlington, TX; Detroit-Warren-Livonia, MI; Houston–Sugar Land–Baytown, TX; Los Angeles–Long Beach–Santa Ana, CA; Minneapolis–St. Paul–Bloomington, MN-WI; New York–Northern New Jersey–Long Island, NY-NJ-PA; Philadelphia-Camden-Wilmington, PA-NJ-DE-MD; San Francisco–Oakland–Fremont, CA; Washington-Arlington-Alexandria, DC-VA-MD-WV.

Real Estate Brokers

Operate real estate office or work for commercial real estate firm, overseeing real estate transactions. Other duties usually include selling real estate or renting properties and arranging loans. (Also included in the Distributive career track.)

Personality Code: EC

College Majors: Real Estate.

Median Annual Earnings: $58,860

Highly Paid Workforce: Out of a total salaried workforce of 49,270, 12,318 people (25%) earn more than $100,570.

Annual Job Growth Through 2016: 11.1%

Average Annual Job Openings Through 2016: 18,689

Best-Paying Industries: Construction; Real Estate and Rental and Leasing.

Best-Paying Metro Areas: Los Angeles–Long Beach–Santa Ana, CA; Miami–Fort Lauderdale–Miami Beach, FL; New York–Northern New Jersey–Long Island, NY-NJ-PA; Phoenix-Mesa-Scottsdale, AZ; San Francisco–Oakland–Fremont, CA.

Securities, Commodities, and Financial Services Sales Agents

Buy and sell securities in investment and trading firms or call upon businesses and individuals to sell financial services. Provide financial services, such as loan, tax, and securities counseling. May advise securities customers about such things as stocks, bonds, and market conditions. (Also included in the Distributive career track.)

© JIST Works

Personality Code: EC

College Majors: Business and Personal/Financial Services Marketing Operations; Financial Planning and Services; Investments and Securities.

Median Annual Earnings: $68,430

Highly Paid Workforce: Out of a total salaried workforce of 268,480, 134,240 people (50%) earn more than $68,430 and 67,120 (25%) earn more than $122,260.

Annual Job Growth Through 2016: 24.8%

Average Annual Job Openings Through 2016: 47,750

Best-Paying Industries: Administrative Support and Waste Management and Remediation Services; Finance and Insurance; Management of Companies and Enterprises.

Best-Paying Metro Areas: Austin–Round Rock, TX; Baltimore-Towson, MD; Boston-Cambridge-Quincy, MA-NH; Bridgeport-Stamford-Norwalk, CT; Buffalo–Niagara Falls, NY; Charlotte-Gastonia-Concord, NC-SC; Chicago-Naperville-Joliet, IL-IN-WI; Dallas–Fort Worth–Arlington, TX; Denver-Aurora, CO; Detroit-Warren-Livonia, MI; Houston–Sugar Land–Baytown, TX; Indianapolis-Carmel, IN; Jacksonville, FL; Kansas City, MO-KS; Los Angeles–Long Beach–Santa Ana, CA; Louisville–Jefferson County, KY-IN; Memphis, TN-MS-AR; Miami–Fort Lauderdale–Miami Beach, FL; Minneapolis–St. Paul–Bloomington, MN-WI; New York–Northern New Jersey–Long Island, NY-NJ-PA; Philadelphia-Camden-Wilmington, PA-NJ-DE-MD; Pittsburgh, PA; Portland-Vancouver-Beaverton, OR-WA; Providence–Fall River–Warwick, RI-MA; Richmond, VA; Salt Lake City, UT; San Diego–Carlsbad–San Marcos, CA; San Francisco–Oakland–Fremont, CA; San Jose–Sunnyvale–Santa Clara, CA; Seattle-Tacoma-Bellevue, WA; Trenton-Ewing, NJ.

Training and Development Managers

Plan, direct, or coordinate the training and development activities and staff of an organization. (Also included in the Managerial career track.)

Personality Code: ES

College Majors: Human Resources Development; Human Resources Management/Personnel Administration, General.

Median Annual Earnings: $84,340

Highly Paid Workforce: Out of a total salaried workforce of 28,170, 14,085 people (50%) earn more than $84,340 and 7,043 (25%) earn more than $111,240.

Annual Job Growth Through 2016: 15.6%

Average Annual Job Openings Through 2016: 3,759

Best-Paying Industries: Finance and Insurance; Health Care and Social Assistance; Information; Management of Companies and Enterprises; Manufacturing; Professional, Scientific, and Technical Services.

Best-Paying Metro Areas: Chicago-Naperville-Joliet, IL-IN-WI; New York–Northern New Jersey–Long Island, NY-NJ-PA.

Six-Figure Niche-Industry Jobs

(At least 10% of workers in the best-paying industries earn more than $100,000.)

Accountants and Auditors

Examine, analyze, and interpret accounting records for the purpose of giving advice or preparing statements. Install or advise on systems of recording costs or other financial and budgetary data. (Also included in the Bachelor's-in-Business career track.)

Personality Code: CEI

College Majors: Accounting; Accounting and Business/Management; Accounting and Computer Science; Accounting and Finance; Auditing; Taxation.

Median Annual Earnings: $57,060

Highly Paid Workforce: Out of a total salaried workforce of 1,115,010, 111,501 people (10%) earn more than $98,220.

Annual Job Growth Through 2016: 17.7%

Average Annual Job Openings Through 2016: 134,463

Best-Paying Industries: Professional, Scientific, and Technical Services.

Administrative Services Managers

Plan, direct, or coordinate supportive services of an organization, such as recordkeeping, mail distribution, telephone operator/receptionist, and

© JIST Works

other office support services. May oversee facilities planning and maintenance and custodial operations. (Also included in the Managerial career
track.)

Personality Code: EC

College Majors: Business Administration and Management, General;
Business/Commerce, General; Medical/Health Management and
Clinical Assistant/Specialist Training; Public Administration; Purchasing,
Procurement/Acquisitions and Contracts Management; Transportation/
Transportation Management.

Median Annual Earnings: $70,990

Highly Paid Workforce: Out of a total salaried workforce of 239,360,
59,840 people (25%) earn more than $94,970.

Annual Job Growth Through 2016: 11.7%

Average Annual Job Openings Through 2016: 19,513

Best-Paying Industries: Administrative Support and Waste Management
and Remediation Services; Arts, Entertainment, and Recreation;
Construction; Educational Services; Federal, State, and Local Government;
Finance and Insurance; Health Care and Social Assistance; Information;
Management of Companies and Enterprises; Manufacturing; Mining;
Other Services (Except Public Administration); Professional, Scientific,
and Technical Services; Real Estate and Rental and Leasing; Retail Trade;
Transportation and Warehousing; Utilities; Wholesale Trade.

Employment, Recruitment, and Placement Specialists

Recruit and place workers. (Also included in the Bachelor's-in-Business
career track.)

Personality Code: ESC

College Majors: Human Resources Management/Personnel
Administration, General; Labor and Industrial Relations.

Median Annual Earnings: $44,380

Highly Paid Workforce: Out of a total salaried workforce of 193,620,
19,362 people (10%) earn more than $85,410.

Annual Job Growth Through 2016: 18.4%

Average Annual Job Openings Through 2016: 33,588

Best-Paying Industries: Professional, Scientific, and Technical Services.

Financial Examiners

Enforce or ensure compliance with laws and regulations governing financial and securities institutions and financial and real estate transactions. May examine, verify correctness of, or establish authenticity of records. (Also included in the Bachelor's-in-Business career track.)

Personality Code: EC

College Majors: Accounting; Taxation.

Median Annual Earnings: $66,670

Highly Paid Workforce: Out of a total salaried workforce of 25,510, 6,378 people (25%) earn more than $93,650 and 2,551 (10%) earn more than $122,050.

Annual Job Growth Through 2016: 10.7%

Average Annual Job Openings Through 2016: 2,449

Best-Paying Industries: Federal, State, and Local Government; Finance and Insurance; Management of Companies and Enterprises; Professional, Scientific, and Technical Services.

Logisticians

Analyze and coordinate the logistical functions of a firm or organization. Responsible for the entire life cycle of a product, including acquisition, distribution, internal allocation, delivery, and final disposal of resources. (Also included in the Bachelor's-in-Business career track.)

Personality Code: EC

College Majors: Logistics and Materials Management; Operations Management and Supervision; Transportation/Transportation Management.

Median Annual Earnings: $64,250

Highly Paid Workforce: Out of a total salaried workforce of 90,340, 9,034 people (10%) earn more than $98,680.

Annual Job Growth Through 2016: 17.3%

© JIST Works

Average Annual Job Openings Through 2016: 9,671

Best-Paying Industries: Federal, State, and Local Government; Information; Management of Companies and Enterprises; Professional, Scientific, and Technical Services; Wholesale Trade.

Management Analysts

Conduct organizational studies and evaluations, design systems and procedures, conduct work simplifications and measurement studies, and prepare operations and procedures manuals to assist management in operating more efficiently and effectively. Includes program analysts and management consultants. (Also included in the Bachelor's-in-Business career track.)

Personality Code: IEC

College Majors: Business Administration and Management, General; Business/Commerce, General.

Median Annual Earnings: $71,150

Highly Paid Workforce: Out of a total salaried workforce of 499,640, 124,910 people (25%) earn more than $96,400 and 49,964 (10%) earn more than $131,870.

Annual Job Growth Through 2016: 21.9%

Average Annual Job Openings Through 2016: 125,669

Best-Paying Industries: Administrative Support and Waste Management and Remediation Services; Construction; Educational Services; Finance and Insurance; Information; Management of Companies and Enterprises; Manufacturing; Mining; Other Services (except Public Administration); Professional, Scientific, and Technical Services; Real Estate and Rental and Leasing; Retail Trade; Transportation and Warehousing; Utilities; Wholesale Trade.

Market Research Analysts

Research market conditions in local, regional, or national areas to determine potential sales of a product or service. May gather information on competitors, prices, sales, and methods of marketing and distribution. May use survey results to create a marketing campaign based on regional preferences and buying habits. (Also included in the Bachelor's-in-Business career track.)

Personality Code: IEC

College Majors: Applied Economics; Business/Managerial Economics; Econometrics and Quantitative Economics; Economics, General; International Economics; Marketing Research.

Median Annual Earnings: $60,300

Highly Paid Workforce: Out of a total salaried workforce of 220,740, 55,185 people (25%) earn more than $85,760 and 22,074 (10%) earn more than $113,390.

Annual Job Growth Through 2016: 20.1%

Average Annual Job Openings Through 2016: 45,015

Best-Paying Industries: Administrative Support and Waste Management and Remediation Services; Construction; Finance and Insurance; Information; Management of Companies and Enterprises; Manufacturing; Professional, Scientific, and Technical Services; Utilities; Wholesale Trade.

Medical and Health Services Managers

Plan, direct, or coordinate medicine and health services in hospitals, clinics, managed care organizations, public health agencies, or similar organizations. (Also included in the Managerial career track.)

Personality Code: ECS

College Majors: Community Health and Preventive Medicine; Health and Medical Administrative Services, Other; Health Information/ Medical Records Administration/Administrator Training; Health Services Administration; Health Unit Manager/Ward Supervisor Training; Health/ Health Care Administration/Management; Hospital and Health Care Facilities Administration/Management; Medical Staff Services Technology/ Technician Training; Nursing Administration (MSN, MS, PhD); Public Health, General (MPH, DPH).

Median Annual Earnings: $76,990

Highly Paid Workforce: Out of a total salaried workforce of 242,640, 60,660 people (25%) earn more than $99,680.

Annual Job Growth Through 2016: 16.4%

Average Annual Job Openings Through 2016: 31,877

© JIST Works

Best-Paying Industries: Administrative Support and Waste Management and Remediation Services; Educational Services; Federal, State, and Local Government; Finance and Insurance; Health Care and Social Assistance; Management of Companies and Enterprises; Professional, Scientific, and Technical Services.

Operations Research Analysts

Formulate and apply mathematical modeling and other optimizing methods, using a computer to develop and interpret information that assists management with decision making, policy formulation, or other managerial functions. May develop related software, service, or products. Frequently concentrates on collecting and analyzing data and developing decision support software. May develop and supply optimal time, cost, or logistics networks for program evaluation, review, or implementation. (Also included in the Scientific career track.)

Personality Code: ICE

College Majors: Educational Evaluation and Research; Educational Statistics and Research Methods; Management Science, General; Management Sciences and Quantitative Methods, Other; Operations Research.

Median Annual Earnings: $66,950

Highly Paid Workforce: Out of a total salaried workforce of 58,750, 14,688 people (25%) earn more than $89,560 and 5,875 (10%) earn more than $113,080.

Annual Job Growth Through 2016: 10.6%

Average Annual Job Openings Through 2016: 5,727

Best-Paying Industries: Administrative Support and Waste Management and Remediation Services; Federal, State, and Local Government; Finance and Insurance; Information; Management of Companies and Enterprises; Manufacturing; Professional, Scientific, and Technical Services; Wholesale Trade.

Real Estate Sales Agents

Rent, buy, or sell property for clients. Perform duties such as studying property listings, interviewing prospective clients, accompanying clients to property site, discussing conditions of sale, and drawing up real estate contracts. Includes agents who represent buyer. (Also included in the Distributive career track.)

Personality Code: EC

College Majors: Real Estate.

Median Annual Earnings: $40,600

Highly Paid Workforce: Out of a total salaried workforce of 172,030, 17,203 people (10%) earn more than $106,790.

Annual Job Growth Through 2016: 10.6%

Average Annual Job Openings Through 2016: 61,232

Best-Paying Industries: Administrative Support and Waste Management and Remediation Services; Construction; Finance and Insurance; Management of Companies and Enterprises; Mining; Real Estate and Rental and Leasing.

Transportation, Storage, and Distribution Managers

Plan, direct, or coordinate transportation, storage, or distribution activities in accordance with governmental policies and regulations. Includes logistics managers. (Also included in the Managerial career track.)

Personality Code: EC

College Majors: Aeronautics/Aviation/Aerospace Science and Technology, General; Aviation/Airway Management and Operations; Business Administration and Management, General; Logistics and Materials Management; Public Administration; Transportation/Transportation Management.

Median Annual Earnings: $76,310

Highly Paid Workforce: Out of a total salaried workforce of 92,790, 23,198 people (25%) earn more than $97,920 and 9,279 (10%) earn more than $126,440.

Annual Job Growth Through 2016: 8.3%

Average Annual Job Openings Through 2016: 6,994

Best-Paying Industries: Administrative Support and Waste Management and Remediation Services; Educational Services; Federal, State, and Local Government; Information; Management of Companies and Enterprises; Manufacturing; Professional, Scientific, and Technical Services; Real Estate

© JIST Works

and Rental and Leasing; Retail Trade; Transportation and Warehousing; Wholesale Trade.

Six-Figure Niche-Location Jobs

(At least 10% of workers in the best-paying metro areas earn more than $100,000.)

Insurance Sales Agents

Sell life, property, casualty, health, automotive, or other types of insurance. May refer clients to independent brokers, work as independent broker, or be employed by an insurance company. (Also included in the Distributive career track.)

Personality Code: ECS

College Majors: Insurance.

Median Annual Earnings: $44,110

Highly Paid Workforce: Out of a total salaried workforce of 321,920, 80,480 people (25%) earn more than $67,510 and 32,192 (10%) earn more than $113,190.

Annual Job Growth Through 2016: 12.9%

Average Annual Job Openings Through 2016: 64,162

Best-Paying Metro Areas: Albany-Schenectady-Troy, NY; Atlanta–Sandy Springs–Marietta, GA; Baltimore-Towson, MD; Birmingham-Hoover, AL; Boston-Cambridge-Quincy, MA-NH; Bridgeport-Stamford-Norwalk, CT; Charlotte-Gastonia-Concord, NC-SC; Chicago-Naperville-Joliet, IL-IN-WI; Cincinnati-Middletown, OH-KY-IN; Cleveland-Elyria-Mentor, OH; Dallas–Fort Worth–Arlington, TX; Denver-Aurora, CO; Detroit-Warren-Livonia, MI; Grand Rapids–Wyoming, MI; Hartford–West Hartford–East Hartford, CT; Indianapolis-Carmel, IN; Kansas City, MO-KS; Las Vegas–Paradise, NV; Los Angeles–Long Beach–Santa Ana, CA; Louisville–Jefferson County, KY-IN; Memphis, TN-MS-AR; Milwaukee–Waukesha–West Allis, WI; Minneapolis–St. Paul–Bloomington, MN-WI; New York–Northern New Jersey–Long Island, NY-NJ-PA; Orlando-Kissimmee, FL; Philadelphia-Camden-Wilmington, PA-NJ-DE-MD; Phoenix-Mesa-Scottsdale, AZ; Pittsburgh, PA; Portland-Vancouver-Beaverton, OR-WA; Riverside–San Bernardino–Ontario, CA; Sacramento–Arden-Arcade–Roseville, CA; Salt Lake City, UT; San Diego–Carlsbad–San Marcos,

CA; San Francisco–Oakland–Fremont, CA; San Jose–Sunnyvale–Santa Clara, CA; Seattle-Tacoma-Bellevue, WA; St. Louis, MO-IL; Tampa–St. Petersburg–Clearwater, FL; Tulsa, OK; Virginia Beach–Norfolk–Newport News, VA-NC; Washington-Arlington-Alexandria, DC-VA-MD-WV.

Property, Real Estate, and Community Association Managers

Plan, direct, or coordinate selling, buying, leasing, or governance activities of commercial, industrial, or residential real estate properties. (Also included in the Managerial career track.)

Personality Code: EC

College Majors: Real Estate.

Median Annual Earnings: $43,670

Highly Paid Workforce: Out of a total salaried workforce of 159,660, 15,966 people (10%) earn more than $97,890.

Annual Job Growth Through 2016: 15.1%

Average Annual Job Openings Through 2016: 49,916

Best-Paying Metro Areas: Atlanta–Sandy Springs–Marietta, GA; Baltimore-Towson, MD; Boston-Cambridge-Quincy, MA-NH; Chicago-Naperville-Joliet, IL-IN-WI; Denver-Aurora, CO; Detroit-Warren-Livonia, MI; Miami–Fort Lauderdale–Miami Beach, FL; New York–Northern New Jersey–Long Island, NY-NJ-PA; Orlando-Kissimmee, FL; Philadelphia-Camden-Wilmington, PA-NJ-DE-MD; Phoenix-Mesa-Scottsdale, AZ; San Francisco–Oakland–Fremont, CA; Seattle-Tacoma-Bellevue, WA; St. Louis, MO-IL; Tampa–St. Petersburg–Clearwater, FL; Washington-Arlington-Alexandria, DC-VA-MD-WV.

© JIST Works

Chapter 10

The Information Technology Career Track to a $100,000 Job

Information technology (IT) has become almost as important a part of our economy as electric power and tap water, so the Information Technology career track offers many opportunities, some of them in high-earning jobs.

These workers learn about how computers work, usually as part of a bachelor's degree program. They learn computer languages, methods of organizing data, and how to send and retrieve data within systems and over networks. They may specialize in software engineering, networks, security, animation, or use of information from business or science. (Computer Hardware Engineers are covered in chapter 8, about the Engineering career track.)

Some of them work in businesses that create new software or apply existing applications to solve business needs. These range in size from one-person consulting businesses to giant corporations like Microsoft. Others work in the information technology department of a business with another mission. A few teach and do research in the IT field.

Your Strategy for Getting on the Information Technology Career Track

Realistic, Investigative, and Conventional

All 12 of the Information Technology jobs have Investigative as a primary or secondary personality type. This section focuses on those seven jobs for which Investigative is the primary type; on the six jobs that have Realistic as a secondary type, all of which also have Conventional as another secondary type; and on the two jobs that have Conventional as their primary type: Computer and Information Scientists, Research; Computer Programmers; Computer Software Engineers, Applications; Computer Software Engineers, Systems Software; Computer Specialists, All Other; Computer Systems Analysts; Database Administrators; Network and Computer Systems Administrators; and Network Systems and Data Communications Analysts. (For Multi-Media Artists and Animators, see the **Artistic** section of this chapter. For Computer and Information Systems Managers, see the **Enterprising** section. For Computer Science Teachers, Postsecondary, see the Academic career track, chapter 5.)

High school students interested in these jobs should take college-prep courses, especially math and computer science. Especially for the two engineering jobs, take at least one advanced science class and the highest level of math available. People who tend toward the Realistic type may also want to study electronics as a course or a hobby; it will not be the primary focus of your college major or of your work, but it is useful to know and may help if you decide later to switch to the Engineering career track.

As a *college student,* enroll in a four-year program. A two-year degree is suitable for some jobs as Computer Programmers, but these are the lowest-paying jobs and the most likely to be lost to overseas workers. Many software vendors offer certification courses in their applications (for example, network management), and these can be useful credentials, but they are not a substitute for a degree. Major in computer science, software engineering, information science, or management information systems (MIS). Students particularly interested in business or scientific applications may choose to major in a business or technical subject and take several courses in computer science. You may be able to work as a software engineer with a nonengineering degree, but a degree in engineering teaches certain skills and approaches to problems that employers value. To teach in college or do research, you usually need a graduate degree.

Experienced workers need to update their skills constantly to keep up with advances in technology. Cutting-edge skills often are not covered by formal classes and must be self-taught. Best opportunities for job security and advancement may be in positions in which you work collaboratively—for example, with sales staff or as part of a team that reengineers business processes or develops new products. Work of this kind can teach you new business skills and make you more knowledgeable about your industry, thus paving the way for advancement to project manager, chief information officer, or high-priced consultant.

© JIST Works

Artistic

The one Artistic job in the Information Technology career track is Multi-Media Artists and Animators. It is possible to pursue this occupation using low technology, but the high-paying jobs are in computer-based animation.

High school students should take art, math, and computer science courses. In your free time, experiment with graphics and animation programs.

College students should major in animation, if possible. Some technical schools offer a two-year associate degree program, but a bachelor's degree is likely to lead to a better-paying job and is a necessity if you want to work in architectural, mechanical, or medical animation. If a bachelor's program in animation is not available, study art, graphic design, or computer science. If you are interested in scientific or engineering applications of animation, you may want to major in one of these subjects with additional courses in animation. From coursework, internships, and summer jobs you should assemble a portfolio and demo reel of animations that you can show prospective employers.

Your first job out of college may involve minor, repetitive tasks as part of a team. *Experienced workers* can advance to more creative roles in the team and may eventually be able to direct a team of animators. Animators with an impressive demo reel, a good network of contacts, and a flair for self-promotion may be able to work as freelancers. Workers in other computer-intensive or graphic-design jobs sometimes can move into the field of animation if they have acquired the right skills on the job.

Social

Only one Information Technology job has Social as a primary or secondary personality type: Computer Science Teachers, Postsecondary. This occupation is also included in the Academic career track, so for detailed suggestions, turn to chapter 5.

Enterprising

The only Enterprising job in the Information Technology career track is Computer and Information Systems Managers.

High school students may take one or two business-related subjects such as accounting, but college-prep courses are more important, especially in math and computer science. Summer work in a business setting is helpful, especially if the work involves computers.

College students should aim for a bachelor's degree in a computer-related subject, but a master's in business management (MBA) with a concentration in technology will accelerate your advancement. Some universities offer degrees in management information systems. These degrees blend technical subjects with business, accounting, and communications courses. Summer jobs in computer-related work can be helpful, and an appropriate internship is especially important as a way to gain experience and make contacts.

You may not be hired into a managerial position fresh out of college, but *experienced workers* may be able to take on some supervisory tasks and gain the necessary skills. Even workers without a college degree may be able to make this career move if they have the right skills. Certification from a software vendor advances your technical skills but is not a substitute for a college degree or for managerial experience. (For more suggestions, see the Managerial track, chapter 11.)

Achieving Six Figures in the Information Technology Track

To stay employed in the Information Technology track, let alone earn the big bucks, you need to keep abreast of the constant and rapid changes in IT. Classes often are not available for the very latest developments, so you should make a habit of learning where technology is headed. You also need to keep up with developments in your industry (for example, finance, manufacturing, or communications); even the IT industry has business issues that are separate from technical developments. For high earnings, try to find work where you collaborate with other highly skilled workers, whether you are part of a team of IT professionals or the computer-skilled member of a team with a nontechnical business mission. It also helps to have expertise in a niche field that's in high demand.

Even with the most up-to-date technical skills, your earnings may hit a ceiling if you continue to focus solely on IT tasks. You can improve your earnings by acquiring and using other skills that can take you into more lucrative career tracks: management, sales, or entrepreneurship. Some companies, as a way of justifying higher pay, give IT professionals managerial titles without requiring supervisory responsibilities. This may sound like a sweet deal, but it can lead to problems later if you try to land a managerial job elsewhere without any relevant achievements you can point to.

© JIST Works

Moving On to Other Career Tracks

People with the right skills and interests can move from this career track to the Managerial track by taking on supervisory tasks, such as evaluating the work of lower-level programmers or developing departmental budgets. Talented workers can advance to leader of a development team, departmental manager, and chief information officer. Getting a master's degree in business administration (MBA) can help with advancement.

The Entrepreneurial track is also an option. Start-up software companies require a smaller initial investment than many other kinds of businesses.

College students who discover they are more interested in hardware than software may want to switch to the Engineering career track, perhaps in graduate school. Software engineering is also an option for college and for work, but in fact most people who work as software engineers have degrees in computer science, not engineering, so the Information Technology track is more appropriate.

People who are especially interested in research may want to get a master's or doctoral degree in computer science or operations research and move into either the Academic track as college teachers or the Scientific track as Operations Research Analysts or Computer and Information Scientists, Research.

Characteristics of Six-Figure Information Technology Jobs

Highest-Level Skills

Programming; Systems Analysis; Technology Design; Troubleshooting; Operations Analysis.

Highest-Level Work Activities

Interacting with Computers; Thinking Creatively; Analyzing Data or Processing Information; Processing Information; Updating and Using Relevant Knowledge.

Most Important Knowledges

Computers and Electronics; Telecommunications; Design; Engineering and Technology; Mathematics.

© JIST Works

Most Important Work Contexts

Electronic Mail; Face-to-Face Discussions; Telephone; Indoors, Environmentally Controlled; Spend Time Sitting.

Most Important Work Needs

Creativity; Ability Utilization; Working Conditions; Autonomy; Responsibility.

Most Important Work Styles

Attention to Detail; Analytical Thinking; Dependability; Adaptability/ Flexibility; Initiative.

Facts About Six-Figure Information Technology Jobs

Six-Figure Occupations

(At least 25% of the workers earn more than $100,000.)

Computer and Information Scientists, Research

Conduct research into fundamental computer and information science as theorists, designers, or inventors. Solve or develop solutions to problems in the field of computer hardware and software. (Also included in the Scientific career track.)

Personality Code: IRC

College Majors: Artificial Intelligence and Robotics; Computer and Information Sciences and Support Services, Other; Computer and Information Sciences, General; Computer Science; Computer Systems Analysis/Analyst Training; Information Science/Studies; Medical Informatics.

Median Annual Earnings: $97,970

Highly Paid Workforce: Out of a total salaried workforce of 28,720, 14,360 people (50%) earn more than $97,970 and 7,180 (25%) earn more than $123,900.

Annual Job Growth Through 2016: 21.5%

© JIST Works

Average Annual Job Openings Through 2016: 2,901

Best-Paying Industries: Federal, State, and Local Government; Information; Manufacturing; Professional, Scientific, and Technical Services; Wholesale Trade.

Best-Paying Metro Areas: Austin–Round Rock, TX; Boston-Cambridge-Quincy, MA-NH; Chicago-Naperville-Joliet, IL-IN-WI; New York–Northern New Jersey–Long Island, NY-NJ-PA; San Francisco–Oakland–Fremont, CA; San Jose–Sunnyvale–Santa Clara, CA; Washington-Arlington-Alexandria, DC-VA-MD-WV.

Computer and Information Systems Managers

Plan, direct, or coordinate activities in such fields as electronic data processing, information systems, systems analysis, and computer programming.

Personality Code: ECI

College Majors: Computer and Information Sciences, General; Computer Science; Information Resources Management/CIO Training; Information Science/Studies; Knowledge Management; Management Information Systems, General; Operations Management and Supervision; System Administration/Administrator Training.

Median Annual Earnings: $108,070

Highly Paid Workforce: Out of a total salaried workforce of 264,990, 132,495 people (50%) earn more than $108,070.

Annual Job Growth Through 2016: 16.4%

Average Annual Job Openings Through 2016: 30,887

Best-Paying Industries: Administrative and Support and Waste Management and Remediation Services; Educational Services; Federal, State, and Local Government; Finance and Insurance; Health Care and Social Assistance; Information; Management of Companies and Enterprises; Manufacturing; Other Services (Except Public Administration); Professional, Scientific, and Technical Services; Real Estate and Rental and Leasing; Retail Trade; Transportation and Warehousing; Utilities; Wholesale Trade.

Best-Paying Metro Areas: Albany-Schenectady-Troy, NY; Atlanta–Sandy Springs–Marietta, GA; Austin–Round Rock, TX; Baltimore-Towson, MD;

Boston-Cambridge-Quincy, MA-NH; Bridgeport-Stamford-Norwalk, CT; Charlotte-Gastonia-Concord, NC-SC; Chicago-Naperville-Joliet, IL-IN-WI; Cincinnati-Middletown, OH-KY-IN; Cleveland-Elyria-Mentor, OH; Columbus, OH; Dallas–Fort Worth–Arlington, TX; Denver-Aurora, CO; Detroit-Warren-Livonia, MI; Durham, NC; Hartford–West Hartford–East Hartford, CT; Houston–Sugar Land–Baytown, TX; Indianapolis-Carmel, IN; Kansas City, MO-KS; Los Angeles–Long Beach–Santa Ana, CA; Louisville–Jefferson County, KY-IN; Miami–Fort Lauderdale–Miami Beach, FL; Milwaukee–Waukesha–West Allis, WI; Minneapolis–St. Paul–Bloomington, MN-WI; Nashville-Davidson-Murfreesboro, TN; New York–Northern New Jersey–Long Island, NY-NJ-PA; Philadelphia-Camden-Wilmington, PA-NJ-DE-MD; Phoenix-Mesa-Scottsdale, AZ; Pittsburgh, PA; Portland-Vancouver-Beaverton, OR-WA; Providence–Fall River–Warwick, RI-MA; Raleigh-Cary, NC; Richmond, VA; Rochester, NY; Sacramento–Arden-Arcade–Roseville, CA; Salt Lake City, UT; San Antonio, TX; San Diego–Carlsbad–San Marcos, CA; San Francisco–Oakland–Fremont, CA; San Jose–Sunnyvale–Santa Clara, CA; Seattle-Tacoma-Bellevue, WA; St. Louis, MO-IL; Tampa–St. Petersburg–Clearwater, FL; Trenton-Ewing, NJ; Washington-Arlington-Alexandria, DC-VA-MD-WV.

Computer Software Engineers, Applications

Develop, create, and modify general computer applications software or specialized utility programs. Analyze user needs and develop software solutions. Design software or customize software for client use with the aim of optimizing operational efficiency. May analyze and design databases within an application area, working individually or coordinating database development as part of a team.

Personality Code: IRC

College Majors: Artificial Intelligence and Robotics; Bioinformatics; Computer Engineering Technologies/Technician Training, Other; Computer Engineering, General; Computer Science; Computer Software Engineering; Information Technology; Medical Illustration and Informatics, Other; Medical Informatics.

Median Annual Earnings: $83,130

Highly Paid Workforce: Out of a total salaried workforce of 495,810, 123,953 people (25%) earn more than $102,710.

Annual Job Growth Through 2016: 44.6%

© JIST Works

Average Annual Job Openings Through 2016: 58,690

Best-Paying Industries: Finance and Insurance; Information; Management of Companies and Enterprises; Manufacturing; Other Services (Except Public Administration); Professional, Scientific, and Technical Services; Real Estate and Rental and Leasing; Transportation and Warehousing; Wholesale Trade.

Best-Paying Metro Areas: Austin–Round Rock, TX; Baltimore-Towson, MD; Boston-Cambridge-Quincy, MA-NH; Boulder, CO; Bridgeport-Stamford-Norwalk, CT; Charlotte-Gastonia-Concord, NC-SC; Chicago-Naperville-Joliet, IL-IN-WI; Dallas–Fort Worth–Arlington, TX; Denver-Aurora, CO; Durham, NC; Houston–Sugar Land–Baytown, TX; Jacksonville, FL; Los Angeles–Long Beach–Santa Ana, CA; New York–Northern New Jersey–Long Island, NY-NJ-PA; Oxnard–Thousand Oaks–Ventura, CA; Philadelphia-Camden-Wilmington, PA-NJ-DE-MD; Portland-Vancouver-Beaverton, OR-WA; Raleigh-Cary, NC; Riverside–San Bernardino–Ontario, CA; San Diego–Carlsbad–San Marcos, CA; San Francisco–Oakland–Fremont, CA; San Jose–Sunnyvale–Santa Clara, CA; Seattle-Tacoma-Bellevue, WA; Trenton-Ewing, NJ; Tucson, AZ; Washington-Arlington-Alexandria, DC-VA-MD-WV; Worcester, MA-CT.

Computer Software Engineers, Systems Software

Research, design, develop, and test operating systems-level software, compilers, and network distribution software for medical, industrial, military, communications, aerospace, business, scientific, and general computing applications. Set operational specifications and formulate and analyze software requirements. Apply principles and techniques of computer science, engineering, and mathematical analysis.

Personality Code: ICR

College Majors: Artificial Intelligence and Robotics; Computer Engineering Technologies/Technician Training, Other; Computer Engineering, General; Computer Science; Information Science/Studies; Information Technology; System, Networking, and LAN/WAN Management/Manager Training.

Median Annual Earnings: $89,070

Highly Paid Workforce: Out of a total salaried workforce of 349,140, 87,285 people (25%) earn more than $109,320.

Annual Job Growth Through 2016: 28.2%

© JIST Works

Average Annual Job Openings Through 2016: 33,139

Best-Paying Industries: Administrative and Support and Waste Management and Remediation Services; Finance and Insurance; Information; Management of Companies and Enterprises; Manufacturing; Professional, Scientific, and Technical Services; Retail Trade; Wholesale Trade.

Best-Paying Metro Areas: Albuquerque, NM; Austin–Round Rock, TX; Baltimore-Towson, MD; Boise City–Nampa, ID; Boston-Cambridge-Quincy, MA-NH; Boulder, CO; Bridgeport-Stamford-Norwalk, CT; Charlotte-Gastonia-Concord, NC-SC; Chicago-Naperville-Joliet, IL-IN-WI; Dallas–Fort Worth–Arlington, TX; Dayton, OH; Denver-Aurora, CO; Durham, NC; Hartford–West Hartford–East Hartford, CT; Houston–Sugar Land–Baytown, TX; Huntsville, AL; Los Angeles–Long Beach–Santa Ana, CA; Minneapolis–St. Paul–Bloomington, MN-WI; New York–Northern New Jersey–Long Island, NY-NJ-PA; Orlando-Kissimmee, FL; Palm Bay–Melbourne–Titusville, FL; Philadelphia-Camden-Wilmington, PA-NJ-DE-MD; Portland-Vancouver-Beaverton, OR-WA; Providence–Fall River–Warwick, RI-MA; Raleigh-Cary, NC; Richmond, VA; San Diego–Carlsbad–San Marcos, CA; San Francisco–Oakland–Fremont, CA; San Jose–Sunnyvale–Santa Clara, CA; Seattle-Tacoma-Bellevue, WA; Washington-Arlington-Alexandria, DC-VA-MD-WV.

Six-Figure Niche-Industry Jobs

(At least 10% of workers in the best-paying industries earn more than $100,000.)

Computer Programmers

Convert project specifications and statements of problems and procedures to detailed logical flow charts for coding into computer language. Develop and write computer programs to store, locate, and retrieve specific documents, data, and information. May program Web sites.

Personality Code: IC

College Majors: Artificial Intelligence and Robotics; Bioinformatics; Computer Graphics; Computer Programming, Specific Applications; Computer Programming, Vendor/Product Certification; Computer Programming/Programmer, General; E-Commerce/Electronic Commerce; Management Information Systems, General; Medical Informatics; Medical Office Computer Specialist/Assistant Training; Web Page, Digital/

© JIST Works

Multimedia and Information Resources Design; Web/Multimedia Management and Webmaster Training.

Median Annual Earnings: $68,080

Highly Paid Workforce: Out of a total salaried workforce of 394,710, 39,471 people (10%) earn more than $109,720.

Annual Job Growth Through 2016: –4.1%

Average Annual Job Openings Through 2016: 27,937

Best-Paying Industries: Administrative and Support and Waste Management and Remediation Services; Finance and Insurance; Information; Management of Companies and Enterprises; Manufacturing; Professional, Scientific, and Technical Services; Real Estate and Rental and Leasing; Retail Trade; Utilities; Wholesale Trade.

Computer Science Teachers, Postsecondary

Teach courses in computer science. May specialize in a field of computer science, such as the design and function of computers or operations and research analysis. Includes both teachers primarily engaged in teaching and those who do a combination of both teaching and research. (Also included in the Academic career track.)

Personality Code: SIC

College Majors: Computer and Information Sciences, General; Computer Programming/Programmer, General; Computer Science; Computer Systems Analysis/Analyst Training; Information Science/Studies.

Median Annual Earnings: $62,020

Highly Paid Workforce: Out of a total salaried workforce of 33,840, 8,460 people (25%) earn more than $88,390 and 3,384 (10%) earn more than $116,460.

Annual Job Growth Through 2016: 22.9%

Average Annual Job Openings Through 2016: 5,820

Best-Paying Industries: Educational Services.

Computer Specialists, All Other

This includes several computer specializations: Software Quality Assurance Engineers and Testers develop and execute software test plans in order to

© JIST Works

identify software problems and their causes. Computer Systems Engineers/ Architects design and develop solutions to complex applications problems, system administration issues, or network concerns; they perform systems management and integration functions. Network Designers determine user requirements and design specifications for computer networks; they plan and implement network upgrades. Web Developers design Web applications and Web sites; they create and specify architectural and technical parameters and direct Web site content creation, enhancement and maintenance. Web Administrators manage Web environment design, deployment, development, and maintenance activities; they perform testing and quality assurance of Web sites and Web applications.

Personality Code: CIR

College Majors: Bioinformatics; Biomathematics and Bioinformatics, Other; Computer and Information Sciences and Support Services, Other; Computer and Information Sciences, General; Computer Science; Computer Software Engineering; Computer Systems Networking and Telecommunications; Data Processing and Data Processing Technology/ Technician Training; E-Commerce/Electronic Commerce; Information Science/Studies; Information Technology; Management Information Systems and Services, Other; System, Networking, and LAN/WAN Management/Manager; Web Page, Digital/Multimedia and Information Resources Design; Web/Multimedia Management and Webmaster.

Median Annual Earnings: $71,510

Highly Paid Workforce: Out of a total salaried workforce of 182,690, 18,269 people (10%) earn more than $108,140.

Annual Job Growth Through 2016: 15.1%

Average Annual Job Openings Through 2016: 14,374

Best-Paying Industries: Administrative and Support and Waste Management and Remediation Services; Federal, State, and Local Government; Finance and Insurance; Information; Management of Companies and Enterprises; Manufacturing; Mining; Professional, Scientific, and Technical Services; Wholesale Trade.

Computer Systems Analysts

Analyze science, engineering, business, and all other data-processing problems for application to electronic data processing systems. Analyze user requirements, procedures, and problems to automate or improve existing

© JIST Works

systems and review computer system capabilities, workflow, and scheduling limitations. May analyze or recommend commercially available software. May supervise computer programmers.

Personality Code: ICR

College Majors: Computer and Information Sciences, General; Computer Systems Analysis/Analyst Training; Information Technology; Web/ Multimedia Management and Webmaster Training.

Median Annual Earnings: $73,090

Highly Paid Workforce: Out of a total salaried workforce of 464,440, 116,110 people (25%) earn more than $92,420 and 46,444 (10%) earn more than $113,670.

Annual Job Growth Through 2016: 29.0%

Average Annual Job Openings Through 2016: 63,166

Best-Paying Industries: Administrative and Support and Waste Management and Remediation Services; Construction; Finance and Insurance; Information; Management of Companies and Enterprises; Manufacturing; Other Services (Except Public Administration); Professional, Scientific, and Technical Services; Real Estate and Rental and Leasing; Retail Trade; Utilities; Wholesale Trade.

Database Administrators

Coordinate changes to computer databases; test and implement the database, applying knowledge of database management systems. May plan, coordinate, and implement security measures to safeguard computer databases.

Personality Code: CI

College Majors: Computer and Information Sciences, General; Computer and Information Systems Security; Computer Systems Analysis/Analyst Training; Data Modeling/Warehousing and Database Administration; Management Information Systems, General.

Median Annual Earnings: $67,250

Highly Paid Workforce: Out of a total salaried workforce of 116,340, 11,634 people (10%) earn more than $106,860.

Annual Job Growth Through 2016: 28.6%

© JIST Works

Average Annual Job Openings Through 2016: 8,258

Best-Paying Industries: Administrative and Support and Waste Management and Remediation Services; Finance and Insurance; Information; Management of Companies and Enterprises; Manufacturing; Professional, Scientific, and Technical Services; Transportation and Warehousing; Wholesale Trade.

Multi-Media Artists and Animators

Create special effects, animation, or other visual images, using film, video, computers, or other electronic tools and media, for use in products or creations such as computer games, movies, music videos, and commercials. (Also included in the Technician/Artisan career track.)

Personality Code: AI

College Majors: Animation, Interactive Technology, Video Graphics and Special Effects; Drawing; Graphic Design; Intermedia/Multimedia; Painting; Printmaking; Web Page, Digital/Multimedia, and Information Resources Design.

Median Annual Earnings: $54,550

Highly Paid Workforce: Out of a total salaried workforce of 29,440, 2,944 people (10%) earn more than $98,050.

Annual Job Growth Through 2016: 25.8%

Average Annual Job Openings Through 2016: 13,182

Best-Paying Industries: Information.

Network and Computer Systems Administrators

Install, configure, and support an organization's local area network (LAN), wide area network (WAN), and Internet system or a segment of a network system. Maintain network hardware and software. Monitor network to ensure network availability to all system users and perform necessary maintenance to support network availability. May supervise other network support and client server specialists and plan, coordinate, and implement network security measures.

Personality Code: ICR

College Majors: Computer and Information Sciences and Support Services, Other; Computer and Information Sciences, General; Computer

© JIST Works

and Information Systems Security; Computer Systems Analysis/Analyst Training; Computer Systems Networking and Telecommunications; Information Science/Studies; System Administration/Administrator Training; System, Networking, and LAN/WAN Management/Manager Training.

Median Annual Earnings: $64,690

Highly Paid Workforce: Out of a total salaried workforce of 309,660, 30,966 people (10%) earn more than $101,520.

Annual Job Growth Through 2016: 27.0%

Average Annual Job Openings Through 2016: 37,010

Best-Paying Industries: Administrative and Support and Waste Management and Remediation Services; Finance and Insurance; Information; Management of Companies and Enterprises; Professional, Scientific, and Technical Services; Utilities.

Network Systems and Data Communications Analysts

Analyze, design, test, and evaluate network systems, such as local area networks (LAN); wide area networks (WAN); and Internet, intranet, and other data communications systems. Perform network modeling, analysis, and planning. Research and recommend network and data communications hardware and software. Includes telecommunications specialists who deal with the interfacing of computer and communications equipment. May supervise computer programmers.

Personality Code: IC

College Majors: Computer and Information Sciences, General; Computer and Information Systems Security; Computer Systems Analysis/Analyst Training; Computer Systems Networking and Telecommunications; Information Technology; System, Networking, and LAN/WAN Management/Manager Training.

Median Annual Earnings: $68,220

Highly Paid Workforce: Out of a total salaried workforce of 216,050, 21,605 people (10%) earn more than $105,980.

Annual Job Growth Through 2016: 53.4%

Average Annual Job Openings Through 2016: 35,086

© JIST Works

Best-Paying Industries: Administrative and Support and Waste Management and Remediation Services; Finance and Insurance; Information; Management of Companies and Enterprises; Manufacturing; Other Services (Except Public Administration); Professional, Scientific, and Technical Services; Real Estate and Rental and Leasing; Utilities; Wholesale Trade.

Six-Figure Niche-Location Jobs

None.

© JIST Works

Chapter 11

The Managerial Career Track to a $100,000 Job

In every business or other organization, managers are needed to coordinate the necessary resources: workers, money, technology, time, and communications, among others. Managers make plans and monitor the fulfillment of plans.

Because managers are so important to the success of businesses, they tend to earn higher income than many other kinds of workers. That's why so many six-figure jobs belong in the Managerial career track. It also explains why people in other career tracks often find that switching to the Managerial track is a good route to higher earnings.

Your Strategy for Getting on the Managerial Career Track

Realistic

Two of the Managerial jobs included in this book have Realistic as a secondary personality type. (Enterprising is the primary type for all Managerial jobs.) One of these, Engineering Managers, is covered in the **Investigative** section of this chapter. This section focuses on the other one: Construction Managers. Those who want to manage construction usually get a college degree in the subject, and that is the preparation route described in this section. For details about how to begin as a construction worker and learn management later, see the **Realistic** section of chapter 14, about the Technician/Artisan track.

High school students should include a good helping of math and science in their curriculum. A course in accounting is also helpful. College-prep courses are suggested, plus summer jobs as a construction laborer or office worker in a construction business.

College students should major in construction management or in a related subject such as construction science or civil engineering.

New *college graduates* may begin as first-line managers, performing day-to-day, on-site supervision. *Experienced workers* are entrusted with larger projects and deal more with planning and monitoring projects. Some set up their own contracting businesses.

Investigative

Three of the Managerial jobs have Investigative as a secondary personality type: Computer and Information Systems Managers, Engineering Managers, and Natural Sciences Managers. For each of these occupations, the preparation route leads first through a different track: Information Technology (see chapter 10), Engineering (see chapter 8), or Scientific (see chapter 13). (Enterprising is the primary type for all Managerial jobs.)

High school students should take as much math and science as possible, including computer science. Independent research projects are useful experience.

College students should major in computer science, another science, or engineering. Those who want to be Natural Sciences Managers may need a master's or doctoral degree, plus perhaps postdoctoral study, to establish research credentials. Those who want to be Engineering Managers may get a master's in business administration (MBA) or in engineering management (MEM). The MBA is also a good stepping stone for Computer and Information Systems Managers, but the program should be focused on technology.

An advanced degree by itself is unlikely to qualify you for one of these managerial jobs; employers usually expect you to have relevant work experience. *Experienced workers* may be given a chance to demonstrate managerial skill by taking on simple supervisory tasks for their team, such as monitoring budgets or directing research assistants. If successful, they may advance to team leader for a project, department head, and possibly a high-level technical title, such as chief information officer. Managers who demonstrate good business skills may be promoted to manage a nontechnical department such as marketing or human resources because in high-tech firms an understanding of technical issues is helpful in those areas. Some managers may start up their own business that offers consulting or does research and development.

© JIST Works

Artistic

Two of the Managerial jobs have Artistic as a secondary personality type: Public Relations Managers and Advertising and Promotions Managers. Both require skill with using writing or various art forms (graphics, music, acting) to communicate the company's message to consumers or to various segments of the public. (Enterprising is the primary type for all Managerial jobs.)

High school students should take college-prep courses, including several to improve writing and speaking skills. Courses in the arts are also useful. Summer jobs in business settings provide helpful experience.

College students may major in advertising, public relations, or journalism. A master's in business administration (MBA) with a concentration in public relations or advertising can lead more quickly to a managerial job. It is important to gain experience by working in advertising, public relations, or journalism as a summer job or intern. Other opportunities for experience are available at the campus newspaper or radio station or in any student organization that needs publicity.

Recent *college graduates* of a four-year program may have to remain in jobs appropriate to the Bachelor's-in-Business track until they gain either experience, a master's degree, or some other kind of training in managerial skills. *Experienced workers* in the public relations or advertising department of a large company, or those who work in a service company that focuses on these functions, may be able to learn managerial skills on the job. Some associations offer certification programs that managers may find particularly valuable in a competitive job market. Company training programs and professional conferences can also help. As these managers advance, they may be put in charge of larger campaigns, become public affairs director for a large organization, move into more general managerial roles, or open their own advertising or public relations firm.

Social

Eight of the Managerial jobs have Social as a secondary personality type. All of these are covered by the **Enterprising and Conventional** section of this chapter except for the two that *do not* have Conventional as a secondary type: Social and Community Service Managers and Training and Development Managers. These two occupations are very different in many ways, but both involve a lot of work with people and attract workers who enjoy meeting people's needs. (Enterprising is the primary type for all Managerial jobs.)

© JIST Works

High school students should take college-prep courses and be sure to develop their communication skills. They may gain experience by working part-time or in summers, as either a volunteer or a paid worker, in a tutoring program or social-service agency.

College students aiming to be Social and Community Service Managers may want to major in general business management or public administration, including courses in management of nonprofits. The master's in public administration (MPA) is an option for those with a bachelor's in a non-managerial field. Another route is to train for one of the services that social and community agencies offer, such as social work or counseling, with the goal of gaining experience in a social service role before moving into management. (Social workers usually need a master's degree.) Those intending to be Training and Development Managers should major in human resources or in a general humanities curriculum with some courses in psychology, education, and business, especially human resources. Some specialized knowledge, such as a foreign language or technology, may later be useful. Students in all majors should continue to improve their communications skills and try to find summer jobs or internships related to their career goal—or at least with opportunities to work with people.

Experienced workers from a variety of backgrounds may step up to these Managerial jobs without targeted degrees. Social and Community Service Managers may have worked in a nonprofit agency in almost any capacity—for example, as a professional such as a social worker or as a business specialist such as an accountant. They may learn management skills formally, through night classes, or informally. Some Training and Development Managers have worked as training specialists after a related bachelor's in business; a teaching career; or work in a specialization that business people want to learn, such as word processing. Many trainers document their professionalism by achieving certification through the American Society for Training and Development (ASTD). Then they learn managerial skills either on the job, through a formal company training program, or through night classes.

Enterprising and Conventional

All 24 Managerial jobs have Enterprising as their primary personality type. This section focuses on 15 of these that have Conventional as a secondary type: Administrative Services Managers; Chief Executives; Compensation and Benefits Managers; Education Administrators, Elementary and Secondary School; Education Administrators, Postsecondary; Financial

© JIST Works

Managers; First-Line Supervisors/Managers of Non-Retail Sales Workers; General and Operations Managers; Industrial Production Managers; Marketing Managers; Medical and Health Services Managers; Property, Real Estate, and Community Association Managers; Purchasing Managers; Sales Managers; and Transportation, Storage, and Distribution Managers. (Three others are discussed elsewhere in this chapter: Construction Managers in the **Realistic** section, Computer and Information Systems Managers in the **Investigative** section, and Advertising and Promotions Managers in the **Artistic** section.)

Although a college education is not always necessary for managerial success, *high school students* should prepare for college and take no more than a few business-related courses, such as accounting. Summer jobs in business settings can provide valuable experience. Facility with productivity software such as spreadsheets is also useful. Good communications skills are important and should be cultivated through extracurricular activities.

College students from a variety of majors may end up in the Managerial track at some point in their careers, but to aim directly for this track as an undergraduate you should select a managerial major, such as business management or public administration. Another strategy is to complete a bachelor's degree in a nonmanagerial field and then earn a master's degree in management. Graduate school may be the only level at which to study some managerial fields, such as higher education administration or health-care administration. Sometimes an appropriate nonmanagerial bachelor's is expected—for example, in a computer-related subject as preparation for a master's in computer systems management. Summer work in business, cooperative education experience, or an internship is very important for acquiring practical skills and building a network of business contacts.

Recent *college graduates*, even though they may have a degree in a managerial field, may not be hired immediately into a managerial position, especially if they have little work experience. Instead, they may be assigned a role in a specialized function such as sales or accounting, in which they can learn about the organization and the industry. However, these grads are likely to be promoted into management more quickly than *experienced workers* who lack an appropriate degree. These workers may need to demonstrate their skill with administrative responsibilities by first taking on low-level tasks such as monitoring budgets or supervising clerical staff. Some workers who lack opportunities to demonstrate supervisory skills at work may be able to convince their bosses to give them a chance based on a track record of success at managing complex nonwork efforts, such as a charity fund drive

© JIST Works

or a community-service project. Managers often advance to positions of greater responsibility by participating in company training programs, taking courses sponsored by industry or trade associations, or attending management conferences. They may have to move from one firm to another to enlarge their responsibilities—and their earnings.

Achieving Six Figures in the Managerial Track

Managers' earnings depend on several factors: the size of the department or organization they manage (in terms of staff, budget, or territory), the industry they work in, and their reputation for getting results. Their pay is also affected by their mastery of the functions they supervise; the two Managerial jobs with the highest average pay are Engineering Managers and Computer and Information Systems Managers. Sometimes compensation includes stock options, which bring higher rewards when the company is successful. The stories of "golden parachutes" for failed CEOs are the exception rather than the rule.

Managers in large organizations have two routes for advancement up the organizational chart: "line" and "staff." Line managers are responsible for accomplishing the organization's main mission; for example, the vice president for production would be a line manager. Staff managers provide support and advice to line managers regarding some aspect of running the business; for example, the comptroller would be a staff manager. Line managers can advance to a higher position in the line, such as president or CEO, or can move to another organization where their equivalent position in the line carries greater responsibility. Staff managers may advance to the top of their department, for example becoming vice president of human resources. For most staff functions, a professional organization offers training and certification that can be helpful for advancement. Staff managers with lot of experience in the business or industry and a broad array of skills are sometimes are promoted to a line position. Others stay in a staff function but advance by moving to another organization where the same department is larger or the industry is higher paying.

Moving On to Other Career Tracks

The Entrepreneurial track is a route some managers take to gain greater income, or at least greater independence. They form a start-up company in an industry that they know well. This is easiest to do in service industries

© JIST Works

that do not require a lot of physical assets such as factories and warehouses. Some focus on purely managerial services and do consulting work as Management Analysts.

Most managers have at least some working knowledge of specialized business functions such as accounting, personnel management, sales, or public relations; in fact, some managers came from a background in one of those functions. Therefore, managers who want to reduce their supervisory tasks may decide to shift to the Bachelor's-in-Business or Distributive track, although this move may represent a lowering of income. A similar U-turn is sometimes possible for managers who earlier advanced from the Scientific or Engineering tracks, but it is less likely because their research or technical skills are likely to be dated.

Those who earn a doctoral degree may move into the Academic track, teaching business subjects and doing research in a college or university. They typically earn more than most workers in the Academic track and often supplement their earnings by doing consulting work.

Characteristics of Six-Figure Managerial Jobs

Highest-Level Skills

Management of Financial Resources; Management of Personnel Resources; Management of Material Resources; Negotiation; Systems Analysis.

Highest-Level Work Activities

Monitoring and Controlling Resources; Guiding, Directing, and Motivating Subordinates; Staffing Organizational Units; Resolving Conflicts and Negotiating with Others; Scheduling Work and Activities.

Most Important Knowledges

Economics and Accounting; Personnel and Human Resources; Administration and Management; Sales and Marketing; Clerical Practices.

Most Important Work Contexts

Telephone; Face-to-Face Discussions; Contact with Others; Electronic Mail; Freedom to Make Decisions.

© JIST Works

Most Important Work Needs
Authority; Creativity; Autonomy; Responsibility; Working Conditions.

Most Important Work Styles
Integrity; Dependability; Leadership; Initiative; Attention to Detail.

Facts About Six-Figure Managerial Jobs

Six-Figure Occupations
(At least 25% of the workers earn more than $100,000.)

Advertising and Promotions Managers

Plan and direct advertising policies and programs or produce collateral materials, such as posters, contests, coupons, or giveaways, to create extra interest in the purchase of a product or service for a department, for an entire organization, or on an account basis. (Also included in the Distributive career track.)

Personality Code: EAC

College Majors: Advertising; Marketing/Marketing Management, General; Public Relations/Image Management.

Median Annual Earnings: $78,250

Highly Paid Workforce: Out of a total salaried workforce of 36,300, 18,150 people (50%) earn more than $78,250 and 9,075 (25%) earn more than $115,910.

Annual Job Growth Through 2016: 6.2%

Average Annual Job Openings Through 2016: 2,955

Best-Paying Industries: Finance and Insurance; Information; Management of Companies and Enterprises; Manufacturing; Other Services (Except Public Administration); Professional, Scientific, and Technical Services; Wholesale Trade.

Best-Paying Metro Areas: Atlanta–Sandy Springs–Marietta, GA; Chicago-Naperville-Joliet, IL-IN-WI; Los Angeles–Long Beach–Santa Ana, CA; New York–Northern New Jersey–Long Island, NY-NJ-PA.

© JIST Works

Chief Executives

Determine and formulate policies and provide the overall direction of companies or private and public sector organizations within the guidelines set up by a board of directors or similar governing body. Plan, direct, or coordinate operational activities at the highest level of management with the help of subordinate executives and staff managers. (Also included in the Entrepreneurial career track.)

Personality Code: EC

College Majors: Business Administration/Management; Business/Commerce, General; Entrepreneurship/Entrepreneurial Studies; International Business/Trade/Commerce; International Relations and Affairs; Public Administration; Public Administration and Services, Other; Public Policy Analysis; Transportation/Transportation Management.

Median Annual Earnings: More than $145,600

Highly Paid Workforce: Out of a total salaried workforce of 299,160, 224,370 people (75%) earn more than $97,960 and 149,580 (50%) earn more than $125,600.

Annual Job Growth Through 2016: 2.0%

Average Annual Job Openings Through 2016: 21,209

Best-Paying Industries: Accommodation and Food Service; Administrative and Support and Waste Management and Remediation Services; Arts, Entertainment, and Recreation; Construction; Educational Services; Federal, State, and Local Government; Finance and Insurance; Health Care and Social Assistance; Information; Management of Companies and Enterprises; Manufacturing; Mining; Other Services (Except Public Administration); Professional, Scientific, and Technical Services; Real Estate and Rental and Leasing; Retail Trade; Transportation and Warehousing; Utilities; Wholesale Trade.

Best-Paying Metro Areas: Albany-Schenectady-Troy, NY; Atlanta–Sandy Springs–Marietta, GA; Austin–Round Rock, TX; Baltimore-Towson, MD; Birmingham-Hoover, AL; Boise City–Nampa, ID; Boston-Cambridge-Quincy, MA-NH; Charleston–North Charleston, SC; Charlotte-Gastonia-Concord, NC-SC; Chicago-Naperville-Joliet, IL-IN-WI; Cincinnati-Middletown, OH-KY-IN; Cleveland-Elyria-Mentor, OH; Columbia, SC; Columbus, OH; Dallas–Fort Worth–Arlington, TX; Denver-Aurora, CO; Detroit-Warren-Livonia, MI; Grand Rapids–Wyoming, MI; Greenville, SC; Hartford–West Hartford–East Hartford, CT; Honolulu,

HI; Houston–Sugar Land–Baytown, TX; Indianapolis-Carmel, IN; Jackson, MS; Jacksonville, FL; Kansas City, MO-KS; Knoxville, TN; Los Angeles–Long Beach–Santa Ana, CA; Louisville–Jefferson County, KY-IN; Memphis, TN-MS-AR; Miami–Fort Lauderdale–Miami Beach, FL; Milwaukee–Waukesha–West Allis, WI; Minneapolis–St. Paul–Bloomington, MN-WI; Nashville-Davidson-Murfreesboro, TN; New York–Northern New Jersey–Long Island, NY-NJ-PA; Oklahoma City, OK; Orlando-Kissimmee, FL; Philadelphia-Camden-Wilmington, PA-NJ-DE-MD; Phoenix-Mesa-Scottsdale, AZ; Pittsburgh, PA; Portland-Vancouver-Beaverton, OR-WA; Providence–Fall River–Warwick, RI-MA; Riverside–San Bernardino–Ontario, CA; Sacramento–Arden-Arcade–Roseville, CA; Salt Lake City, UT; San Diego–Carlsbad–San Marcos, CA; San Francisco–Oakland–Fremont, CA; San Jose–Sunnyvale–Santa Clara, CA; San Juan–Caguas–Guaynabo, PR; Seattle-Tacoma-Bellevue, WA; Springfield, MA-CT; St. Louis, MO-IL; Tampa–St. Petersburg–Clearwater, FL; Tulsa, OK; Washington-Arlington-Alexandria, DC-VA-MD-WV; Wichita, KS; Worcester, MA-CT.

Compensation and Benefits Managers

Plan, direct, or coordinate compensation and benefits activities and staff of an organization. (Also included in the Entrepreneurial career track.)

Personality Code: ECS

College Majors: Labor and Industrial Relations.

Median Annual Earnings: $81,410

Highly Paid Workforce: Out of a total salaried workforce of 41,780, 10,445 people (25%) earn more than $107,370.

Annual Job Growth Through 2016: 12.0%

Average Annual Job Openings Through 2016: 6,121

Best-Paying Industries: Administrative and Support and Waste Management and Remediation Services; Educational Services; Finance and Insurance; Information; Management of Companies and Enterprises; Manufacturing; Professional, Scientific, and Technical Services; Wholesale Trade.

Best-Paying Metro Areas: Boston-Cambridge-Quincy, MA-NH; Dallas–Fort Worth–Arlington, TX; Los Angeles–Long Beach–Santa Ana, CA; New York–Northern New Jersey–Long Island, NY-NJ-PA; Philadelphia-

© JIST Works

Camden-Wilmington, PA-NJ-DE-MD; Washington-Arlington-Alexandria, DC-VA-MD-WV.

Computer and Information Systems Managers

Plan, direct, or coordinate activities in such fields as electronic data processing, information systems, systems analysis, and computer programming. (Also included in the Information Technology career track.)

Personality Code: ECI

College Majors: Computer and Information Sciences, General; Computer Science; Information Resources Management/CIO Training; Information Science/Studies; Knowledge Management; Management Information Systems, General; Operations Management and Supervision; System Administration/Administrator Training.

Median Annual Earnings: $108,070

Highly Paid Workforce: Out of a total salaried workforce of 264,990, 132,495 people (50%) earn more than $108,070.

Annual Job Growth Through 2016: 16.4%

Average Annual Job Openings Through 2016: 30,887

Best-Paying Industries: Administrative and Support and Waste Management and Remediation Services; Educational Services; Federal, State, and Local Government; Finance and Insurance; Health Care and Social Assistance; Information; Management of Companies and Enterprises; Manufacturing; Other Services (Except Public Administration); Professional, Scientific, and Technical Services; Real Estate and Rental and Leasing; Retail Trade; Transportation and Warehousing; Utilities; Wholesale Trade.

Best-Paying Metro Areas: Albany-Schenectady-Troy, NY; Atlanta–Sandy Springs–Marietta, GA; Austin–Round Rock, TX; Baltimore-Towson, MD; Boston-Cambridge-Quincy, MA-NH; Bridgeport-Stamford-Norwalk, CT; Charlotte-Gastonia-Concord, NC-SC; Chicago-Naperville-Joliet, IL-IN-WI; Cincinnati-Middletown, OH-KY-IN; Cleveland-Elyria-Mentor, OH; Columbus, OH; Dallas–Fort Worth–Arlington, TX; Denver-Aurora, CO; Detroit-Warren-Livonia, MI; Durham, NC; Hartford–West Hartford–East Hartford, CT; Houston–Sugar Land–Baytown, TX; Indianapolis-Carmel, IN; Kansas City, MO-KS; Los Angeles–Long Beach–Santa Ana, CA; Louisville–Jefferson County, KY-IN; Miami–Fort Lauderdale–Miami Beach, FL; Milwaukee–Waukesha–West Allis, WI; Minneapolis–St.

© JIST Works

Paul–Bloomington, MN-WI; Nashville-Davidson-Murfreesboro, TN; New York–Northern New Jersey–Long Island, NY-NJ-PA; Philadelphia-Camden-Wilmington, PA-NJ-DE-MD; Phoenix-Mesa-Scottsdale, AZ; Pittsburgh, PA; Portland-Vancouver-Beaverton, OR-WA; Providence–Fall River–Warwick, RI-MA; Raleigh-Cary, NC; Richmond, VA; Rochester, NY; Sacramento–Arden-Arcade–Roseville, CA; Salt Lake City, UT; San Antonio, TX; San Diego–Carlsbad–San Marcos, CA; San Francisco–Oakland–Fremont, CA; San Jose–Sunnyvale–Santa Clara, CA; Seattle-Tacoma-Bellevue, WA; St. Louis, MO-IL; Tampa–St. Petersburg–Clearwater, FL; Trenton-Ewing, NJ; Washington-Arlington-Alexandria, DC-VA-MD-WV.

Construction Managers

Plan, direct, coordinate, or budget, usually through subordinate supervisory personnel, activities concerned with the construction and maintenance of structures, facilities, and systems. Participate in the conceptual development of a construction project and oversee its organization, scheduling, and implementation. (Also included in the Entrepreneurial career track.)

Personality Code: ERC

College Majors: Business Administration and Management, General; Business/Commerce, General; Construction Engineering Technology/Technician Training; Construction Management; Operations Management and Supervision.

Median Annual Earnings: $76,230

Highly Paid Workforce: Out of a total salaried workforce of 216,120, 54,030 people (25%) earn more than $102,190.

Annual Job Growth Through 2016: 15.7%

Average Annual Job Openings Through 2016: 44,158

Best-Paying Industries: Administrative and Support and Waste Management and Remediation Services; Construction; Management of Companies and Enterprises; Manufacturing; Professional, Scientific, and Technical Services; Real Estate and Rental and Leasing.

Best-Paying Metro Areas: Baltimore-Towson, MD; Boston-Cambridge-Quincy, MA-NH; Chicago-Naperville-Joliet, IL-IN-WI; Cincinnati-Middletown, OH-KY-IN; Columbus, OH; Detroit-Warren-Livonia, MI; Las Vegas–Paradise, NV; Los Angeles–Long Beach–Santa Ana, CA; Miami–Fort Lauderdale–Miami Beach, FL; Minneapolis–St.

Paul–Bloomington, MN-WI; New York–Northern New Jersey–Long Island, NY-NJ-PA; Philadelphia-Camden-Wilmington, PA-NJ-DE-MD; Phoenix-Mesa-Scottsdale, AZ; Riverside–San Bernardino–Ontario, CA; Sacramento–Arden-Arcade–Roseville, CA; San Diego–Carlsbad–San Marcos, CA; San Francisco–Oakland–Fremont, CA; Seattle-Tacoma-Bellevue, WA; Virginia Beach–Norfolk–Newport News, VA-NC; Washington-Arlington-Alexandria, DC-VA-MD-WV.

Education Administrators, Postsecondary

Plan, direct, or coordinate research, instructional, student administration and services, and other educational activities at postsecondary institutions, including universities, colleges, and junior and community colleges.

Personality Code: ECS

College Majors: Community College Education; Educational Administration and Supervision, Other; Educational Leadership and Administration, General; Educational, Instructional, and Curriculum Supervision; Higher Education/Higher Education Administration.

Median Annual Earnings: $75,780

Highly Paid Workforce: Out of a total salaried workforce of 101,160, 25,290 people (25%) earn more than $105,320.

Annual Job Growth Through 2016: 14.2%

Average Annual Job Openings Through 2016: 17,121

Best-Paying Industries: Educational Services.

Best-Paying Metro Areas: Baltimore-Towson, MD; Boston-Cambridge-Quincy, MA-NH; Chicago-Naperville-Joliet, IL-IN-WI; Detroit-Warren-Livonia, MI; New York–Northern New Jersey–Long Island, NY-NJ-PA; Philadelphia-Camden-Wilmington, PA-NJ-DE-MD; Phoenix-Mesa-Scottsdale, AZ; Washington-Arlington-Alexandria, DC-VA-MD-WV.

Engineering Managers

Plan, direct, or coordinate activities in such fields as architecture and engineering or research and development in these fields. (Also included in the Entrepreneurial career track.)

Personality Code: ERI

College Majors: Aerospace Engineering; Agricultural/Biological Engineering; Architectural Engineering; Biomedical Engineering; Ceramic

Sciences and Engineering; City/Urban, Community and Regional Planning; Civil Engineering, General; Computer Engineering, General; Electrical, Electronics and Communications Engineering; Engineering, General; Industrial Engineering; Materials Engineering; Mechanical Engineering; Metallurgical Engineering; Nuclear Engineering; Ocean Engineering; Petroleum Engineering; others.

Median Annual Earnings: $111,020

Highly Paid Workforce: Out of a total salaried workforce of 184,410, 138,308 people (75%) earn more than $88,350 and 92,205 (50%) earn more than $111,020.

Annual Job Growth Through 2016: 7.3%

Average Annual Job Openings Through 2016: 7,404

Best-Paying Industries: Administrative and Support and Waste Management and Remediation Services; Construction; Federal, State, and Local Government; Information; Management of Companies and Enterprises; Manufacturing; Mining; Professional, Scientific, and Technical Services; Transportation and Warehousing; Utilities; Wholesale Trade.

Best-Paying Metro Areas: Atlanta–Sandy Springs–Marietta, GA; Austin–Round Rock, TX; Baltimore-Towson, MD; Boston-Cambridge-Quincy, MA-NH; Charlotte-Gastonia-Concord, NC-SC; Chicago-Naperville-Joliet, IL-IN-WI; Cincinnati-Middletown, OH-KY-IN; Cleveland-Elyria-Mentor, OH; Dallas–Fort Worth–Arlington, TX; Denver-Aurora, CO; Detroit-Warren-Livonia, MI; Hartford–West Hartford–East Hartford, CT; Houston–Sugar Land–Baytown, TX; Huntsville, AL; Indianapolis-Carmel, IN; Kansas City, MO-KS; Los Angeles–Long Beach–Santa Ana, CA; Miami–Fort Lauderdale–Miami Beach, FL; Milwaukee–Waukesha–West Allis, WI; Minneapolis–St. Paul–Bloomington, MN-WI; New York–Northern New Jersey–Long Island, NY-NJ-PA; Philadelphia-Camden-Wilmington, PA-NJ-DE-MD; Phoenix-Mesa-Scottsdale, AZ; Pittsburgh, PA; Raleigh-Cary, NC; Riverside–San Bernardino–Ontario, CA; Rochester, NY; Sacramento–Arden-Arcade–Roseville, CA; San Diego–Carlsbad–San Marcos, CA; San Francisco–Oakland–Fremont, CA; San Jose–Sunnyvale–Santa Clara, CA; St. Louis, MO-IL; Washington-Arlington-Alexandria, DC-VA-MD-WV.

© JIST Works

Financial Managers

Plan, direct, and coordinate accounting, investing, banking, insurance, securities, and other financial activities of a branch, office, or department of an establishment. (Also included in the Entrepreneurial career track.)

Personality Code: EC

College Majors: Accounting and Business/Management; Accounting and Finance; Credit Management; Finance and Financial Management Services, Other; Finance, General; International Finance; Public Finance.

Median Annual Earnings: $95,310

Highly Paid Workforce: Out of a total salaried workforce of 484,390, 242,195 people (50%) earn more than $95,310 and 242,195 (25%) earn more than $130,860.

Annual Job Growth Through 2016: 12.6%

Average Annual Job Openings Through 2016: 57,589

Best-Paying Industries: Accommodation and Food Service; Administrative and Support and Waste Management and Remediation Services; Arts, Entertainment, and Recreation; Construction; Educational Services; Federal, State, and Local Government; Finance and Insurance; Health Care and Social Assistance; Information; Management of Companies and Enterprises; Manufacturing; Mining; Other Services (Except Public Administration); Professional, Scientific, and Technical Services; Real Estate and Rental and Leasing; Retail Trade; Transportation and Warehousing; Utilities; Wholesale Trade.

Best-Paying Metro Areas: Albany-Schenectady-Troy, NY; Atlanta–Sandy Springs–Marietta, GA; Austin–Round Rock, TX; Baltimore-Towson, MD; Birmingham-Hoover, AL; Boston-Cambridge-Quincy, MA-NH; Bridgeport-Stamford-Norwalk, CT; Buffalo–Niagara Falls, NY; Charlotte-Gastonia-Concord, NC-SC; Chattanooga, TN-GA; Chicago-Naperville-Joliet, IL-IN-WI; Cincinnati-Middletown, OH-KY-IN; Cleveland-Elyria-Mentor, OH; Columbia, SC; Columbus, OH; Dallas–Fort Worth–Arlington, TX; Dayton, OH; Denver-Aurora, CO; Des Moines–West Des Moines, IA; Detroit-Warren-Livonia, MI; Durham, NC; Greensboro–High Point, NC; Hartford–West Hartford–East Hartford, CT; Honolulu, HI; Houston–Sugar Land–Baytown, TX; Indianapolis-Carmel, IN; Jacksonville, FL; Kansas City, MO-KS; Las Vegas–Paradise, NV; Lexington-Fayette, KY; Los Angeles–Long Beach–Santa Ana, CA; Louisville–Jefferson County, KY-IN; Madison, WI; Memphis, TN-MS-

AR; Miami–Fort Lauderdale–Miami Beach, FL; Milwaukee–Waukesha–
West Allis, WI; Minneapolis–St. Paul–Bloomington, MN-WI; New
Haven, CT; New Orleans–Metairie–Kenner, LA; New York–Northern
New Jersey–Long Island, NY-NJ-PA; Omaha–Council Bluffs, NE-IA;
Orlando-Kissimmee, FL; Oxnard–Thousand Oaks–Ventura, CA;
Philadelphia-Camden-Wilmington, PA-NJ-DE-MD; Phoenix-Mesa-
Scottsdale, AZ; Pittsburgh, PA; Portland-Vancouver-Beaverton, OR-WA;
Providence–Fall River–Warwick, RI-MA; Raleigh-Cary, NC; Richmond,
VA; Riverside–San Bernardino–Ontario, CA; Rochester, NY; Sacramento–
Arden-Arcade–Roseville, CA; Salt Lake City, UT; San Antonio, TX; San
Diego–Carlsbad–San Marcos, CA; San Francisco–Oakland–Fremont,
CA; San Jose–Sunnyvale–Santa Clara, CA; Seattle-Tacoma-Bellevue,
WA; Springfield, MA-CT; St. Louis, MO-IL; Syracuse, NY; Tampa–St.
Petersburg–Clearwater, FL; Trenton-Ewing, NJ; Virginia Beach–Norfolk–
Newport News, VA-NC; Washington-Arlington-Alexandria, DC-VA-MD-
WV; Winston-Salem, NC; Worcester, MA-CT.

General and Operations Managers

Plan, direct, or coordinate the operations of companies or public and private sector organizations. Duties and responsibilities include formulating
policies, managing daily operations, and planning the use of materials and
human resources, but are too diverse and general in nature to be classified
in any one functional area of management or administration, such as personnel, purchasing, or administrative services. Includes owners and managers who head small business establishments whose duties are primarily
managerial. (Also included in the Entrepreneurial career track.)

Personality Code: ECS

College Majors: Business Administration and Management, General;
Business/Commerce, General; Entrepreneurship/Entrepreneurial Studies;
International Business/Trade/Commerce; Public Administration.

Median Annual Earnings: $88,700

Highly Paid Workforce: Out of a total salaried workforce of 1,655,410,
827,705 people (50%) earn more than $88,700 and 413,853 (25%) earn
more than $133,570.

Annual Job Growth Through 2016: 1.5%

Average Annual Job Openings Through 2016: 112,072

© JIST Works

Best-Paying Industries: Administrative and Support and Waste Management and Remediation Services; Agriculture, Forestry, Fishing, and Hunting; Arts, Entertainment, and Recreation; Construction; Educational Services; Federal, State, and Local Government; Finance and Insurance; Health Care and Social Assistance; Information; Management of Companies and Enterprises; Manufacturing; Mining; Other Services (Except Public Administration); Professional, Scientific, and Technical Services; Real Estate and Rental and Leasing; Retail Trade; Transportation and Warehousing; Utilities; Wholesale Trade.

Best-Paying Metro Areas: Akron, OH; Albany-Schenectady-Troy, NY; Albuquerque, NM; Alexandria, LA; Allentown-Bethlehem-Easton, PA-NJ; Amarillo, TX; Ann Arbor, MI; Appleton, WI; Asheville, NC; Atlanta–Sandy Springs–Marietta, GA; Augusta–Richmond County, GA-SC; Austin–Round Rock, TX; Bakersfield, CA; Baltimore-Towson, MD; Barnstable Town, MA; Baton Rouge, LA; Beaumont–Port Arthur, TX; Binghamton, NY; Birmingham-Hoover, AL; Boston-Cambridge-Quincy, MA-NH; Boulder, CO; Bridgeport-Stamford-Norwalk, CT; Buffalo–Niagara Falls, NY; Canton-Massillon, OH; Cape Coral–Fort Myers, FL; Charleston–North Charleston, SC; Charlotte-Gastonia-Concord, NC-SC; Chattanooga, TN-GA; Chicago-Naperville-Joliet, IL-IN-WI; Cincinnati-Middletown, OH-KY-IN; Cleveland-Elyria-Mentor, OH; College Station–Bryan, TX; Colorado Springs, CO; Columbia, SC; Columbus, OH; Corpus Christi, TX; Dallas–Fort Worth–Arlington, TX; Dalton, GA; Danbury, CT; Davenport–Moline–Rock Island, IA-IL; Dayton, OH; Denver-Aurora, CO; Des Moines–West Des Moines, IA; Detroit-Warren-Livonia, MI; Duluth, MN-WI; Durham, NC; El Paso, TX; Elkhart-Goshen, IN; Eugene-Springfield, OR; Evansville, IN-KY; Fargo, ND-MN; Fayetteville, NC; Fayetteville-Springdale-Rogers, AR-MO; Florence, SC; Fort Collins–Loveland, CO; Fort Wayne, IN; Fresno, CA; Grand Rapids–Wyoming, MI; Greeley, CO; Green Bay, WI; Greensboro–High Point, NC; Greenville, SC; Gulfport-Biloxi, MS; Hagerstown-Martinsburg, MD-WV; Harrisburg-Carlisle, PA; Hartford–West Hartford–East Hartford, CT; Hickory-Lenior-Morganton, NC; Honolulu, HI; Houma–Bayou Cane–Thibodaux, LA; Houston–Sugar Land–Baytown, TX; Huntsville, AL; Indianapolis-Carmel, IN; Jackson, MS; Jacksonville, FL; Kalamazoo-Portage, MI; Kansas City, MO-KS; Knoxville, TN; Lafayette, LA; Lake Charles, LA; Lakeland, FL; Lancaster, PA; Lansing–East Lansing, MI; Laredo, TX; Las Vegas–Paradise, NV; Lexington-Fayette, KY; Lincoln, NE; Little Rock–North Little Rock, AR; Longview, TX; Los Angeles–Long Beach–Santa Ana, CA; Louisville–Jefferson County, KY-IN; Lubbock, TX; Madison,

187

WI; Manchester, NH; Memphis, TN-MS-AR; Miami–Fort Lauderdale–Miami Beach, FL; Midland, TX; Milwaukee–Waukesha–West Allis, WI; Minneapolis–St. Paul–Bloomington, MN-WI; Mobile, AL; Modesto, CA; Montgomery, AL; Napa, CA; Naples–Marco Island, FL; Nashville-Davidson-Murfreesboro, TN; New Haven, CT; New Orleans–Metairie–Kenner, LA; New York–Northern New Jersey–Long Island, NY-NJ-PA; Norwich–New London, CT-RI; Odessa, TX; Omaha–Council Bluffs, NE-IA; Orlando-Kissimmee, FL; Oxnard–Thousand Oaks–Ventura, CA; Palm Bay–Melbourne–Titusville, FL; Pensacola–Ferry Pass–Brent, FL; Peoria, IL; Philadelphia-Camden-Wilmington, PA-NJ-DE-MD; Phoenix-Mesa-Scottsdale, AZ; Pittsburgh, PA; Portland–South Portland–Biddeford, ME; Portland-Vancouver-Beaverton, OR-WA; Poughkeepsie-Newburgh-Middletown, NY; Providence–Fall River–Warwick, RI-MA; Provo-Orem, UT; Raleigh-Cary, NC; Reading, PA; Redding, CA; Reno-Sparks, NV; Richmond, VA; Riverside–San Bernardino–Ontario, CA; Roanoke, VA; Rochester, NY; Rockford, IL; Sacramento–Arden-Arcade–Roseville, CA; Salem, OR; Salinas, CA; Salt Lake City, UT; San Antonio, TX; San Diego–Carlsbad–San Marcos, CA; San Francisco–Oakland–Fremont, CA; San Jose–Sunnyvale–Santa Clara, CA; San Juan–Caguas–Guaynabo, PR; San Luis Obispo–Paso Robles, CA; Santa Barbara–Santa Maria, CA; Santa Cruz–Watsonville, CA; Santa Rosa–Petaluma, CA; Sarasota-Bradenton-Venice, FL; Scranton–Wilkes-Barre, PA; Seattle-Tacoma-Bellevue, WA; Shreveport–Bossier City, LA; Sioux Falls, SD; South Bend–Mishawaka, IN-MI; Spartanburg, SC; Spokane, WA; Springfield, MA-CT; Springfield, MO; St. Cloud, MN; St. Louis, MO-IL; Stockton, CA; Syracuse, NY; Tallahassee, FL; Tampa–St. Petersburg–Clearwater, FL; Toledo, OH; Trenton-Ewing, NJ; Tucson, AZ; Tuscaloosa, AL; Tyler, TX; Utica-Rome, NY; Vallejo-Fairfield, CA; Virginia Beach–Norfolk–Newport News, VA-NC; Visalia-Porterville, CA; Waco, TX; Washington-Arlington-Alexandria, DC-VA-MD-WV; Waterbury, CT; Wilmington, NC; Winston-Salem, NC; Worcester, MA-CT; York-Hanover, PA; Youngstown-Warren-Boardman, OH-PA.

Industrial Production Managers

Plan, direct, or coordinate the work activities and resources necessary for manufacturing products in accordance with cost, quality, and quantity specifications. (Also included in the Entrepreneurial career track.)

Personality Code: EC

College Majors: Business Administration and Management, General; Business/Commerce, General; Operations Management and Supervision.

© JIST Works

Median Annual Earnings: $80,560

Highly Paid Workforce: Out of a total salaried workforce of 152,870, 38,218 people (25%) earn more than $104,860.

Annual Job Growth Through 2016: −5.9%

Average Annual Job Openings Through 2016: 14,889

Best-Paying Industries: Administrative and Support and Waste Management and Remediation Services; Information; Management of Companies and Enterprises; Manufacturing; Mining; Professional, Scientific, and Technical Services; Utilities; Wholesale Trade.

Best-Paying Metro Areas: Baltimore-Towson, MD; Boston-Cambridge-Quincy, MA-NH; Chicago-Naperville-Joliet, IL-IN-WI; Cincinnati-Middletown, OH-KY-IN; Cleveland-Elyria-Mentor, OH; Dallas–Fort Worth–Arlington, TX; Detroit-Warren-Livonia, MI; Hartford–West Hartford–East Hartford, CT; Houston–Sugar Land–Baytown, TX; Los Angeles–Long Beach–Santa Ana, CA; Minneapolis–St. Paul–Bloomington, MN-WI; New York–Northern New Jersey–Long Island, NY-NJ-PA; Philadelphia-Camden-Wilmington, PA-NJ-DE-MD; Phoenix-Mesa-Scottsdale, AZ; Portland-Vancouver-Beaverton, OR-WA; San Diego–Carlsbad–San Marcos, CA; San Francisco–Oakland–Fremont, CA; San Jose–Sunnyvale–Santa Clara, CA; Seattle-Tacoma-Bellevue, WA; St. Louis, MO-IL.

Marketing Managers

Determine the demand for products and services offered by a firm and its competitors and identify potential customers. Develop pricing strategies with the goal of maximizing the firm's profits or share of the market while ensuring that the firm's customers are satisfied. Oversee product development or monitor trends that indicate the need for new products and services.

Personality Code: EC

College Majors: Apparel and Textile Marketing Management; Consumer Merchandising/Retailing Management; International Marketing; Marketing Research; Marketing, Other; Marketing/Marketing Management, General.

Median Annual Earnings: $104,400

Highly Paid Workforce: Out of a total salaried workforce of 165,240, 82,620 people (50%) earn more than $104,400.

© JIST Works

Annual Job Growth Through 2016: 14.4%

Average Annual Job Openings Through 2016: 20,189

Best-Paying Industries: Accommodation and Food Service; Administrative and Support and Waste Management and Remediation Services; Arts, Entertainment, and Recreation; Construction; Educational Services; Finance and Insurance; Information; Management of Companies and Enterprises; Manufacturing; Other Services (Except Public Administration); Professional, Scientific, and Technical Services; Real Estate and Rental and Leasing; Retail Trade; Transportation and Warehousing; Utilities; Wholesale Trade.

Best-Paying Metro Areas: Atlanta–Sandy Springs–Marietta, GA; Austin–Round Rock, TX; Baltimore-Towson, MD; Boston-Cambridge-Quincy, MA-NH; Bridgeport-Stamford-Norwalk, CT; Charlotte-Gastonia-Concord, NC-SC; Chicago-Naperville-Joliet, IL-IN-WI; Cincinnati-Middletown, OH-KY-IN; Dallas–Fort Worth–Arlington, TX; Denver-Aurora, CO; Detroit-Warren-Livonia, MI; Hartford–West Hartford–East Hartford, CT; Houston–Sugar Land–Baytown, TX; Indianapolis-Carmel, IN; Kansas City, MO-KS; Las Vegas–Paradise, NV; Los Angeles–Long Beach–Santa Ana, CA; Memphis, TN-MS-AR; Miami–Fort Lauderdale–Miami Beach, FL; Minneapolis–St. Paul–Bloomington, MN-WI; Nashville-Davidson-Murfreesboro, TN; New York–Northern New Jersey–Long Island, NY-NJ-PA; Philadelphia-Camden-Wilmington, PA-NJ-DE-MD; Phoenix-Mesa-Scottsdale, AZ; Portland-Vancouver-Beaverton, OR-WA; Providence–Fall River–Warwick, RI-MA; Sacramento–Arden-Arcade–Roseville, CA; San Diego–Carlsbad–San Marcos, CA; San Francisco–Oakland–Fremont, CA; San Jose–Sunnyvale–Santa Clara, CA; Seattle-Tacoma-Bellevue, WA; St. Louis, MO-IL; Tampa–St. Petersburg–Clearwater, FL; Washington-Arlington-Alexandria, DC-VA-MD-WV.

Natural Sciences Managers

Plan, direct, or coordinate activities in such fields as life sciences, physical sciences, mathematics, and statistics and research and development in these fields. (Also included in the Scientific career track.)

Personality Code: EI

College Majors: Analytical Chemistry; Astronomy; Biology/Biological Sciences; Botany/Plant Biology; Chemistry, General; Entomology; Geology/Earth Science; Inorganic Chemistry; Marine Biology and Biological Oceanography; Mathematics, General; Meteorology;

© JIST Works

Microbiology; Molecular Biology; Nutrition Sciences; Oceanography, Organic Chemistry; Paleontology; Physics, General; Plant Pathology/ Phytopathology; Statistics, General; Theoretical and Mathematical Physics; Toxicology; Virology; Zoology; others.

Median Annual Earnings: $104,040

Highly Paid Workforce: Out of a total salaried workforce of 39,370, 19,685 people (50%) earn more than $104,040.

Annual Job Growth Through 2016: 11.4%

Average Annual Job Openings Through 2016: 3,661

Best-Paying Industries: Educational Services; Federal, State, and Local Government; Management of Companies and Enterprises; Manufacturing; Professional, Scientific, and Technical Services.

Best-Paying Metro Areas: Boston-Cambridge-Quincy, MA-NH; Los Angeles–Long Beach–Santa Ana, CA; Minneapolis–St. Paul–Bloomington, MN-WI; New York–Northern New Jersey–Long Island, NY-NJ-PA; Philadelphia-Camden-Wilmington, PA-NJ-DE-MD; San Diego–Carlsbad– San Marcos, CA; San Francisco–Oakland–Fremont, CA; Washington-Arlington-Alexandria, DC-VA-MD-WV.

Public Relations Managers

Plan and direct public relations programs designed to create and maintain a favorable public image for employer or client or, if engaged in fundraising, plan and direct activities to solicit and maintain funds for special projects and nonprofit organizations. (Also included in the Entrepreneurial career track.)

Personality Code: EA

College Majors: Public Relations/Image Management.

Median Annual Earnings: $86,470

Highly Paid Workforce: Out of a total salaried workforce of 47,210, 23,605 people (50%) earn more than $86,470 and 11,803 (25%) earn more than $121,500.

Annual Job Growth Through 2016: 16.9%

Average Annual Job Openings Through 2016: 5,781

Best-Paying Industries: Arts, Entertainment, and Recreation; Educational Services; Federal, State, and Local Government; Finance and Insurance;

Information; Management of Companies and Enterprises; Manufacturing; Other Services (Except Public Administration); Professional, Scientific, and Technical Services.

Best-Paying Metro Areas: Boston-Cambridge-Quincy, MA-NH; Chicago-Naperville-Joliet, IL-IN-WI; Los Angeles–Long Beach–Santa Ana, CA; New York–Northern New Jersey–Long Island, NY-NJ-PA; Philadelphia-Camden-Wilmington, PA-NJ-DE-MD; San Francisco–Oakland–Fremont, CA; Washington-Arlington-Alexandria, DC-VA-MD-WV.

Purchasing Managers

Plan, direct, or coordinate the activities of buyers, purchasing officers, and related workers involved in purchasing materials, products, and services. (Also included in the Entrepreneurial career track.)

Personality Code: EC

College Majors: Purchasing, Procurement/Acquisitions and Contracts Management.

Median Annual Earnings: $85,440

Highly Paid Workforce: Out of a total salaried workforce of 65,600, 32,800 people (50%) earn more than $85,440 and 16,400 (25%) earn more than $111,240.

Annual Job Growth Through 2016: 3.4%

Average Annual Job Openings Through 2016: 7,243

Best-Paying Industries: Administrative and Support and Waste Management and Remediation Services; Construction; Educational Services; Federal, State, and Local Government; Health Care and Social Assistance; Management of Companies and Enterprises; Manufacturing; Professional, Scientific, and Technical Services; Wholesale Trade.

Best-Paying Metro Areas: Atlanta–Sandy Springs–Marietta, GA; Boston-Cambridge-Quincy, MA-NH; Chicago-Naperville-Joliet, IL-IN-WI; Dallas–Fort Worth–Arlington, TX; Detroit-Warren-Livonia, MI; Houston–Sugar Land–Baytown, TX; Los Angeles–Long Beach–Santa Ana, CA; Minneapolis–St. Paul–Bloomington, MN-WI; New York–Northern New Jersey–Long Island, NY-NJ-PA; Philadelphia-Camden-Wilmington, PA-NJ-DE-MD; San Francisco–Oakland–Fremont, CA; Washington-Arlington-Alexandria, DC-VA-MD-WV.

© JIST Works

Sales Managers

Direct the actual distribution or movement of a product or service to the customer. Coordinate sales distribution by establishing sales territories, quotas, and goals and establish training programs for sales representatives. Analyze sales statistics gathered by staff to determine sales potential and inventory requirements and monitor the preferences of customers.

Personality Code: EC

College Majors: Business Administration and Management, General; Business/Commerce, General; Consumer Merchandising/Retailing Management; Marketing, Other; Marketing/Marketing Management, General.

Median Annual Earnings: $94,910

Highly Paid Workforce: Out of a total salaried workforce of 322,170, 161,085 people (50%) earn more than $94,910 and 80,542 (25%) earn more than $138,280.

Annual Job Growth Through 2016: 10.2%

Average Annual Job Openings Through 2016: 36,392

Best-Paying Industries: Administrative and Support and Waste Management and Remediation Services; Arts, Entertainment, and Recreation; Construction; Finance and Insurance; Health Care and Social Assistance; Information; Management of Companies and Enterprises; Manufacturing; Other Services (Except Public Administration); Professional, Scientific, and Technical Services; Real Estate and Rental and Leasing; Retail Trade; Transportation and Warehousing; Wholesale Trade.

Best-Paying Metro Areas: Atlanta–Sandy Springs–Marietta, GA; Austin–Round Rock, TX; Baltimore-Towson, MD; Birmingham-Hoover, AL; Boston-Cambridge-Quincy, MA-NH; Bridgeport-Stamford-Norwalk, CT; Charlotte-Gastonia-Concord, NC-SC; Chicago-Naperville-Joliet, IL-IN-WI; Cincinnati-Middletown, OH-KY-IN; Cleveland-Elyria-Mentor, OH; Columbus, OH; Dallas–Fort Worth–Arlington, TX; Denver-Aurora, CO; Detroit-Warren-Livonia, MI; Grand Rapids–Wyoming, MI; Greensboro–High Point, NC; Greenville, SC; Hartford–West Hartford–East Hartford, CT; Honolulu, HI; Houston–Sugar Land–Baytown, TX; Indianapolis-Carmel, IN; Jacksonville, FL; Kansas City, MO-KS; Los Angeles–Long Beach–Santa Ana, CA; Louisville–Jefferson County, KY-IN; Memphis, TN-MS-AR; Miami–Fort Lauderdale–Miami Beach, FL; Milwaukee–Waukesha–West Allis, WI; Minneapolis–St. Paul–Bloomington, MN-WI;

Nashville-Davidson-Murfreesboro, TN; New Orleans–Metairie–Kenner, LA; New York–Northern New Jersey–Long Island, NY-NJ-PA; Oklahoma City, OK; Orlando-Kissimmee, FL; Oxnard–Thousand Oaks–Ventura, CA; Philadelphia-Camden-Wilmington, PA-NJ-DE-MD; Phoenix-Mesa-Scottsdale, AZ; Pittsburgh, PA; Portland-Vancouver-Beaverton, OR-WA; Providence–Fall River–Warwick, RI-MA; Raleigh-Cary, NC; Riverside–San Bernardino–Ontario, CA; Sacramento–Arden-Arcade–Roseville, CA; Salt Lake City, UT; San Antonio, TX; San Diego–Carlsbad–San Marcos, CA; San Francisco–Oakland–Fremont, CA; San Jose–Sunnyvale–Santa Clara, CA; Seattle-Tacoma-Bellevue, WA; St. Louis, MO-IL; Tampa–St. Petersburg–Clearwater, FL; Tulsa, OK; Washington-Arlington-Alexandria, DC-VA-MD-WV.

Training and Development Managers

Plan, direct, or coordinate the training and development activities and staff of an organization. (Also included in the Entrepreneurial career track.)

Personality Code: ES

College Majors: Human Resources Development; Human Resources Management/Personnel Administration, General.

Median Annual Earnings: $84,340

Highly Paid Workforce: Out of a total salaried workforce of 28,170, 14,085 people (50%) earn more than $84,340 and 7,043 (25%) earn more than $111,240.

Annual Job Growth Through 2016: 15.6%

Average Annual Job Openings Through 2016: 3,759

Best-Paying Industries: Finance and Insurance; Health Care and Social Assistance; Information; Management of Companies and Enterprises; Manufacturing; Professional, Scientific, and Technical Services.

Best-Paying Metro Areas: Chicago-Naperville-Joliet, IL-IN-WI; New York–Northern New Jersey–Long Island, NY-NJ-PA.

© JIST Works

Six-Figure Niche-Industry Jobs

(At least 10% of workers in the best-paying industries earn more than $100,000.)

Administrative Services Managers

Plan, direct, or coordinate supportive services of an organization, such as recordkeeping, mail distribution, telephone operator/receptionist, and other office support services. May oversee facilities planning and maintenance and custodial operations. (Also included in the Entrepreneurial career track.)

Personality Code: EC

College Majors: Business Administration and Management, General; Business/Commerce, General; Medical/Health Management and Clinical Assistant/Specialist Training; Public Administration; Purchasing, Procurement/Acquisitions and Contracts Management; Transportation/Transportation Management.

Median Annual Earnings: $70,990

Highly Paid Workforce: Out of a total salaried workforce of 239,360, 59,840 people (25%) earn more than $94,970.

Annual Job Growth Through 2016: 11.7%

Average Annual Job Openings Through 2016: 19,513

Best-Paying Industries: Administrative and Support and Waste Management and Remediation Services; Arts, Entertainment, and Recreation; Construction; Educational Services; Federal, State, and Local Government; Finance and Insurance; Health Care and Social Assistance; Information; Management of Companies and Enterprises; Manufacturing; Mining; Other Services (Except Public Administration); Professional, Scientific, and Technical Services; Real Estate and Rental and Leasing; Retail Trade; Transportation and Warehousing; Utilities; Wholesale Trade.

Education Administrators, Elementary and Secondary School

Plan, direct, or coordinate the academic, clerical, or auxiliary activities of public or private elementary or secondary-level schools.

Personality Code: ESC

© JIST Works

College Majors: Educational Administration and Supervision, Other; Educational Leadership and Administration, General; Educational, Instructional, and Curriculum Supervision; Elementary and Middle School Administration/Principalship; Secondary School Administration/Principalship.

Median Annual Earnings: $80,580

Highly Paid Workforce: Out of a total salaried workforce of 218,820, 54,705 people (25%) earn more than $98,480 and 21,882 (10%) earn more than $117,740.

Annual Job Growth Through 2016: 7.6%

Average Annual Job Openings Through 2016: 27,143

Best-Paying Industries: Educational Services; Federal, State, and Local Government.

First-Line Supervisors/Managers of Non-Retail Sales Workers

Directly supervise and coordinate activities of sales workers other than retail sales workers. May perform duties such as budgeting, accounting, and personnel work in addition to supervisory duties. (Also included in the Distributive career track.)

Personality Code: ECS

College Majors: Business, Management, Marketing, and Related Support Services, Other; General Merchandising, Sales, and Related Marketing Operations, Other; Special Products Marketing Operations; Specialized Merchandising, Sales, and Related Marketing Operations, Other.

Median Annual Earnings: $67,020

Highly Paid Workforce: Out of a total salaried workforce of 280,770, 70,193 people (25%) earn more than $96,240 and 28,077 (10%) earn more than $133,910.

Annual Job Growth Through 2016: 3.7%

Average Annual Job Openings Through 2016: 48,883

Best-Paying Industries: Accommodation and Food Service; Administrative and Support and Waste Management and Remediation Services; Arts, Entertainment, and Recreation; Construction; Finance and

© JIST Works

Insurance; Health Care and Social Assistance; Information; Management of Companies and Enterprises; Manufacturing; Other Services (Except Public Administration); Professional, Scientific, and Technical Services; Real Estate and Rental and Leasing; Retail Trade; Wholesale Trade.

Medical and Health Services Managers

Plan, direct, or coordinate medicine and health services in hospitals, clinics, managed care organizations, public health agencies, or similar organizations. (Also included in the Entrepreneurial career track.)

Personality Code: ECS

College Majors: Community Health and Preventive Medicine; Health and Medical Administrative Services, Other; Health Information/ Medical Records Administration/Administrator Training; Health Services Administration; Health Unit Manager/Ward Supervisor Training; Health/ Health Care Administration/Management; Hospital and Health Care Facilities Administration/Management; Medical Staff Services Technology/ Technician Training; Nursing Administration (MSN, MS, PhD); Public Health, General (MPH, DPH).

Median Annual Earnings: $76,990

Highly Paid Workforce: Out of a total salaried workforce of 242,640, 60,660 people (25%) earn more than $99,680.

Annual Job Growth Through 2016: 16.4%

Average Annual Job Openings Through 2016: 31,877

Best-Paying Industries: Administrative and Support and Waste Management and Remediation Services; Educational Services; Federal, State, and Local Government; Finance and Insurance; Health Care and Social Assistance; Management of Companies and Enterprises; Professional, Scientific, and Technical Services.

Social and Community Service Managers

Plan, organize, or coordinate the activities of a social service program or community outreach organization. Oversee the program or organization's budget and policies regarding participant involvement, program requirements, and benefits. Work may involve directing social workers, counselors, or probation officers.

Personality Code: ES

© JIST Works

College Majors: Business Administration and Management, General; Business, Management, Marketing, and Related Support Services, Other; Business/Commerce, General; Community Organization and Advocacy; Entrepreneurship/Entrepreneurial Studies; Human Services, General; Non-Profit/Public/Organizational Management; Public Administration.

Median Annual Earnings: $54,530

Highly Paid Workforce: Out of a total salaried workforce of 112,330, 11,233 people (10%) earn more than $93,810.

Annual Job Growth Through 2016: 24.7%

Average Annual Job Openings Through 2016: 23,788

Best-Paying Industries: Educational Services; Federal, State, and Local Government.

Transportation, Storage, and Distribution Managers

Plan, direct, or coordinate transportation, storage, or distribution activities in accordance with governmental policies and regulations. Includes logistics managers. (Also included in the Entrepreneurial career track.)

Personality Code: EC

College Majors: Aeronautics/Aviation/Aerospace Science and Technology, General; Aviation/Airway Management and Operations; Business Administration and Management, General; Logistics and Materials Management; Public Administration; Transportation/Transportation Management.

Median Annual Earnings: $76,310

Highly Paid Workforce: Out of a total salaried workforce of 92,790, 23,198 people (25%) earn more than $97,920 and 9,279 (10%) earn more than $126,440.

Annual Job Growth Through 2016: 8.3%

Average Annual Job Openings Through 2016: 6,994

Best-Paying Industries: Administrative and Support and Waste Management and Remediation Services; Educational Services; Federal, State, and Local Government; Information; Management of Companies and Enterprises; Manufacturing; Professional, Scientific, and Technical Services; Real Estate and Rental and Leasing; Retail Trade; Transportation and Warehousing; Wholesale Trade.

© JIST Works

Six-Figure Niche-Location Jobs

(At least 10% of workers in the best-paying metro areas earn more than $100,000.)

Property, Real Estate, and Community Association Managers

Plan, direct, or coordinate selling, buying, leasing, or governance activities of commercial, industrial, or residential real estate properties. (Also included in the Entrepreneurial career track.)

Personality Code: EC

College Majors: Real Estate.

Median Annual Earnings: $43,670

Highly Paid Workforce: Out of a total salaried workforce of 159,660, 15,966 people (10%) earn more than $97,890.

Annual Job Growth Through 2016: 15.1%

Average Annual Job Openings Through 2016: 49,916

Best-Paying Metro Areas: Atlanta–Sandy Springs–Marietta, GA; Baltimore-Towson, MD; Boston-Cambridge-Quincy, MA-NH; Chicago-Naperville-Joliet, IL-IN-WI; Denver-Aurora, CO; Detroit-Warren-Livonia, MI; Miami–Fort Lauderdale–Miami Beach, FL; New York–Northern New Jersey–Long Island, NY-NJ-PA; Orlando-Kissimmee, FL; Philadelphia-Camden-Wilmington, PA-NJ-DE-MD; Phoenix-Mesa-Scottsdale, AZ; San Francisco–Oakland–Fremont, CA; Seattle-Tacoma-Bellevue, WA; St. Louis, MO-IL; Tampa–St. Petersburg–Clearwater, FL; Washington-Arlington-Alexandria, DC-VA-MD-WV.

© JIST Works

Chapter 12

The Professional Career Track to a $100,000 Job

Professional jobs require an advanced degree from a properly accredited program in a graduate or professional school. With these credentials and the knowledge you acquire in the program (perhaps supplemented by some studying afterward), you are eligible to sit for a licensing or certification exam. These jobs have such steep requirements because the workers make decisions that can profoundly affect people's lives. The jobs carry great responsibilities, but they also offer great rewards, including high income.

This chapter focuses on Professional careers in health care, the law, and architecture. You may be surprised to find several health-care occupations here that used to be considered "allied health" jobs. In fact, several of the jobs covered by this chapter technically do not require a graduate degree, but most people who go into these jobs get at least five years of education beyond high school, and to work at the six-figure income level they probably need to have a master's degree. The overall level of professionalism in these careers, rather than their minimum entry requirements, is what justifies their presence in this chapter. (Professional engineers do not always need a graduate degree, and the career pathway is so specialized that it is discussed in chapter 8, on the Engineering track.)

Your Strategy for Getting on the Professional Career Track

Realistic and Investigative

Fifteen of the Professional jobs have Investigative as their primary personality type. One of these, Pharmacists, is covered in the **Conventional** section of this chapter. The remaining 14 combine Investigative with Social, Realistic, or both as secondary types, and all are related to health care. This section includes these 14 jobs, plus Oral and Maxillofacial Surgeons (coded RSI).

High school students should take as much math and science as possible. Good communication skills are also important, so courses in English and public speaking are helpful. Volunteer work in a health-care facility is valuable experience.

College students do not need to major in a pre-med or pre-professional program as long as their program includes courses in physics, chemistry, and biology (including laboratories), English, mathematics, and the social sciences. Many students major in a science, such as biology or chemistry. Most complete a four-year degree, although some who enter dental or optometry school have completed three years and receive their bachelor's while in professional school. Veterinary schools vary on how much previous college coursework they require, but most students enter with a bachelor's. The professional schools for dentistry, medicine (including osteopathy), optometry, and veterinary science all require a specific entrance exam. For dentistry, this is the Dental Admissions Test (DAT); for medicine or osteopathy, the Medical College Admission Test (MCAT); for optometry, the Optometry Admissions Test (OAT); and for veterinary, the Graduate Record Examination (GRE, the one most often required), the Veterinary College Admission Test (VCAT), or the Medical College Admission Test (MCAT). Admission to all of these professional schools is highly competitive.

The professional schools all begin by emphasizing courses about theory and end with emphasis on clinical experience. Students spend time practicing all the important aspects of clinical care. Courses in practice management may be included. After medical school, medical doctors (M.D.s) enter a residency program, usually at a hospital, which is a form of graduate education that is accomplished through paid on-the-job training for a few years. Most new osteopaths (D.O.s) do a one-year internship before doing a residency. Doctors of veterinary medicine (D.V.M.s) may do one or both. Similarly, optometrists (D.O.s) may choose to learn advanced skills through a residency. About 65 percent of graduates of dentistry school enroll in residencies, some of which are for general dentistry and others for dental specializations such as oral and maxillofacial surgery, orthodontia, and prosthodontia.

Licensure in all of these professions requires a degree from an accredited school plus passing one or more exams. *Experienced workers* need to get continuing education to maintain their licensure. Professionals who want to learn a specialization and be certified by the appropriate professional board (for example, M.D.s who want to do plastic surgery) may spend several

© JIST Works

years in residency and have to pass another exam. Some professionals work as a salaried employee in a health-care facility or large practice early in their careers and later start a practice of their own.

Artistic

Of the 24 Professional jobs, one has Artistic as its primary personality type and is the focus of this section: Architects, Except Landscape and Naval. Three other jobs have Artistic as a secondary type: Clinical, Counseling, and School Psychologists; Psychiatrists; and Speech-Language Pathologists. Although the Artistic aspect of architecture is obvious, you may wonder where it resides in these other occupations. Consider that in these jobs workers must have great sensitivity to subtle aspects of interpersonal communication, a skill that belongs at the intersection of the Artistic and Social types. **Social** is a secondary type for all three of these jobs, and Speech-Language Pathologists is covered in that section of this chapter. The two psychological jobs have **Investigative** as their primary type and are covered in that section.

High school students aiming for a career in architecture should take college-prep courses, focusing on science, math, and the visual arts. Summer work as a construction laborer or helping a surveying team is useful experience.

Most *college students* who study architecture enter a five-year bachelor of Architecture (B. Arch.) program, but note that the coursework is so specialized that those who do not complete the program may have difficulty transferring to a different major. Another route is to get a bachelor of science in architecture (which is not a professional degree), or in a related field such as civil engineering, followed by a two-year master's in architecture. Students with a bachelor's in an unrelated field may need three or four years to complete the master's. Most architecture firms do not pay higher salaries to architects who have a master's, the exception being the larger firms.

Those who hold the professional degree need to gain work experience through an internship in an architectural firm, usually lasting at least three years, before they can sit for the licensing exams. Sometimes they complete a portion of the internship requirement while still students. Even after being licensed, *experienced workers* in most states are required to get continuing education to keep their skills up to date. Many seek certification by the National Council of Architectural Registration Boards, based on independent verification of their educational transcripts, employment record, and professional references. Certification makes it easier for them

© JIST Works

to be licensed in multiple states and often results in a raise in pay. As they gain experience, architects are given greater responsibility for projects and may become partners (part-owners) in established firms or set up their own practices.

Social

Four of the Professional jobs have Social as their primary personality type: Physical Therapists, Physician Assistants, Registered Nurses, and Speech-Language Pathologists. All of these jobs used to be considered "allied health" occupations, but academic requirements for them have been upgraded, causing them to gain professionalism. (Sixteen other jobs in this chapter have Social as a secondary type.)

High school students need a good background in college-prep math and science, especially biology. Volunteer work in a hospital or health-care facility is valuable experience.

College students can either study one of these health-care specializations as part of a bachelor's program or major in some other subject, perhaps taking coursework in biology and chemistry, with the goal of getting a professional degree in the field after the bachelor's. All of the professional degree programs begin by covering science and the theory behind health care and then transition to supervised clinical training in real health-care settings. Practitioners almost always are required to get continuing education to keep their licenses.

Those who get a bachelor's in physical therapy need to continue studying the subject for about one year extra at the master's level, and the doctorate (an additional year) is becoming increasingly important. Those with a bachelor's in a different field require additional years of study to complete a graduate degree. Licensure requires a degree from an accredited school and passing scores on national and state exams.

Physician Assistants may earn an associate degree from their preparatory program or may have military training, but most of them enter the two-year program with a bachelor's in hand, or at least two years of college plus some work experience, and these more seasoned students usually are awarded a master's. Some programs offer a Doctor of Science Physician Assistant (DScPA) degree. Even with the most professional-sounding degrees, PAs must practice under the supervision of a physician.

Nurses need to pass a national licensing exam to be licensed (that is, "registered"), and some do this after completing an associate degree program or a certificate program at a hospital. However, those with less than a bachelor's are limited in the work they can do and, therefore, their earning potential. Those experienced nurses who earn a master's or certificate in nursing (often in a specialized field) are usually called advanced practice nurses, an umbrella term that includes nurse practitioners (NP), clinical nurse specialists (CNS), certified nurse-midwives (CNM), and nurse anesthetists (CRNA). These nurses work with considerable independence, can prescribe medications, and can command high salaries.

Bachelor's programs in speech-language pathology are rare and do not qualify graduates to work as Speech-Language Pathologists. Most earn their credentials in a master's degree program, gain nine months of additional clinical experience, and then pass an exam to be licensed or registered. In most states, providing speech services in public schools usually requires a teaching license instead.

Experienced workers in these health-care specializations can advance to supervisory roles. Physical Therapists, Speech-Language Pathologists, and advanced practice nurses may open their own practices. Those with advanced degrees may pursue research or college teaching.

Enterprising

Three of the Professional jobs have Enterprising as their primary personality type: Administrative Law Judges, Adjudicators, and Hearing Officers; Judges, Magistrate Judges, and Magistrates; and Lawyers. (No jobs in this chapter have Enterprising as a secondary type.) These three occupations all require law school for most jobs that offer opportunities at the six-figure level.

High school students should prepare for college and develop their communication skills by taking courses such as English and public speaking.

Although some *college students* take a "pre-law" curriculum as a major, there are no standards for what such a program should include, nor is it necessary to have this major on your transcript. Instead, good preparation is a range of courses in the humanities and social sciences taken as part of a bachelor's degree program. Some courses may help prepare for a particular branch of the law: for example, engineering or science for those interested in patent law or accounting for those interested in tax law. Admission to law school is often competitive and depends on a mixture of factors: college grades, scores on the Law School Admission Test (LSAT), work experience, and perhaps an interview. Law school usually takes three years full

© JIST Works

time. Law students learn about important principles of the law and how to do legal research. They may get practical experience by participating in school-sponsored legal clinics, arguing appeals in moot courts, or researching and writing for the school's law review. Part-time or summer clerkships in law firms, government agencies, and corporate legal departments also provide valuable experience. After receiving the *juris doctor* (J.D.) degree, lawyers become licensed by passing the bar exam of the state where they intend to practice. The exam measures knowledge of the law and may be accompanied by exams covering practical skills and ethical standards. In almost all jurisdictions, lawyers must participate in continuing education to remain licensed.

Lawyers usually begin in salaried positions in law firms, government agencies, or the legal departments of companies. *Experienced workers* may be asked to become partners, which means they are partial owners of the firm, or go into practice for themselves. Others advance to higher positions in a legal department, such as general counsel. Judges and magistrates are appointed or elected, which means they need to build political support. Some judges, administrative law judges, and other hearing officials are not law school graduates, but these are usually in positions with limited jurisdiction and comparatively low pay. Federal administrative law judges pass a competitive exam administered by the U.S. Office of Personnel Management. Newly appointed or elected judges complete a brief orientation program lasting no more than a few weeks, but they often must take continuing education courses while serving on the bench.

Conventional

The only Professional job with Conventional as a personality type is Pharmacists, coded ICS.

High school students should take as much chemistry as possible, plus math and other college-prep courses. Volunteer work in a health-care facility is useful experience.

College students need to have completed at least two years of college before being admitted to a pharmacy school. (Most have completed three or more years.) Some colleges offer a "pre-pharmacy" major, but any program will suffice as long as it includes courses in the following sciences, including laboratory components: biology, general chemistry, organic chemistry, and physics. It should also include English, anatomy and physiology, microbiology, and calculus. Most pharmacy schools require you to take the Pharmacy College Admissions Test (PCAT). The Doctor of Pharmacy

(Pharm.D.) program usually takes four years and includes courses in theory and clinical practice. Some students continue their studies to earn a master's or PhD degree, especially to prepare for work in research or college teaching. Those who want to practice in hospitals may want or need to do a one- or two-year residency program that usually includes a research project. Those who want to own or manage a pharmacy may get a master's in business administration (MBA).

Licensure requires graduation from an accredited school of pharmacy, plus passing two exams: the North American Pharmacist Licensure Exam (NAPLEX), which tests pharmacy skills and knowledge, plus another exam about pharmacy law. *Experienced workers* in hospital pharmacies, drugstores, or pharmaceutical research companies may advance to administrative positions. Some get a graduate degree in management or at least some coursework in management. Others learn managerial skills on the job by taking over low-level supervisory tasks and gradually gaining broader responsibilities.

Achieving Six Figures in the Professional Track

It is difficult to generalize about jobs in the Professional track because they are so diverse. The three conventional routes to high pay are to specialize, to acquire a stake in one's professional practice, or to take on administrative duties.

Doctors and dentists specialize by getting clinical training and passing the board certification exam for a particularly well-compensated branch of medicine or dentistry, such as anesthesiology, cardiology, radiology, orthopedic surgery, urology, or orthodontia. Other professions have their own high-paying specializations.

Professionals often start their own practices, perhaps in partnership with other professionals, or they may be offered a partnership stake in an existing practice, perhaps after some years in which they demonstrate their productivity as salaried workers. In some cases, a professional practice can create income streams apart from direct professional service to patients or clients. For example, a veterinary practice may include a kennel for boarding pets.

Most professionals take on at least some managerial duties because they usually supervise the work of paraprofessionals and technicians: Doctors work with nurses and physician assistants; physician assistants and nurses

© JIST Works

work with orderlies and medical assistants; dentists work with hygienists and assistants; lawyers work with paralegals; judges work with law clerks; architects work with drafters and technicians. Having a large number of assistants can allow a professional to work more efficiently and therefore bring in higher earnings. Some professionals move to the Managerial track by taking on work roles in which supervisory tasks dominate. Usually this means an increase in earnings.

Moving On to Other Career Tracks

Because these workers hold advanced degrees, they often can move easily into the Academic career track. In fact, some people who earn a professional degree go directly into academia rather than pursue a career as a professional. This track would be a good shift for someone interested primarily in teaching and research. Teachers in professional schools are among the best-paid workers in the Academic track.

The Scientific track offers another pathway for health-care professionals interested primarily in research rather than in seeing patients. Companies that produce health-care products and services, such as pharmaceuticals, medical appliances, and medical information systems, need professionals on their research staffs.

For experienced workers, the Managerial track is often a route to higher income. Many professionals gain managerial experience by working in teams or supervising paraprofessionals and clerical support staff. Others earn a master's in business administration (MBA) or in a specialized field such as legal or medical administration (MLA or MMA).

Many professionals pursue the Entrepreneurial track by starting their own practice, perhaps in partnership with other practitioners. Some health-care professionals team with engineers in start-up companies to create new medical devices. Lawyers sometimes start advocacy or lobbying organizations.

Some professionals enter the Distributive track by taking a job in sales. Because of their training and experience, they are able to sell specialized equipment, supplies, and services to their fellow professionals or to organizations (such as hospitals or law practices) in their field.

© JIST Works

Characteristics of Six-Figure Professional Jobs

Highest-Level Skills

Negotiation; Persuasion; Social Perceptiveness; Service Orientation; Speaking.

Highest-Level Work Activities

Assisting and Caring for Others; Performing for or Working Directly with the Public; Identifying Objects, Actions, and Events; Documenting/Recording Processing Information; Updating and Using Relevant Knowledge.

Most Important Knowledges

Medicine and Dentistry; Therapy and Counseling; Psychology; Biology; Sociology and Anthropology.

Most Important Work Contexts

Telephone; Contact with Others; Face-to-Face Discussions; Indoors, Environmentally Controlled; Importance of Being Exact or Accurate.

Most Important Work Needs

Social Service; Ability Utilization; Achievement; Social Status; Co-workers.

Most Important Work Styles

Integrity; Dependability; Attention to Detail; Stress Tolerance; Concern for Others.

© JIST Works

Facts About Six-Figure Professional Jobs

Six-Figure Occupations

(At least 25% of the workers earn more than $100,000.)

Administrative Law Judges, Adjudicators, and Hearing Officers

Conduct hearings to decide or recommend decisions on claims concerning government programs or other government-related matters and prepare decisions. Determine penalties or the existence and the amount of liability or recommend the acceptance or rejection of claims or compromise settlements.

Personality Code: EIS

College Majors: Law (LL.B., J.D.); Legal Professions and Studies, Other.

Median Annual Earnings: $74,170

Highly Paid Workforce: Out of a total salaried workforce of 14,100, 3,525 people (25%) earn more than $104,350.

Annual Job Growth Through 2016: 0.1%

Average Annual Job Openings Through 2016: 794

Best-Paying Industries: Federal, State, and Local Government.

Best-Paying Metro Areas: No metro area has a large number of six-figure workers.

Anesthesiologists

Administer anesthetics during surgery or other medical procedures.

Personality Code: IRS

College Majors: Anesthesiology; Critical Care Anesthesiology.

Median Annual Earnings: More than $145,600

Highly Paid Workforce: Out of a total salaried workforce of 31,030, 27,927 people (90%) earn more than $118,320.

Annual Job Growth Through 2016: 14.2%

Average Annual Job Openings Through 2016: 38,027

Best-Paying Industries: Health Care and Social Assistance.

Best-Paying Metro Areas: Chicago-Naperville-Joliet, IL-IN-WI; New York–Northern New Jersey–Long Island, NY-NJ-PA.

Dentists, General

Diagnose and treat diseases, injuries, and malformations of teeth and gums and related oral structures. May treat diseases of nerve, pulp, and other dental tissues affecting vitality of teeth.

Personality Code: IRS

College Majors: Advanced General Dentistry (Cert, MS, PhD); Dental Clinical Sciences, General (MS, PhD); Dental Materials (MS, PhD); Dental Public Health and Education (Cert, MS/MPH, PhD/DPH); Dental Public Health Specialty; Dentistry (DDS, DMD); Oral Biology and Oral Pathology (MS, PhD); Pediatric Dentistry/Pedodontics (Cert, MS, PhD); Pedodontics Specialty.

Median Annual Earnings: $137,630

Highly Paid Workforce: Out of a total salaried workforce of 85,260, 63,945 people (75%) earn more than $100,040.

Annual Job Growth Through 2016: 9.2%

Average Annual Job Openings Through 2016: 7,106

Best-Paying Industries: Federal, State, and Local Government; Health Care and Social Assistance.

Best-Paying Metro Areas: Atlanta–Sandy Springs–Marietta, GA; Baltimore-Towson, MD; Boston-Cambridge-Quincy, MA-NH; Chicago-Naperville-Joliet, IL-IN-WI; Dallas–Fort Worth–Arlington, TX; Detroit-Warren-Livonia, MI; Houston–Sugar Land–Baytown, TX; Los Angeles–Long Beach–Santa Ana, CA; Miami–Fort Lauderdale–Miami Beach, FL; Minneapolis–St. Paul–Bloomington, MN-WI; New York–Northern New Jersey–Long Island, NY-NJ-PA; Philadelphia-Camden-Wilmington, PA-NJ-DE-MD; Phoenix-Mesa-Scottsdale, AZ; San Francisco–Oakland–Fremont, CA; Seattle-Tacoma-Bellevue, WA; Washington-Arlington-Alexandria, DC-VA-MD-WV.

© JIST Works

Family and General Practitioners

Diagnose, treat, and help prevent diseases and injuries that commonly occur in the general population.

Personality Code: IS

College Majors: Family Medicine; Medicine (MD); Osteopathic Medicine/Osteopathy (DO).

Median Annual Earnings: More than $145,600

Highly Paid Workforce: Out of a total salaried workforce of 113,250, 101,925 people (90%) earn more than $67,400 and 84,938 (75%) earn more than $113,480.

Annual Job Growth Through 2016: 14.2%

Average Annual Job Openings Through 2016: 38,027

Best-Paying Industries: Educational Services; Federal, State, and Local Government; Health Care and Social Assistance.

Best-Paying Metro Areas: Boston-Cambridge-Quincy, MA-NH; Chicago-Naperville-Joliet, IL-IN-WI; Columbus, OH; Dallas–Fort Worth–Arlington, TX; Detroit-Warren-Livonia, MI; Houston–Sugar Land–Baytown, TX; Kansas City, MO-KS; Los Angeles–Long Beach–Santa Ana, CA; Miami–Fort Lauderdale–Miami Beach, FL; Milwaukee–Waukesha–West Allis, WI; Minneapolis–St. Paul–Bloomington, MN-WI; New York–Northern New Jersey–Long Island, NY-NJ-PA; Omaha–Council Bluffs, NE-IA; Philadelphia-Camden-Wilmington, PA-NJ-DE-MD; Pittsburgh, PA; San Francisco–Oakland–Fremont, CA; Seattle-Tacoma-Bellevue, WA; St. Louis, MO-IL; Washington-Arlington-Alexandria, DC-VA-MD-WV.

Internists, General

Diagnose and provide non-surgical treatment of diseases and injuries of internal organ systems. Provide care mainly for adults who have a wide range of problems associated with the internal organs.

Personality Code: ISR

College Majors: Cardiology; Critical Care Medicine; Endocrinology and Metabolism; Gastroenterology; Geriatric Medicine; Hematology; Infectious Disease; Internal Medicine; Nephrology; Neurology; Nuclear Medicine; Oncology; Pulmonary Disease; Rheumatology.

© JIST Works

Median Annual Earnings: More than $145,600

Highly Paid Workforce: Out of a total salaried workforce of 46,260, 41,634 people (90%) earn more than $89,130 and 34,695 (75%) earn more than $130,750.

Annual Job Growth Through 2016: 14.2%

Average Annual Job Openings Through 2016: 38,027

Best-Paying Industries: Educational Services; Health Care and Social Assistance.

Best-Paying Metro Areas: Atlanta–Sandy Springs–Marietta, GA; Baltimore-Towson, MD; Boston-Cambridge-Quincy, MA-NH; Chicago-Naperville-Joliet, IL-IN-WI; Los Angeles–Long Beach–Santa Ana, CA; New York–Northern New Jersey–Long Island, NY-NJ-PA; Philadelphia-Camden-Wilmington, PA-NJ-DE-MD.

Judges, Magistrate Judges, and Magistrates

Arbitrate, advise, adjudicate, or administer justice in a court of law. May sentence defendant in criminal cases according to government statutes. May determine liability of defendant in civil cases. May issue marriage licenses and perform wedding ceremonies.

Personality Code: ES

College Majors: Law (LL.B., J.D.); Legal Professions and Studies, Other.

Median Annual Earnings: $107,230

Highly Paid Workforce: Out of a total salaried workforce of 25,500, 12,750 people (50%) earn more than $107,230.

Annual Job Growth Through 2016: 5.1%

Average Annual Job Openings Through 2016: 1,567

Best-Paying Industries: Federal, State, and Local Government.

Best-Paying Metro Areas: New York–Northern New Jersey–Long Island, NY-NJ-PA.

Lawyers

Represent clients in criminal and civil litigation and other legal proceedings, draw up legal documents, and manage or advise clients on legal transactions. May specialize in a single area or may practice broadly in many areas of law.

© JIST Works

Personality Code: EI

College Majors: American/U.S. Law/Legal Studies/Jurisprudence (LL.M., M.C.J., J.S.D./S.J.D.); Banking, Corporate, Finance, and Securities Law (LL.M., J.S.D./S.J.D.); Comparative Law (LL.M., M.C.L., J.S.D./S.J.D.); Energy, Environment, and Natural Resources Law (LL.M., M.S., J.S.D./S.J.D.); Health Law (LL.M., M.J., J.S.D./S.J.D.); International Law and Legal Studies (LL.M., J.S.D./S.J.D.); Law (LL.B., J.D.); Programs for Foreign Lawyers (LL.M., M.C.L.); Tax Law/Taxation (LL.M., J.S.D./S.J.D.); others.

Median Annual Earnings: $106,120

Highly Paid Workforce: Out of a total salaried workforce of 555,770, 277,885 people (50%) earn more than $106,120.

Annual Job Growth Through 2016: 11.0%

Average Annual Job Openings Through 2016: 49,445

Best-Paying Industries: Administrative and Support and Waste Management and Remediation Services; Educational Services; Federal, State, and Local Government; Finance and Insurance; Information; Management of Companies and Enterprises; Manufacturing; Other Services (Except Public Administration); Professional, Scientific, and Technical Services; Real Estate and Rental and Leasing; Transportation and Warehousing; Utilities; Wholesale Trade.

Best-Paying Metro Areas: Akron, OH; Albany-Schenectady-Troy, NY; Albuquerque, NM; Atlanta–Sandy Springs–Marietta, GA; Austin–Round Rock, TX; Baltimore-Towson, MD; Baton Rouge, LA; Birmingham-Hoover, AL; Boise City–Nampa, ID; Boston-Cambridge-Quincy, MA-NH; Bridgeport-Stamford-Norwalk, CT; Buffalo–Niagara Falls, NY; Charlotte-Gastonia-Concord, NC-SC; Chicago-Naperville-Joliet, IL-IN-WI; Cincinnati-Middletown, OH-KY-IN; Cleveland-Elyria-Mentor, OH; Columbia, SC; Columbus, OH; Dallas–Fort Worth–Arlington, TX; Denver-Aurora, CO; Des Moines–West Des Moines, IA; Detroit-Warren-Livonia, MI; Fresno, CA; Grand Rapids–Wyoming, MI; Harrisburg-Carlisle, PA; Hartford–West Hartford–East Hartford, CT; Honolulu, HI; Houston–Sugar Land–Baytown, TX; Indianapolis-Carmel, IN; Jackson, MS; Jacksonville, FL; Kansas City, MO-KS; Knoxville, TN; Las Vegas–Paradise, NV; Little Rock–North Little Rock, AR; Los Angeles–Long Beach–Santa Ana, CA; Louisville–Jefferson County, KY-IN; Madison, WI; Memphis, TN-MS-AR; Miami–Fort Lauderdale–Miami Beach, FL;

© JIST Works

Milwaukee–Waukesha–West Allis, WI; Minneapolis–St. Paul–Bloomington, MN-WI; Nashville-Davidson-Murfreesboro, TN; New Haven, CT; New Orleans–Metairie–Kenner, LA; New York–Northern New Jersey–Long Island, NY-NJ-PA; Oklahoma City, OK; Omaha–Council Bluffs, NE-IA; Orlando-Kissimmee, FL; Philadelphia-Camden-Wilmington, PA-NJ-DE-MD; Phoenix-Mesa-Scottsdale, AZ; Pittsburgh, PA; Portland–South Portland–Biddeford, ME; Portland-Vancouver-Beaverton, OR-WA; Providence–Fall River–Warwick, RI-MA; Raleigh-Cary, NC; Richmond, VA; Riverside–San Bernardino–Ontario, CA; Rochester, NY; Sacramento–Arden-Arcade–Roseville, CA; Salt Lake City, UT; San Antonio, TX; San Diego–Carlsbad–San Marcos, CA; San Francisco–Oakland–Fremont, CA; San Jose–Sunnyvale–Santa Clara, CA; Sarasota-Bradenton-Venice, FL; St. Louis, MO-IL; Syracuse, NY; Tallahassee, FL; Tampa–St. Petersburg–Clearwater, FL; Toledo, OH; Trenton-Ewing, NJ; Tucson, AZ; Tulsa, OK; Virginia Beach–Norfolk–Newport News, VA-NC; Washington-Arlington-Alexandria, DC-VA-MD-WV.

Obstetricians and Gynecologists

Diagnose, treat, and help prevent diseases of women, especially those affecting the reproductive system and the process of childbirth.

Personality Code: ISR

College Majors: Neonatal-Perinatal Medicine; Obstetrics and Gynecology.

Median Annual Earnings: More than $145,600

Highly Paid Workforce: Out of a total salaried workforce of 21,340, 19,206 people (90%) earn more than $100,770.

Annual Job Growth Through 2016: 14.2%

Average Annual Job Openings Through 2016: 38,027

Best-Paying Industries: Health Care and Social Assistance.

Best-Paying Metro Areas: New York–Northern New Jersey–Long Island, NY-NJ-PA.

Optometrists

Diagnose, manage, and treat conditions and diseases of the human eye and visual system. Examine eyes and visual system, diagnose problems or impairments, prescribe corrective lenses, and provide treatment. May prescribe therapeutic drugs to treat specific eye conditions.

© JIST Works

Personality Code: ISR

College Majors: Optometry (OD).

Median Annual Earnings: $93,800

Highly Paid Workforce: Out of a total salaried workforce of 24,900, 12,450 people (50%) earn more than $93,800 and 6,225 (25%) earn more than $121,910.

Annual Job Growth Through 2016: 11.3%

Average Annual Job Openings Through 2016: 1,789

Best-Paying Industries: Health Care and Social Assistance; Retail Trade.

Best-Paying Metro Areas: Chicago-Naperville-Joliet, IL-IN-WI; New York–Northern New Jersey–Long Island, NY-NJ-PA.

Oral and Maxillofacial Surgeons

Perform surgery on mouth, jaws, and related head and neck structure to execute difficult and multiple extractions of teeth, to remove tumors and other abnormal growths, to correct abnormal jaw relations by mandibular or maxillary revision, to prepare mouth for insertion of dental prosthesis, or to treat fractured jaws.

Personality Code: RSI

College Majors: Dental/Oral Surgery Specialty; Oral/Maxillofacial Surgery (Cert, MS, PhD).

Median Annual Earnings: More than $145,600

Highly Paid Workforce: Out of a total salaried workforce of 5,040, 4,536 people (90%) earn more than $63,850 and 3,780 (75%) earn more than $142,690.

Annual Job Growth Through 2016: 9.1%

Average Annual Job Openings Through 2016: 400

Best-Paying Industries: Health Care and Social Assistance.

Best-Paying Metro Areas: No metro area has a large number of six-figure workers.

© JIST Works

Orthodontists

Examine, diagnose, and treat dental malocclusions and oral cavity anomalies. Design and fabricate appliances to realign teeth and jaws to produce and maintain normal function and to improve appearance.

Personality Code: IRS

College Majors: Orthodontics Specialty; Orthodontics/Orthodontology (Cert, MS, PhD).

Median Annual Earnings: More than $145,600

Highly Paid Workforce: Out of a total salaried workforce of 5,350, 4,815 people (90%) earn more than $95,740.

Annual Job Growth Through 2016: 9.2%

Average Annual Job Openings Through 2016: 479

Best-Paying Industries: Health Care and Social Assistance.

Best-Paying Metro Areas: No metro area has a large number of six-figure workers.

Pediatricians, General

Diagnose, treat, and help prevent children's diseases and injuries.

Personality Code: IS

College Majors: Child/Pediatric Neurology; Family Medicine; Neonatal-Perinatal Medicine; Pediatric Cardiology; Pediatric Endocrinology; Pediatric Hemato-Oncology; Pediatric Nephrology; Pediatric Orthopedics; Pediatric Surgery; Pediatrics.

Median Annual Earnings: $140,690

Highly Paid Workforce: Out of a total salaried workforce of 28,890, 21,668 people (75%) earn more than $108,310.

Annual Job Growth Through 2016: 14.2%

Average Annual Job Openings Through 2016: 38,027

Best-Paying Industries: Educational Services; Health Care and Social Assistance.

Best-Paying Metro Areas: Boston-Cambridge-Quincy, MA-NH; Dallas–Fort Worth–Arlington, TX; Los Angeles–Long Beach–Santa Ana, CA; New York–Northern New Jersey–Long Island, NY-NJ-PA.

© JIST Works

Pharmacists

Compound and dispense medications, following prescriptions issued by physicians, dentists, or other authorized medical practitioners.

Personality Code: ICS

College Majors: Clinical and Industrial Drug Development (MS, PhD); Clinical, Hospital, and Managed Care Pharmacy (MS, PhD); Industrial and Physical Pharmacy and Cosmetic Sciences (MS, PhD); Medicinal and Pharmaceutical Chemistry (MS, PhD); Natural Products Chemistry and Pharmacognosy (MS, PhD); Pharmaceutical Economics (MS, PhD); Pharmaceutics and Drug Design (MS, PhD); Pharmacy (PharmD [USA] PharmD, BS/BPharm [Canada]); Pharmacy Administration and Pharmacy Policy and Regulatory Affairs (MS, PhD); others.

Median Annual Earnings: $100,480

Highly Paid Workforce: Out of a total salaried workforce of 253,110, 126,555 people (50%) earn more than $100,480.

Annual Job Growth Through 2016: 21.7%

Average Annual Job Openings Through 2016: 16,358

Best-Paying Industries: Administrative and Support and Waste Management and Remediation Services; Educational Services; Federal, State, and Local Government; Finance and Insurance; Health Care and Social Assistance; Retail Trade; Wholesale Trade.

Best-Paying Metro Areas: Atlanta–Sandy Springs–Marietta, GA; Austin–Round Rock, TX; Baltimore-Towson, MD; Birmingham-Hoover, AL; Boston-Cambridge-Quincy, MA-NH; Buffalo–Niagara Falls, NY; Charlotte-Gastonia-Concord, NC-SC; Chicago-Naperville-Joliet, IL-IN-WI; Cincinnati-Middletown, OH-KY-IN; Cleveland-Elyria-Mentor, OH; Columbus, OH; Dallas–Fort Worth–Arlington, TX; Denver-Aurora, CO; Detroit-Warren-Livonia, MI; Hartford–West Hartford–East Hartford, CT; Honolulu, HI; Houston–Sugar Land–Baytown, TX; Indianapolis-Carmel, IN; Jacksonville, FL; Kansas City, MO-KS; Las Vegas–Paradise, NV; Los Angeles–Long Beach–Santa Ana, CA; Louisville–Jefferson County, KY-IN; Memphis, TN-MS-AR; Miami–Fort Lauderdale–Miami Beach, FL; Milwaukee–Waukesha–West Allis, WI; Minneapolis–St. Paul–Bloomington, MN-WI; Nashville-Davidson-Murfreesboro, TN; New York–Northern New Jersey–Long Island, NY-NJ-PA; Oklahoma City, OK; Orlando-Kissimmee, FL; Philadelphia-Camden-Wilmington, PA-NJ-DE-MD; Phoenix-Mesa-Scottsdale, AZ; Portland-Vancouver-Beaverton, OR-WA;

Providence–Fall River–Warwick, RI-MA; Richmond, VA; Riverside–San Bernardino–Ontario, CA; Sacramento–Arden-Arcade–Roseville, CA; San Antonio, TX; San Diego–Carlsbad–San Marcos, CA; San Francisco–Oakland–Fremont, CA; San Jose–Sunnyvale–Santa Clara, CA; Seattle-Tacoma-Bellevue, WA; St. Louis, MO-IL; Tampa–St. Petersburg–Clearwater, FL; Virginia Beach–Norfolk–Newport News, VA-NC; Washington-Arlington-Alexandria, DC-VA-MD-WV.

Podiatrists

Diagnose and treat diseases and deformities of the human foot.

Personality Code: ISR

College Majors: Podiatric Medicine/Podiatry (DPM).

Median Annual Earnings: $110,510

Highly Paid Workforce: Out of a total salaried workforce of 9,320, 6,990 people (75%) earn more than $71,380 and 4,660 (50%) earn more than $110,510.

Annual Job Growth Through 2016: 9.5%

Average Annual Job Openings Through 2016: 648

Best-Paying Industries: Health Care and Social Assistance.

Best-Paying Metro Areas: New York–Northern New Jersey–Long Island, NY-NJ-PA.

Prosthodontists

Construct oral prostheses to replace missing teeth and other oral structures; to correct natural and acquired deformation of mouth and jaws; to restore and maintain oral function, such as chewing and speaking; and to improve appearance.

Personality Code: IR

College Majors: Prosthodontics Specialty; Prosthodontics/Prosthodontology (Cert, MS, PhD).

Median Annual Earnings: More than $145,600

Highly Paid Workforce: Out of a total salaried workforce of 380, 342 people (90%) earn more than $75,450 and 285 (75%) earn more than $122,440.

© JIST Works

Annual Job Growth Through 2016: 10.7%

Average Annual Job Openings Through 2016: 54

Best-Paying Industries: No industry has a large number of six-figure workers.

Best-Paying Metro Areas: No metro area has a large number of six-figure workers.

Psychiatrists

Diagnose, treat, and help prevent disorders of the mind.

Personality Code: ISA

College Majors: Child Psychiatry; Physical Medical and Rehabilitation/ Psychiatry; Psychiatry.

Median Annual Earnings: More than $145,600

Highly Paid Workforce: Out of a total salaried workforce of 21,790, 16,343 people (75%) earn more than $104,410.

Annual Job Growth Through 2016: 14.2%

Average Annual Job Openings Through 2016: 38,027

Best-Paying Industries: Federal, State, and Local Government; Health Care and Social Assistance.

Best-Paying Metro Areas: Los Angeles–Long Beach–Santa Ana, CA; New York–Northern New Jersey–Long Island, NY-NJ-PA.

Surgeons

Treat diseases, injuries, and deformities by invasive methods, such as manual manipulation, or by using instruments and appliances.

Personality Code: IRS

College Majors: Adult Reconstructive Orthopedics (Orthopedic Surgery); Colon and Rectal Surgery; Critical Care Surgery; General Surgery; Hand Surgery; Neurological Surgery/Neurosurgery; Orthopedic Surgery of the Spine; Orthopedics/Orthopedic Surgery; Otolaryngology; Pediatric Orthopedics; Pediatric Surgery; Plastic Surgery; Sports Medicine; Thoracic Surgery; Urology; Vascular Surgery.

Median Annual Earnings: More than $145,600

© JIST Works

Highly Paid Workforce: Out of a total salaried workforce of 50,260, 45,234 people (90%) earn more than $104,410.

Annual Job Growth Through 2016: 14.2%

Average Annual Job Openings Through 2016: 38,027

Best-Paying Industries: Educational Services; Health Care and Social Assistance.

Best-Paying Metro Areas: Boston-Cambridge-Quincy, MA-NH; Chicago-Naperville-Joliet, IL-IN-WI; Dallas–Fort Worth–Arlington, TX; Houston–Sugar Land–Baytown, TX; Los Angeles–Long Beach–Santa Ana, CA; Minneapolis–St. Paul–Bloomington, MN-WI; New York–Northern New Jersey–Long Island, NY-NJ-PA; Philadelphia-Camden-Wilmington, PA-NJ-DE-MD.

Six-Figure Niche-Industry Jobs

(At least 10% of workers in the best-paying industries earn more than $100,000.)

Architects, Except Landscape and Naval

Plan and design structures, such as private residences, office buildings, theaters, factories, and other structural property.

Personality Code: AI

College Majors: Architectural History and Criticism, General; Architecture (BArch, BA/BS, MArch, MA/MS, PhD); Architecture and Related Services, Other; Environmental Design/Architecture.

Median Annual Earnings: $67,620

Highly Paid Workforce: Out of a total salaried workforce of 106,830, 26,708 people (25%) earn more than $88,360 and 10,683 (10%) earn more than $112,990.

Annual Job Growth Through 2016: 17.7%

Average Annual Job Openings Through 2016: 11,324

Best-Paying Industries: Construction; Federal, State, and Local Government; Professional, Scientific, and Technical Services.

© JIST Works

Clinical, Counseling, and School Psychologists

Diagnose and treat mental disorders; learning disabilities; and cognitive, behavioral, and emotional problems, using individual, child, family, and group therapies. May design and implement behavior modification programs.

Personality Code: ISA

College Majors: Clinical Child Psychology; Clinical Psychology; Counseling Psychology; Developmental and Child Psychology; Educational Assessment, Testing, and Measurement; Psychoanalysis and Psychotherapy; Psychology, General; School Psychology.

Median Annual Earnings: $62,210

Highly Paid Workforce: Out of a total salaried workforce of 95,120, 9,512 people (10%) earn more than $104,520.

Annual Job Growth Through 2016: 15.8%

Average Annual Job Openings Through 2016: 8,309

Best-Paying Industries: Federal, State, and Local Government; Health Care and Social Assistance.

Physical Therapists

Assess, plan, organize, and participate in rehabilitative programs that improve mobility, relieve pain, increase strength, and decrease or prevent deformity of patients suffering from disease or injury.

Personality Code: SIR

College Majors: Kinesiotherapy/Kinesiotherapist Training; Physical Therapy/Therapist Training.

Median Annual Earnings: $69,760

Highly Paid Workforce: Out of a total salaried workforce of 161,850, 16,185 people (10%) earn more than $100,080.

Annual Job Growth Through 2016: 27.1%

Average Annual Job Openings Through 2016: 12,072

Best-Paying Industries: Administrative and Support and Waste Management and Remediation Services; Health Care and Social Assistance.

Physician Assistants

Under the supervision of a physician, provide health-care services typically performed by a physician. Conduct complete physicals, provide treatment, and counsel patients. May, in some cases, prescribe medication. Must graduate from an accredited educational program for physician assistants.

Personality Code: SIR

College Majors: Physician Assistant Training.

Median Annual Earnings: $78,450

Highly Paid Workforce: Out of a total salaried workforce of 67,160, 6,716 people (10%) earn more than $105,680.

Annual Job Growth Through 2016: 27.0%

Average Annual Job Openings Through 2016: 7,147

Best-Paying Industries: Administrative and Support and Waste Management and Remediation Services; Health Care and Social Assistance.

Speech–Language Pathologists

Assess and treat persons with speech, language, voice, and fluency disorders. May select alternative communication systems and teach their use. May perform research related to speech and language problems.

Personality Code: SIA

College Majors: Audiology/Audiologist and Speech-Language Pathology/ Pathologist Training; Communication Disorders Sciences and Services, Other; Communication Disorders, General; Speech-Language Pathology/ Pathologist Training.

Median Annual Earnings: $60,690

Highly Paid Workforce: Out of a total salaried workforce of 103,810, 10,381 people (10%) earn more than $94,740.

Annual Job Growth Through 2016: 10.6%

Average Annual Job Openings Through 2016: 11,160

Best-Paying Industries: Health Care and Social Assistance.

© JIST Works

Veterinarians

Diagnose and treat diseases and dysfunctions of animals. May engage in a particular function, such as research and development, consultation, administration, technical writing, sale or production of commercial products, or rendering of technical services to commercial firms or other organizations. Includes veterinarians who inspect livestock.

Personality Code: IR

College Majors: Comparative and Laboratory Animal Medicine; Laboratory Animal Medicine; Veterinary Anatomy (Cert, MS, PhD); Veterinary Anesthesiology; Veterinary Dentistry; Veterinary Emergency and Critical Care Medicine; Veterinary Internal Medicine; Veterinary Medicine (DVM); Veterinary Nutrition; Veterinary Pathology; Veterinary Preventive Medicine; Veterinary Radiology; Veterinary Surgery; Veterinary Toxicology; Veterinary Toxicology and Pharmacology (Cert, MS, PhD); Zoological Medicine; others.

Median Annual Earnings: $75,230

Highly Paid Workforce: Out of a total salaried workforce of 50,790, 12,698 people (25%) earn more than $98,450.

Annual Job Growth Through 2016: 35.0%

Average Annual Job Openings Through 2016: 5,301

Best-Paying Industries: Federal, State, and Local Government; Professional, Scientific, and Technical Services.

Six-Figure Niche-Location Jobs

(At least 10% of workers in the best-paying metro areas earn more than $100,000.)

Registered Nurses

Assess patient health problems and needs, develop and implement nursing care plans, and maintain medical records. Administer nursing care to ill, injured, convalescent, or disabled patients. May advise patients on health maintenance and disease prevention or provide case management. Licensing or registration required. Includes advance practice nurses, such as nurse practitioners, clinical nurse specialists, certified nurse midwives, and certified registered nurse anesthetists. Advanced practice nursing is practiced by RNs who have specialized formal, post-basic education and who function in highly autonomous and specialized roles.

Personality Code: SIC

College Majors: Adult Health Nurse Training/Nursing; Clinical Nurse Specialist Training; Critical Care Nursing; Maternal/Child Health and Neonatal Nursing; Nurse Anesthetist Training; Nurse Practitioner Training; Nursing Midwifery; Nursing Science (MS, PhD); Nursing/Registered Nurse Training (RN, ASN, BSN, MSN); Occupational and Environmental Health Nursing; Pediatric Nursing; Perioperative/Operating Room and Surgical Nurse Training/Nursing; Psychiatric/Mental Health Nurse Training/Nursing; Public Health/Community Nurse Training/Nursing; others.

Median Annual Earnings: $60,010

Highly Paid Workforce: Out of a total salaried workforce of 2,468,340, 246,834 people (10%) earn more than $87,310.

Annual Job Growth Through 2016: 23.5%

Average Annual Job Openings Through 2016: 233,499

Best-Paying Metro Areas: Boston-Cambridge-Quincy, MA-NH; Lexington-Fayette, KY; Los Angeles–Long Beach–Santa Ana, CA; Midland, TX; Modesto, CA; Naples–Marco Island, FL; New York–Northern New Jersey–Long Island, NY-NJ-PA; Sacramento–Arden-Arcade–Roseville, CA; Salinas, CA; San Francisco–Oakland–Fremont, CA; San Jose–Sunnyvale–Santa Clara, CA; Santa Rosa–Petaluma, CA; Worcester, MA-CT.

© JIST Works

Chapter 13

The Scientific Career Track to a $100,000 Job

Much of our economy is based on technology, and scientific research is what creates and improves technologies. Scientists are also needed for the quantitative research that businesses and government depend on to understand how to maximize their services and their profits. Finally, scientists increase the fund of human knowledge so we have a better understanding of our place in the universe.

Although a few Scientific careers are open to college graduates with a bachelor's degree, a master's or doctoral degree is usually more appropriate (and more lucrative) because it teaches advanced research skills.

Your Strategy for Getting on the Scientific Career Track

Realistic

Of the 15 Scientific jobs included in this book, 8 have Realistic as a secondary personality type; they provide opportunities for hands-on research in the laboratory, field, or observatory. Three of these (Astronomers; Biochemists and Biophysicists; and Medical Scientists, Except Epidemiologists) are discussed in the **Artistic** section of this chapter. Chapter 10, about the Information Technology track, has suggestions for those who want to be Computer and Information Scientists, Research. This section focuses on Chemists; Environmental Scientists and Specialists, Including Health; Geoscientists, Except Hydrologists and Geographers; and Physicists. The suggestions here also apply to Natural Sciences Managers, which is coded EI.

High school students should take as much math and science as possible, including computer science. Independent research projects can provide good experience; for those interested in geology or environmental science, this should include work in the field.

College students should major in their chosen specialization as undergraduates. Chemists may need only a bachelor's degree; a master's is usually required for Environmental Scientists and Specialists, Including Health, and for Geoscientists, Except Hydrologists and Geographers. Physicists usually need a doctorate. In all Scientific fields, an advanced degree or postdoctoral research can improve your career prospects, especially if you focus on a topic that is vital to the economy. Geoscientists and environmental scientists usually blend field work and lab work but may specialize more in one or the other. In all fields it may be possible to specialize in applications of research tools such as statistics and computers or in commercial applications such as pharmaceuticals, consumer electronics, or environmental-risk assessments. Some graduate programs allow students to include courses in management.

Experienced workers with the appropriate degree usually advance by gaining experience with research, perhaps documented by publications, conference presentations, or patents. They may gain greater independence or take on supervision of research assistants. Workers who have studied management as part of their graduate training, have completed a master's in business administration (MBA), or have acquired supervisory skills through work experience may become Natural Science Managers. Some graduates of programs in a field such as geology, meteorology, or biology acquire credentials as environmental scientists through experience in environmental-related research. Consulting is often an option for experienced scientists. As scientific knowledge advances, scientists and their managers must keep abreast of current developments.

Investigative

With two exceptions (Actuaries and Natural Sciences Managers), all of the Scientific jobs have Investigative as their primary personality type. (For Natural Sciences Managers, it is the secondary type.) Consider what secondary types might best characterize you and look at the sections of this chapter that focus on them.

Artistic

Six of the Scientific jobs covered in this book have Artistic as a secondary personality type. Writing skill is important in some of these jobs, such as Industrial-Organizational Psychologists and Political Scientists. Visualization of concepts is important in other jobs, such as Mathematicians and Astronomers. Finding new rules, rather than

© JIST Works

conforming to existing ones, is important for jobs such as Medical Scientists, Except Epidemiologists, and Biochemists and Biophysicists.

High school students should take math and science courses up to the highest levels available. Independent research projects can provide good experience.

College students should concentrate in their chosen scientific field as undergraduates and should expect to earn at least a master's degree in the field. Psychology and political science may sometimes be considered "applied" sciences, but they require mastery of statistics, and good computer skills are also important. Those in the hard sciences should earn a doctorate and perhaps do postdoctoral research to learn advanced skills and establish their credentials. Internships and postdoc positions also can lead to job offers.

Experienced workers in other fields rarely can work as scientists without the appropriate degrees. Scientists generally advance by gaining greater independence in their work, larger budgets, or tenure in university positions. Some do consulting work. Many rely on grants to support their work; funding can sometimes be hard to find or limit the subjects that researchers can explore. Scientists need to keep up to date with advances in their field.

Social

Only one Scientific job has Social as a secondary personality type: Political Scientists, which is discussed in the **Artistic** section of this chapter.

Enterprising and Conventional

Four Scientific jobs have Enterprising as a secondary type. Three of these also have Conventional as a primary or secondary type: Actuaries, Economists, and Operations Research Analysts. These are jobs that apply scientific methods of analysis to business problems. Natural Sciences Managers is coded EI, but the normal way of preparing for this career is to follow the recommendations in the **Realistic** section of this chapter.

High school students may take one or two business-related subjects such as accounting, but college-prep courses are more important, especially in math and computer science. Summer work in a business setting is helpful.

College students should expect to continue their education beyond the bachelor's degree. Undergraduate majors are available in economics, actuarial

© JIST Works

science, or operations research, or you may choose to do your bachelor's in mathematics, statistics, or computer science with minor course work in the field you intend for your career, followed by graduate study in that field. Dual graduate degrees in operations research and computer science are especially attractive to employers.

Some companies provide actuarial training for *college graduates* of a bachelor's program; to qualify for such a position, it helps to have studied economics, applied statistics, and corporate finance. Actuaries advance in their careers by passing certification exams that take them to higher levels of professionalism, which usually means higher pay. Months of study are needed to prepare for the exams. Operations Research Analysts also need to study to keep abreast of technological advances and improvements in analytical methods. Economists with a bachelor's degree usually qualify for entry-level positions as a research assistant, management trainee, or salesworker. A master's degree usually is required to qualify for more responsible research and administrative positions. A Ph.D. is necessary for top economist positions in many organizations.

Experienced workers from other backgrounds rarely can find work in these occupations; most employers expect specialized theoretical knowledge and research skills that usually are learned in the classroom rather than on the job.

Achieving Six Figures in the Scientific Track

Those who enter the Scientific track because they want to work in science usually do postdoctoral research (often for more than one term) to build up their skills, reputations, and connections. Many are not primarily interested in the money to be earned in science, but rather they enjoy the creativity and the chance to make their own decisions about their work. These often seek academic careers. Those who want the highest earnings instead go to work in industry. Some work in practical applications of scientific knowledge, sometimes competing with workers trained in the Engineering track. Workers in industry may add to their earnings by taking on a supervisory or even entrepreneurial role.

Those who want to apply their skills in a nonscientific field may get a master's in that field or learn on the job. In fields such as finance or computer systems analysis, their mathematical and analytical skills may allow them to

© JIST Works

outcompete workers trained in the Bachelor's-in-Business or Information Technology track.

Moving On to Other Career Tracks

Many scientists work in the Academic career track; they get a master's or, more likely, doctoral degree and teach in a college or university. With the appropriate degree, the Academic track can be an option at any time during your career, especially if you have published your research findings. It often is not the most lucrative career track available, but there are six-figure jobs.

The Engineering track is sometimes an option. Some students who major in a science as undergraduates get a master's degree in an engineering application of their scientific specialization. Others take no formal engineering coursework but get a job working with technological applications and learn engineering skills on the job.

Experienced workers sometimes move into the Managerial track. Getting a master's degree in business (MBA) can help. Some acquire managerial skills through supervising a research department or managing grant funding and become Natural Science Managers. Economists may get experience by working closely with the managers who rely on them for advice about finance or marketing.

The Distributive track is an option for those who have acquired a good scientific background but don't want to make a career of research. One option is working as a Sales Engineer; for sales of some applications, a degree in engineering is not needed.

Some researchers working in a field with important commercial applications may be able to jump to the Entrepreneurial track by forming their own company. Purely theoretical knowledge rarely finds buyers, but patents for products or processes may be worth large sums. Some scientists provide consulting for commercial activities; for example, they may write environmental-impact statements for construction projects or reports with economic projections for investors. (Note that for many of the jobs listed in this chapter, one of the highest-paying industries is Professional, Scientific, and Technical Services.)

© JIST Works

Characteristics of Six-Figure Scientific Jobs

Highest-Level Skills

Science; Programming; Systems Analysis; Mathematics; Complex Problem Solving.

Highest-Level Work Activities

Processing Information; Analyzing Data or Information; Estimating the Quantifiable Characteristics of Products, Events, or Information; Providing Consultation and Advice to Others; Interpreting the Meaning of Information for Others.

Most Important Knowledges

Chemistry; Mathematics; Biology; Engineering and Technology; Physics.

Most Important Work Contexts

Face-to-Face Discussions; Electronic Mail; Telephone; Indoors, Environmentally Controlled; Freedom to Make Decisions.

Most Important Work Needs

Creativity; Autonomy; Ability Utilization; Responsibility; Recognition.

Most Important Work Styles

Analytical Thinking; Integrity; Attention to Detail; Dependability; Initiative.

Facts About Six-Figure Scientific Jobs

Six-Figure Occupations

(At least 25% of the workers earn more than $100,000.)

Actuaries

Analyze statistical data, such as mortality, accident, sickness, disability, and retirement rates, and construct probability tables to forecast risk and liability for payment of future benefits. May ascertain premium rates required and cash reserves necessary to ensure payment of future benefits.

© JIST Works

Personality Code: CIE

College Majors: Actuarial Science.

Median Annual Earnings: $85,690

Highly Paid Workforce: Out of a total salaried workforce of 18,030, 9,015 people (50%) earn more than $85,690 and 4,508 (25%) earn more than $119,820.

Annual Job Growth Through 2016: 23.7%

Average Annual Job Openings Through 2016: 3,245

Best-Paying Industries: Finance and Insurance; Management of Companies and Enterprises; Professional, Scientific, and Technical Services.

Best-Paying Metro Areas: New York–Northern New Jersey–Long Island, NY-NJ-PA; Philadelphia-Camden-Wilmington, PA-NJ-DE-MD.

Astronomers

Observe, research, and interpret celestial and astronomical phenomena to increase basic knowledge and apply such information to practical problems.

Personality Code: IAR

College Majors: Astronomy; Astronomy and Astrophysics, Other; Astrophysics; Planetary Astronomy and Science.

Median Annual Earnings: $99,020

Highly Paid Workforce: Out of a total salaried workforce of 1,520, 760 people (50%) earn more than $99,020 and 380 (25%) earn more than $131,620.

Annual Job Growth Through 2016: 5.6%

Average Annual Job Openings Through 2016: 128

Best-Paying Industries: No industry has a large number of six-figure workers.

Best-Paying Metro Areas: No metro area has a large number of six-figure workers.

© JIST Works

Biochemists and Biophysicists

Study the chemical composition and physical principles of living cells and organisms, their electrical and mechanical energy, and related phenomena. May conduct research to further understanding of the complex chemical combinations and reactions involved in metabolism, reproduction, growth, and heredity. May determine the effects of foods, drugs, serums, hormones, and other substances on tissues and vital processes of living organisms.

Personality Code: IAR

College Majors: Biochemistry/Biophysics and Molecular Biology; Biophysics; Cell/Cellular Biology and Anatomical Sciences, Other; Molecular Biophysics; Soil Chemistry and Physics; Soil Microbiology.

Median Annual Earnings: $79,270

Highly Paid Workforce: Out of a total salaried workforce of 19,490, 4,873 people (25%) earn more than $104,600.

Annual Job Growth Through 2016: 15.9%

Average Annual Job Openings Through 2016: 1,637

Best-Paying Industries: Manufacturing; Professional, Scientific, and Technical Services.

Best-Paying Metro Areas: Boston-Cambridge-Quincy, MA-NH; New York–Northern New Jersey–Long Island, NY-NJ-PA; Philadelphia-Camden-Wilmington, PA-NJ-DE-MD; San Francisco–Oakland–Fremont, CA.

Computer and Information Scientists, Research

Conduct research into fundamental computer and information science as theorists, designers, or inventors. Solve or develop solutions to problems in the field of computer hardware and software. (Also included in the Information Technology career track.)

Personality Code: IRC

College Majors: Artificial Intelligence and Robotics; Computer and Information Sciences and Support Services, Other; Computer and Information Sciences, General; Computer Science; Computer Systems Analysis/Analyst Training; Information Science/Studies; Medical Informatics.

© JIST Works

Median Annual Earnings: $97,970

Highly Paid Workforce: Out of a total salaried workforce of 28,720, 14,360 people (50%) earn more than $97,970 and 7,180 (25%) earn more than $123,900.

Annual Job Growth Through 2016: 21.5%

Average Annual Job Openings Through 2016: 2,901

Best-Paying Industries: Federal, State, and Local Government; Information; Manufacturing; Professional, Scientific, and Technical Services; Wholesale Trade.

Best-Paying Metro Areas: Austin–Round Rock, TX; Boston–Cambridge-Quincy, MA-NH; Chicago-Naperville-Joliet, IL-IN-WI; New York–Northern New Jersey–Long Island, NY-NJ-PA; San Francisco–Oakland–Fremont, CA; San Jose–Sunnyvale–Santa Clara, CA; Washington-Arlington-Alexandria, DC-VA-MD-WV.

Economists

Conduct research, prepare reports, or formulate plans to aid in solution of economic problems arising from production and distribution of goods and services. May collect and process economic and statistical data, using econometric and sampling techniques. (Also included in the Enterprising career track.)

Personality Code: ICE

College Majors: Agricultural Economics; Applied Economics; Business/Managerial Economics; Development Economics and International Development; Econometrics and Quantitative Economics; Economics, General; Economics, Other; International Economics.

Median Annual Earnings: $80,220

Highly Paid Workforce: Out of a total salaried workforce of 12,740, 3,185 people (25%) earn more than $106,200.

Annual Job Growth Through 2016: 7.5%

Average Annual Job Openings Through 2016: 1,555

Best-Paying Industries: Federal, State, and Local Government; Professional, Scientific, and Technical Services.

Best-Paying Metro Areas: Washington-Arlington-Alexandria, DC-VA-MD-WV.

© JIST Works

Geoscientists, Except Hydrologists and Geographers

Study the composition, structure, and other physical aspects of the earth. May use geological, physics, and mathematics knowledge in exploration for oil, gas, minerals, or underground water or in waste disposal, land reclamation, or other environmental problems. May study the earth's internal composition, atmospheres, and oceans and its magnetic, electrical, and gravitational forces. Includes mineralogists, crystallographers, paleontologists, stratigraphers, geodesists, and seismologists.

Personality Code: IR

College Majors: Geochemistry; Geochemistry and Petrology; Geological and Earth Sciences/Geosciences, Other; Geology/Earth Science, General; Geophysics and Seismology; Oceanography, Chemical and Physical; Paleontology.

Median Annual Earnings: $75,800

Highly Paid Workforce: Out of a total salaried workforce of 31,390, 7,848 people (25%) earn more than $106,030.

Annual Job Growth Through 2016: 21.9%

Average Annual Job Openings Through 2016: 2,471

Best-Paying Industries: Mining.

Best-Paying Metro Areas: Dallas–Fort Worth–Arlington, TX; Denver-Aurora, CO; Houston–Sugar Land–Baytown, TX.

Industrial-Organizational Psychologists

Apply principles of psychology to personnel, administration, management, sales, and marketing problems. Activities may include policy planning; employee screening, training, and development; and organizational development and analysis. May work with management to reorganize the work setting to improve worker productivity.

Personality Code: IEA

College Majors: Industrial and Organizational Psychology; Psychology, General.

Median Annual Earnings: $80,820

© JIST Works

Highly Paid Workforce: Out of a total salaried workforce of 1,240, 620 people (50%) earn more than $80,820 and 310 (25%) earn more than $111,180.

Annual Job Growth Through 2016: 21.3%

Average Annual Job Openings Through 2016: 118

Best-Paying Industries: No industry has a large number of six-figure workers.

Best-Paying Metro Areas: No metro area has a large number of six-figure workers.

Mathematicians

Conduct research in fundamental mathematics or in application of mathematical techniques to science, management, and other fields. Solve or direct solutions to problems in various fields by mathematical methods.

Personality Code: ICA

College Majors: Algebra and Number Theory; Analysis and Functional Analysis; Applied Mathematics; Applied Mathematics, Other; Computational Mathematics; Geometry/Geometric Analysis; Logic; Mathematical Statistics and Probability; Mathematics and Statistics, Other; Mathematics, General; Mathematics, Other; Topology and Foundations.

Median Annual Earnings: $90,870

Highly Paid Workforce: Out of a total salaried workforce of 3,160, 1,580 people (50%) earn more than $90,870 and 790 (25%) earn more than $113,800.

Annual Job Growth Through 2016: 10.2%

Average Annual Job Openings Through 2016: 473

Best-Paying Industries: Federal, State, and Local Government; Professional, Scientific, and Technical Services.

Best-Paying Metro Areas: No metro area has a large number of six-figure workers.

Natural Sciences Managers

Plan, direct, or coordinate activities in such fields as life sciences, physical sciences, mathematics, and statistics and research and development in these fields. (Also included in the Managerial career track.)

Personality Code: EI

College Majors: Analytical Chemistry; Astronomy; Biology/Biological Sciences; Botany/Plant Biology; Chemistry, General; Entomology; Geology/Earth Science; Inorganic Chemistry; Marine Biology and Biological Oceanography; Mathematics, General; Meteorology; Microbiology; Molecular Biology; Nutrition Sciences; Oceanography, Organic Chemistry; Paleontology; Physics, General; Plant Pathology/Phytopathology; Statistics, General; Theoretical and Mathematical Physics; Toxicology; Virology; Zoology; others.

Median Annual Earnings: $104,040

Highly Paid Workforce: Out of a total salaried workforce of 39,370, 19,685 people (50%) earn more than $104,040.

Annual Job Growth Through 2016: 11.4%

Average Annual Job Openings Through 2016: 3,661

Best-Paying Industries: Educational Services; Federal, State, and Local Government; Management of Companies and Enterprises; Manufacturing; Professional, Scientific, and Technical Services.

Best-Paying Metro Areas: Boston-Cambridge-Quincy, MA-NH; Los Angeles–Long Beach–Santa Ana, CA; Minneapolis–St. Paul–Bloomington, MN-WI; New York–Northern New Jersey–Long Island, NY-NJ-PA; Philadelphia-Camden-Wilmington, PA-NJ-DE-MD; San Diego–Carlsbad–San Marcos, CA; San Francisco–Oakland–Fremont, CA; Washington-Arlington-Alexandria, DC-VA-MD-WV.

Physicists

Conduct research into the phases of physical phenomena, develop theories and laws on the basis of observation and experiments, and devise methods to apply laws and theories to industry and other fields.

Personality Code: IR

College Majors: Acoustics; Astrophysics; Atomic/Molecular Physics; Elementary Particle Physics; Health/Medical Physics; Nuclear Physics; Optics/Optical Sciences; Physics, General; Physics, Other; Plasma and High-Temperature Physics; Solid State and Low-Temperature Physics; Theoretical and Mathematical Physics.

Median Annual Earnings: $96,850

© JIST Works

Highly Paid Workforce: Out of a total salaried workforce of 13,980, 6,990 people (50%) earn more than $96,850 and 3,495 (25%) earn more than $123,610.

Annual Job Growth Through 2016: 6.8%

Average Annual Job Openings Through 2016: 1,302

Best-Paying Industries: Federal, State, and Local Government; Health Care and Social Assistance; Professional, Scientific, and Technical Services.

Best-Paying Metro Areas: Chicago-Naperville-Joliet, IL-IN-WI; New York–Northern New Jersey–Long Island, NY-NJ-PA; Washington-Arlington-Alexandria, DC-VA-MD-WV.

Political Scientists

Study the origin, development, and operation of political systems. Research a wide range of subjects, such as relations between the United States and foreign countries, the beliefs and institutions of foreign nations, or the politics of small towns or a major metropolis. May study topics such as public opinion, political decision making, and ideology. May analyze the structure and operation of governments, as well as various political entities. May conduct public opinion surveys, analyze election results, or analyze public documents.

Personality Code: IAS

College Majors: American Government and Politics (United States); Canadian Government and Politics; International/Global Studies; Political Science and Government, General; Political Science and Government, Other.

Median Annual Earnings: $91,580

Highly Paid Workforce: Out of a total salaried workforce of 3,940, 1,970 people (50%) earn more than $91,580 and 985 (25%) earn more than $118,310.

Annual Job Growth Through 2016: 5.3%

Average Annual Job Openings Through 2016: 318

Best-Paying Industries: Federal, State, and Local Government.

Best-Paying Metro Areas: Washington-Arlington-Alexandria, DC-VA-MD-WV.

© JIST Works

Six-Figure Niche-Industry Jobs

(At least 10% of workers in the best-paying industries earn more than $100,000.)

Chemists

Conduct qualitative and quantitative chemical analyses or chemical experiments in laboratories for quality or process control or to develop new products or knowledge.

Personality Code: IRC

College Majors: Analytical Chemistry; Chemical Physics; Chemistry, General; Chemistry, Other; Inorganic Chemistry; Organic Chemistry; Physical and Theoretical Chemistry; Polymer Chemistry.

Median Annual Earnings: $63,490

Highly Paid Workforce: Out of a total salaried workforce of 79,860, 7,986 people (10%) earn more than $108,610.

Annual Job Growth Through 2016: 9.1%

Average Annual Job Openings Through 2016: 9,024

Best-Paying Industries: Administrative and Support and Waste Management and Remediation Services; Federal, State, and Local Government; Management of Companies and Enterprises; Manufacturing; Professional, Scientific, and Technical Services; Wholesale Trade.

Environmental Scientists and Specialists, Including Health

Conduct research or perform investigation for the purpose of identifying, abating, or eliminating sources of pollutants or hazards that affect either the environment or the health of the population. Utilizing knowledge of various scientific disciplines, may collect, synthesize, study, report, and take action based on data derived from measurements or observations of air, food, soil, water, and other sources.

Personality Code: IRC

College Majors: Environmental Science; Environmental Studies.

Median Annual Earnings: $58,380

© JIST Works

Highly Paid Workforce: Out of a total salaried workforce of 80,070, 8,007 people (10%) earn more than $99,320.

Annual Job Growth Through 2016: 25.1%

Average Annual Job Openings Through 2016: 6,961

Best-Paying Industries: Professional, Scientific, and Technical Services.

Medical Scientists, Except Epidemiologists

Conduct research dealing with the understanding of human diseases and the improvement of human health. Engage in clinical investigation or other research, production, technical writing, or related activities.

Personality Code: IRA

College Majors: Anatomy; Biochemistry; Biomedical Sciences, General; Biophysics; Biostatistics; Cardiovascular Science; Cell Physiology; Endocrinology; Epidemiology; Human/Medical Genetics; Immunology; Medical Microbiology and Bacteriology; Molecular Biology; Molecular Pharmacology; Neurobiology and Neurophysiology; Oncology and Cancer Biology; Pathology; Pharmacology; Pharmacology and Toxicology; Physiology, General; Reproductive Biology; Toxicology; Vision Science/ Physiological Optics; others.

Median Annual Earnings: $64,200

Highly Paid Workforce: Out of a total salaried workforce of 87,440, 21,860 people (25%) earn more than $91,950 and 8,744 (10%) earn more than $124,480.

Annual Job Growth Through 2016: 20.2%

Average Annual Job Openings Through 2016: 10,596

Best-Paying Industries: Federal, State, and Local Government; Health Care and Social Assistance; Management of Companies and Enterprises; Manufacturing; Professional, Scientific, and Technical Services; Wholesale Trade.

Operations Research Analysts

Formulate and apply mathematical modeling and other optimizing methods, using a computer to develop and interpret information that assists management with decision making, policy formulation, or other managerial functions. May develop related software, service, or products. Frequently concentrates on collecting and analyzing data and developing decision support software. May develop and supply optimal time, cost, or logistics networks for program evaluation, review, or implementation. (Also included in the Enterprising career track.)

Personality Code: ICE

College Majors: Educational Evaluation and Research; Educational Statistics and Research Methods; Management Science, General; Management Sciences and Quantitative Methods, Other; Operations Research.

Median Annual Earnings: $66,950

Highly Paid Workforce: Out of a total salaried workforce of 58,750, 14,688 people (25%) earn more than $89,560 and 5,875 (10%) earn more than $113,080.

Annual Job Growth Through 2016: 10.6%

Average Annual Job Openings Through 2016: 5,727

Best-Paying Industries: Administrative and Support and Waste Management and Remediation Services; Federal, State, and Local Government; Finance and Insurance; Information; Management of Companies and Enterprises; Manufacturing; Professional, Scientific, and Technical Services; Wholesale Trade.

Six-Figure Niche-Location Jobs

None.

© JIST Works

Chapter 14

The Technician/Artisan Career Track to a $100,000 Job

The Technician/Artisan career track covers a very diverse set of jobs. Technicians are highly skilled with a technology, and artisans are highly skilled with a craft, but in fact some crafts involve a lot of technology, and to succeed with some technologies it helps to have a creative flair.

Keep in mind that a few highly skilled technicians and artisans can earn six-figure incomes in fields *other than those* listed in this chapter. Movie stars, master guitar makers, underwater welders, popular talk-radio personalities, crime-scene cleanup contractors, and superstar chefs are just a few examples of workers who achieve high earnings on the Technician/Artisan career track but whose occupational titles are not listed in this chapter. Obviously, these outstanding earners have unique talents or physical gifts and may face a lot of competition for their positions.

This chapter of the book does not cover all the possible options for achieving six figures as a technician or artisan. Instead, it focuses on 18 jobs, of which all but three are niche jobs. The attributes listed in the section headed "Characteristics of Six-Figure Technician/Artisan Jobs" apply only to these 18 jobs. However, many of the ideas in the suggested strategies for this track do apply to jobs other than the 18 covered here. For example, in the section about **Realistic** jobs, the strategy of studying math and science in high school and then learning a skill in an apprenticeship, a vocational-technical school, or the armed forces is a useful plan for entering many hands-on occupations that can lead to six-figure earnings for workers with exceptional skills and motivation (especially for those who use them as a springboard to the Managerial or Entrepreneurial track).

Your Strategy for Getting on the Technician/Artisan Career Track

Realistic

Nine of the Technician/Artisan jobs have Realistic as a primary or secondary personality type. (Three of these are covered in the **Investigative** section of this chapter: Airline Pilots, Copilots, and Flight Engineers; Commercial Pilots; and Transportation Inspectors.)

High school students should include a good helping of math and science in their curriculum. A course in accounting is also helpful. Summer jobs in the targeted industry can be helpful. Certification in CPR is helpful for fire fighting because you almost certainly will need to become certified as an emergency medical technician (EMT) at the basic level.

Apprenticeship is often a route for becoming an electrician, fire fighter, construction worker, mechanic, or production worker. The program typically lasts three or four years and combines on-the-job training with night classes. Apprentices rotate through all the relevant work tasks to learn the full set of skills and work habits. They earn while they learn. At completion of the program, which often takes four years but sometimes more or less time, they earn the status of journey worker (traditionally called "journeyman"), which qualifies them to work in this trade anywhere, and they may also earn an associate degree. Applicants for an apprenticeship may have to pass a written exam (especially for fire fighting) and a test of strength. For construction and mechanical trades, they usually must buy their own basic tools.

Vocational-technical schools, often called "institutes" when they are privately owned, have programs that teach skills in mechanical and construction trades, including Electricians. Some graduates of these programs enter apprenticeships to get additional training and experience and a credential they can take anywhere.

The *armed forces* may be an option for being trained in many trades; in some cases a formal apprenticeship is available. The Navy and Coast Guard are particularly appropriate places to launch a maritime career. See the **Investigative** section of this chapter for additional comments about the military.

College students may enroll in a maritime academy to earn a four-year bachelor of science degree and a Coast Guard license as a deck officer. Many

© JIST Works

colleges offer majors in industrial management or construction management. (For details about the college route to construction management, see the **Realistic** section of chapter 11, about the Managerial track.)

Work experience is important for advancement to management in mechanical, production, and construction trades, and for fire fighting it is virtually the only route. *Experienced workers* in trades who lack a degree in management may be able to learn some managerial skills on the job, but it helps to take night classes in business subjects. Familiarity with computers and software programs for job costing, online collaboration, scheduling, and estimating is important. Some professional organizations have developed educational programs and certification exams for management. First-line managers perform day-to-day, on-site supervision. As managers advance, they are entrusted with larger projects and deal more with planning and monitoring projects. Some set up their own consulting or contracting businesses.

Fire fighters upgrade their skills by studying and taking classes, often at a fire academy. They learn not only advanced fire-fighting techniques, but also building construction, emergency medical technology, writing, public speaking, management and budgeting procedures, and public relations. They demonstrate their skills by taking exams, usually written but sometimes also performance-based. With good performance on the job and on exams, plus seniority, they may advance to engineer, then lieutenant, captain, battalion chief, assistant chief, deputy chief, and, finally, chief. Promotion beyond chief may require a bachelor's degree in fire science or public administration.

Entry-level seamen or deckhands on vessels operating in harbors or on rivers or other waterways do not need a license. All others working on larger, ocean-going vessels do need a Coast Guard license and must pass a drug screen, take a medical exam, and be U.S. citizens. After getting experience and passing exams, deck officers may become captains. Some are able to become owner-operators of boats.

Investigative

Four Technician/Artisan jobs have Investigative as their primary personality type. One, Electricians, is covered in the **Realistic** section of this chapter. The other three jobs are in the transportation industry: Airline Pilots, Copilots, and Flight Engineers; Commercial Pilots; and Transportation Inspectors.

High school students aiming to fly planes for airlines should take college-prep courses, because most job candidates have a college degree. All others should take math and science courses, especially physics.

Many pilots get initial training and acquire flight experience in the *armed forces*. Enlisting depends on meeting certain physical and mental standards, requires a commitment of several years, means giving up certain personal freedoms, and can be hazardous even in peacetime. But in the service you get paid while you are trained and you qualify for many educational benefits after you return to civilian life. The armed forces also provide training in some transportation occupations that may give you experience relevant to a job as a transportation inspector. For detailed information about opportunities in the armed forces and steps you should take when signing up and transitioning out, see *150 Best Jobs Through Military Training* (JIST).

College students intending to be airline pilots may enroll in an aeronautical science major at a few colleges. Flight schools specializing in pilot training are another option. Those who want to be test pilots should get a degree in aeronautical engineering. (See chapter 8, about the Engineering track.) For a high-level career in transportation inspection, it may help to major in transportation management, a concentration available at some colleges.

Experienced workers in the field of transportation inspection, such as those who inspect airports for compliance with safety standards, may command high salaries. Pilots need flight experience to qualify for a license and must pass a written test, plus they must get continuing training and testing with flight simulators to maintain licensure. Airline pilots need to be able to fly at night and by instruments, which means they need additional experience and must pass tests beyond those required for the basic license. Many pilots start with regional or commuter airlines to get the experience they need to be hired by a major airline.

Artistic

Five of the Technician/Artisan jobs have Artistic as their primary personality type: Art Directors; Editors; Film and Video Editors; Multi-Media Artists and Animators (which is covered in greater detail in the Information Technology career track, chapter 10); and Writers and Authors.

High school students should take college-prep courses, plus courses related to either the visual arts or writing. Students can get valuable experience by participating in student activities related to the arts—for example, painting

© JIST Works

stage sets; shooting and editing a YouTube video to promote a candidate for student government; or writing articles or drawing cartoons for the student newspaper or literary magazine.

College students should prepare for the art form in which they plan to work. Those planning to be writers and editors may major in English or in any other subject that gives them experience with writing. Some may choose a career-oriented major such as journalism or communications. Courses in science or business may be useful for those who want to edit technical writing. Student publications and internships can provide valuable writing and editing experience. Those aiming for the visual arts may go to art school or study in the art or cinema department of a liberal arts college or university. Students can gain experience through projects required by courses, internships, or volunteer work with local arts groups.

Recently graduated art majors usually begin as entry-level artists in advertising, publishing, design, and motion picture production firms. *Experienced workers* may be promoted to Art Directors after demonstrating artistic and leadership abilities. Film and Video Editors usually serve a few years of apprenticeship with an experienced editor before they are recognized as fully qualified. Some advance to become directors, perhaps after another apprenticeship.

People with good writing skills may transfer from jobs as technicians, scientists, or engineers into jobs as writers or editors. Some workers start as copy editors, who make sure all the text is correct, and advance to become acquisitions or developmental editors, who decide which articles or books should be published and work with authors to shape the content and style of publications. Writers may begin as freelancers and, after building a reputation for meeting deadlines and doing quality work, may be taken on as staff writers. Writers of larger works, such as novels or screenplays, often use the services of agents to find buyers for their output. New media such as blogs are providing new ways for writers to reach readers and establish reputations.

Social

None of the Technician/Artisan jobs has Social as a primary or personality type, but two have it as a secondary type: First-Line Supervisors/Managers of Police and Detectives and Flight Attendants, both coded ESC.

High school students should take college-prep courses. Applicants for jobs as Flight Attendants do not usually need a college degree, but one can

© JIST Works

be a plus, especially from a college or school that offers flight attendant training. Some police departments require some college or a degree. High school courses in public speaking and foreign language are helpful, and summer jobs that work with the public are good experience.

Some police and flight attendants get training and work experience in the *armed forces*. For details about the military, see the **Investigative** section of this chapter.

College students should major in flight attendant training, if available, or law enforcement. Knowledge of a foreign language can be very helpful or even required in some positions. Training in CPR is also useful and will be required on the job. Participation in sports is recommended for those seeking police work, because fitness is important.

To be accepted for police academy training, you generally must pass a civil service exam, a fitness exam, drug testing, and psychological testing. After several months of training at the police academy, new officers usually serve for a probationary period before they are considered for promotion to detective or specialist in a kind of police work. *Experienced workers* may be promoted to corporal, sergeant, lieutenant, and captain, depending on job performance and passing written exams. Police receive continuing training to be aware of legal and tactical developments.

Applicants for jobs as Flight Attendants have an advantage if they have experience working with the public and some college, especially training in flight attendant skills. They also are screened by a background check. Training by the airline takes three to eight weeks, and trainees are not considered employees until they have completed the program, which includes several performance tests to make sure trainees can handle difficult situations. At completion, they receive the FAA's Certificate of Demonstrated Proficiency, and they must get periodic retraining to maintain certification or if they want to work in a different kind of aircraft. New graduates are on reserve status, which means that they fill in for experienced attendants who are sick or on vacation. After one or several years on reserve, they may bid on regular assignments. *Experienced workers* get higher priority in choosing assignments. Some are promoted to supervisory positions.

Enterprising

Seven of the Technician/Artisan jobs have Enterprising as their primary personality type. Four of these are covered by the **Realistic** section of this chapter: First-Line Supervisors/Managers of Construction Trades and

© JIST Works

Extraction Workers; First-Line Supervisors/Managers of Fire Fighting and Prevention Workers; First-Line Supervisors/Managers of Mechanics, Installers, and Repairers; and First-Line Supervisors/Managers of Production and Operating Workers. Two of the Enterprising jobs are covered by the **Social** section: Flight Attendants and First-Line Supervisors/Managers of Police and Detectives, both coded ESC. The remaining occupation, the only one covered here, is Air Traffic Controllers.

High school students should take college-prep courses, because although a college degree is not required to become an Air Traffic Controller, most job candidates have a bachelor's. Students should become familiar with using computer-based applications.

Some Air Traffic Controllers get initial training and experience in the *armed forces*. For details about the military, see the **Investigative** section.

College students can major in any subject. Job applicants need four years of college, three years of full-time work experience, or a combination, in which one year of college is considered equivalent to nine months of work experience.

Those without military experience need to enroll in an FAA-approved educational program, apply for an advertised job opening, and pass a pre-employment aptitude test. Those who are selected receive 12 weeks of training at the FAA Academy in Oklahoma City, after which they work as trainees for two to four years until they are certified for the positions in their facility. With military experience, this training period takes less time. Workers must pass job-performance exams twice each year and are subject to drug testing.

Experienced workers in other occupations must follow the same entry route as all other job applicants. They must be under 31 years of age to begin training. Experienced Air Traffic Controllers may advance to supervisory positions.

Conventional

Only one of the Technician/Artisan jobs has Conventional as its primary personality type: Cost Estimators. (Three other occupations have Conventional as a secondary type: First-Line Supervisors/Managers of Police and Detectives; Flight Attendants; and Air Traffic Controllers. These are all covered in the **Enterprising** section of this chapter.)

© JIST Works

The college route for Cost Estimators is described in detail in the **Conventional** section of chapter 8, about the Engineering track. Those who are not college-trained usually enter through the construction industry, which employs the largest number of Cost Estimators, although it is not the highest-paying industry. Others start in a manufacturing industry. For details about starting a career in construction or production, see the **Realistic** section of this chapter. Some *experienced workers* in these industries learn how to estimate costs by working with an experienced estimator. Those with no experience reading specifications or blueprints first learn that aspect of the work. Then they may accompany an experienced estimator to the construction site or shop floor, where they observe the work being done, take measurements, or perform other routine tasks. As they become more knowledgeable, estimators learn how to tabulate quantities and dimensions from drawings and how to select the appropriate prices for materials. Night classes in cost-estimating techniques and procedures may be helpful.

Achieving Six Figures in the Technician/Artisan Track

These workers typically increase their earnings either by entering the Managerial track or, more rarely, by improving their technical skills. Note that several of these jobs are already supervisory in nature and therefore allow workers with the right skills (perhaps acquired through an appropriate degree or certification training) to move up the administrative ladder. In large organizations, these supervisory workers are listed as "staff" managers in the organizational chart, as explained in chapter 11, about the Managerial track.

In some of these fields, there is a thin line between outstanding technical skills and native talent, but even those born with great aptitude for tasks such as writing, cartooning, or flying planes need to spend years refining their techniques and studying the work of superstars in their field. Even the most highly skilled workers will not command high earnings unless they seek out employers who appreciate their abilities or a large market in which to sell their output.

Moving On to Other Career Tracks

Experienced technicians and artisans often find the Managerial career track is a good route for advancement. A college degree in business can help,

© JIST Works

and some professional associations offer certification programs that teach managerial skills.

Some workers draw on their experience as a technician or artisan to go into a specialized sales position and thus enter the Distributive track.

Other technicians and artisans enter the Entrepreneurial track by forming their own company. For example, a ship's captain might purchase a luxury yacht and hire a crew, then offer cruises to wealthy customers. A cost estimator might open a consulting business.

Characteristics of Six-Figure Technician/Artisan Jobs

Highest-Level Skills

Operation Monitoring; Management of Personnel Resources; Operation and Control; Repairing; Management of Material Resources.

Highest-Level Work Activities

Guiding, Directing, and Motivating Subordinates; Coordinating the Work and Activities of Others; Scheduling Work and Activities; Developing and Building Teams; Drafting, Laying Out, and Specifying Technical Devices, Parts, and Equipment.

Most Important Knowledges

Mechanical; Building and Construction; Design; Engineering and Technology; Production and Processing.

Most Important Work Contexts

Face-to-Face Discussions; Telephone; Freedom to Make Decisions; Contact with Others; Importance of Being Exact or Accurate.

Most Important Work Needs

Authority; Responsibility; Autonomy; Variety; Co-workers.

Most Important Work Styles

Dependability; Attention to Detail; Integrity; Stress Tolerance; Leadership.

Facts About Six-Figure Technician/ Artisan Jobs

Six-Figure Occupations

(At least 25% of the workers earn more than $100,000.)

Air Traffic Controllers

Control air traffic on and within vicinity of airport and movement of air traffic between altitude sectors and control centers according to established procedures and policies. Authorize, regulate, and control commercial airline flights according to government or company regulations to expedite and ensure flight safety.

Personality Code: EC

College Majors: Air Traffic Controller Training.

Median Annual Earnings: $112,930

Highly Paid Workforce: Out of a total salaried workforce of 24,180, 18,135 people (25%) earn more than $76,550 and 12,090 (50%) earn more than $112,930.

Annual Job Growth Through 2016: 10.2%

Average Annual Job Openings Through 2016: 1,213

Best-Paying Industries: Federal, State, and Local Government; Transportation and Warehousing.

Best-Paying Metro Areas: Washington-Arlington-Alexandria, DC-VA-MD-WV.

Airline Pilots, Copilots, and Flight Engineers

Pilot and navigate the flight of multi-engine aircraft in regularly scheduled service for the transport of passengers and cargo. Requires Federal Air Transport rating and certification in specific aircraft type used.

Personality Code: RCI

College Majors: Airline/Commercial/Professional Pilot and Flight Crew Training; Flight Instructor Training.

Median Annual Earnings: More than $145,600

© JIST Works

Highly Paid Workforce: Out of a total salaried workforce of 78,250, 58,688 people (75%) earn more than $85,340 and 39,125 (50%) earn more than $145,600.

Annual Job Growth Through 2016: 12.9%

Average Annual Job Openings Through 2016: 4,073

Best-Paying Industries: Federal, State, and Local Government; Transportation and Warehousing.

Best-Paying Metro Areas: Atlanta–Sandy Springs–Marietta, GA; Chicago-Naperville-Joliet, IL-IN-WI; Denver-Aurora, CO; Los Angeles–Long Beach–Santa Ana, CA; Miami–Fort Lauderdale–Miami Beach, FL; New York–Northern New Jersey–Long Island, NY-NJ-PA; San Francisco–Oakland–Fremont, CA; St. Louis, MO-IL; Washington-Arlington-Alexandria, DC-VA-MD-WV.

Art Directors

Formulate design concepts and presentation approaches and direct workers engaged in art work, layout design, and copy writing for visual communications media, such as magazines, books, newspapers, and packaging.

Personality Code: AE

College Majors: Graphic Design; Intermedia/Multimedia.

Median Annual Earnings: $72,320

Highly Paid Workforce: Out of a total salaried workforce of 32,290, 8,073 people (25%) earn more than $102,160.

Annual Job Growth Through 2016: 9.0%

Average Annual Job Openings Through 2016: 9,719

Best-Paying Industries: Management of Companies and Enterprises; Professional, Scientific, and Technical Services.

Best-Paying Metro Areas: Boston-Cambridge-Quincy, MA-NH; Los Angeles–Long Beach–Santa Ana, CA; New York–Northern New Jersey–Long Island, NY-NJ-PA; San Francisco–Oakland–Fremont, CA.

© JIST Works

Six-Figure Niche-Industry Jobs

(At least 10% of workers in the best-paying industries earn more than $100,000.)

Captains, Mates, and Pilots of Water Vessels

Command or supervise operations of ships and water vessels, such as tugboats and ferryboats, that travel into and out of harbors, estuaries, straits, and sounds and on rivers, lakes, bays, and oceans. Required to hold license issued by U.S. Coast Guard.

Personality Code: REC

College Majors: Commercial Fishing; Marine Science/Merchant Marine Officer Training; Marine Transportation, Other.

Median Annual Earnings: $57,210

Highly Paid Workforce: Out of a total salaried workforce of 30,540, 3,054 people (10%) earn more than $99,330.

Annual Job Growth Through 2016: 17.9%

Average Annual Job Openings Through 2016: 2,665

Best-Paying Industries: Transportation and Warehousing.

Commercial Pilots

Pilot and navigate the flight of small fixed or rotary winged aircraft primarily for the transport of cargo and passengers. Requires Commercial Rating.

Personality Code: RIE

College Majors: Airline/Commercial/Professional Pilot and Flight Crew Training; Flight Instructor Training.

Median Annual Earnings: $61,640

Highly Paid Workforce: Out of a total salaried workforce of 29,180, 7,295 people (25%) earn more than $86,380 and 2,918 (10%) earn more than $122,550.

Annual Job Growth Through 2016: 13.2%

Average Annual Job Openings Through 2016: 1,425

Best-Paying Industries: Agriculture, Forestry, Fishing, and Hunting; Manufacturing; Transportation and Warehousing.

© JIST Works

Film and Video Editors

Edit motion picture soundtracks, film, and video.

Personality Code: AEI

College Majors: Audiovisual Communications Technologies/
Technician Training, Other; Cinematography and Film/Video Production;
Communications Technology/Technician Training; Photojournalism;
Radio and Television; Radio and Television Broadcasting Technology/
Technician Training.

Median Annual Earnings: $47,870

Highly Paid Workforce: Out of a total salaried workforce of 17,410,
4,353 (25%) people earn more than $77,180 and 1,741 (10%) earn more
than $113,580.

Annual Job Growth Through 2016: 12.7%

Average Annual Job Openings Through 2016: 2,707

Best-Paying Industries: Information.

First-Line Supervisors/Managers of Fire Fighting and Prevention Workers

Supervise and coordinate activities of workers engaged in fire fighting and
fire prevention and control. (Also included in the Managerial career track.)

Personality Code: ER

College Majors: Fire Protection and Safety Technology/Technician
Training; Fire Services Administration.

Median Annual Earnings: $65,040

Highly Paid Workforce: Out of a total salaried workforce of 52,160,
5,216 people (10%) earn more than $101,370.

Annual Job Growth Through 2016: 11.5%

Average Annual Job Openings Through 2016: 3,771

Best-Paying Industries: Federal, State, and Local Government.

© JIST Works

First-Line Supervisors/Managers of Police and Detectives

Supervise and coordinate activities of members of police force.

Personality Code: ESC

College Majors: Corrections; Criminal Justice/Law Enforcement Administration; Criminal Justice/Safety Studies.

Median Annual Earnings: $72,620

Highly Paid Workforce: Out of a total salaried workforce of 91,510, 9,151 people (10%) earn more than $108,480.

Annual Job Growth Through 2016: 9.2%

Average Annual Job Openings Through 2016: 9,373

Best-Paying Industries: Federal, State, and Local Government.

First-Line Supervisors/Managers of Production and Operating Workers

Supervise and coordinate the activities of production and operating workers, such as inspectors, precision workers, machine setters and operators, assemblers, fabricators, and plant and system operators.

Personality Code: ERC

College Majors: Operations Management and Supervision.

Median Annual Earnings: $48,670

Highly Paid Workforce: Out of a total salaried workforce of 666,850, 66,685 people (10%) earn more than $79,050.

Annual Job Growth Through 2016: –4.8%

Average Annual Job Openings Through 2016: 46,144

Best-Paying Industries: Utilities.

Flight Attendants

Provide personal services to ensure the safety and comfort of airline passengers during flight. Greet passengers, verify tickets, explain use of safety equipment, and serve food or beverages.

Personality Code: ESC

© JIST Works

College Majors: Airline Flight Attendant Training.

Median Annual Earnings: $61,120

Highly Paid Workforce: Out of a total salaried workforce of 97,010, 9,701 people (10%) earn more than $102,660.

Annual Job Growth Through 2016: 10.6%

Average Annual Job Openings Through 2016: 10,773

Best-Paying Industries: Transportation and Warehousing.

Multi-Media Artists and Animators

Create special effects, animation, or other visual images, using film, video, computers, or other electronic tools and media, for use in products or creations such as computer games, movies, music videos, and commercials. (Also included in the Information Technology career track.)

Personality Code: AI

College Majors: Animation, Interactive Technology, Video Graphics and Special Effects; Drawing; Graphic Design; Intermedia/Multimedia; Painting; Printmaking; Web Page, Digital/Multimedia and Information Resources Design.

Median Annual Earnings: $54,550

Highly Paid Workforce: Out of a total salaried workforce of 29,440, 2,944 people (10%) earn more than $98,050.

Annual Job Growth Through 2016: 25.8%

Average Annual Job Openings Through 2016: 13,182

Best-Paying Industries: Information.

Transportation Inspectors

Inspect equipment or goods in connection with the safe transport of cargo or people. Includes rail transport inspectors, such as freight inspectors, car inspectors, rail inspectors, and other nonprecision inspectors of other types of transportation vehicles.

Personality Code: RCI

College Majors: Avionics Maintenance Technology/Technician Training. For many specializations, this job is learned through work experience in a related occupation.

Median Annual Earnings: $51,440

Highly Paid Workforce: Out of a total salaried workforce of 24,130, 2,413 people (10%) earn more than $98,170.

Annual Job Growth Through 2016: 16.4%

Average Annual Job Openings Through 2016: 2,122

Best-Paying Industries: Federal, State, and Local Government.

Writers and Authors

Originate and prepare written material, such as scripts, stories, advertisements, and other material.

Personality Code: AEI

College Majors: Broadcast Journalism; Business/Corporate Communications; Communications, Journalism, and Related Fields, Other; Communication Studies/Speech Communication and Rhetoric; Creative Writing; English Composition; Family and Consumer Sciences/Human Sciences Communications; Journalism; Mass Communications/Media Studies; Playwriting and Screenwriting; Technical and Business Writing.

Median Annual Earnings: $50,660

Highly Paid Workforce: Out of a total salaried workforce of 44,310, 4,431 people (10%) earn more than $99,910.

Annual Job Growth Through 2016: 12.8%

Average Annual Job Openings Through 2016: 24,023

Best-Paying Industries: Arts, Entertainment, and Recreation; Professional, Scientific, and Technical Services.

Six-Figure Niche-Location Jobs

(At least 10% of workers in the best-paying metro areas earn more than $100,000.)

Cost Estimators

Prepare cost estimates for product manufacturing, construction projects, or services to aid management in bidding on or determining price of product or service. May specialize according to particular service performed or type of product manufactured. (Also included in the Engineering career track.)

© JIST Works

Personality Code: CE

College Majors: Business Administration and Management, General; Business/Commerce, General; Construction Engineering; Construction Engineering Technology/Technician Training; Manufacturing Engineering; Materials Engineering; Mechanical Engineering.

Median Annual Earnings: $54,920

Highly Paid Workforce: Out of a total salaried workforce of 219,070, 21,907 people (10%) earn more than $91,350.

Annual Job Growth Through 2016: 18.5%

Average Annual Job Openings Through 2016: 38,379

Best-Paying Metro Areas: Boston-Cambridge-Quincy, MA-NH; Chicago-Naperville-Joliet, IL-IN-WI; Detroit-Warren-Livonia, MI; Houston–Sugar Land–Baytown, TX; New York–Northern New Jersey–Long Island, NY-NJ-PA; San Francisco–Oakland–Fremont, CA; San Jose–Sunnyvale–Santa Clara, CA.

Editors

Perform variety of editorial duties, such as laying out, indexing, and revising content of written materials, in preparation for final publication.

Personality Code: AEC

College Majors: Broadcast Journalism; Business/Corporate Communications; Communication, Journalism, and Related Programs, Other; Creative Writing; English; Family and Consumer Sciences/Human Sciences Communication; Journalism; Mass Communication/Media Studies; Publishing; Technical and Business Writing.

Median Annual Earnings: $48,320

Highly Paid Workforce: Out of a total salaried workforce of 105,920, 10,592 people (10%) earn more than $91,390.

Annual Job Growth Through 2016: 2.3%

Average Annual Job Openings Through 2016: 20,193

Best-Paying Metro Areas: Los Angeles–Long Beach–Santa Ana, CA; New York–Northern New Jersey–Long Island, NY-NJ-PA.

Electricians

Install, maintain, and repair electrical wiring, equipment, and fixtures. Ensure that work is in accordance with relevant codes. May install or service street lights, intercom systems, or electrical control systems.

Personality Code: RIC

College Majors: Electrician Training.

Median Annual Earnings: $44,780

Highly Paid Workforce: Out of a total salaried workforce of 624,560, 62,456 people (10%) earn more than $76,000.

Annual Job Growth Through 2016: 7.4%

Average Annual Job Openings Through 2016: 79,083

Best-Paying Metro Areas: Philadelphia-Camden-Wilmington, PA-NJ-DE-MD; San Francisco–Oakland–Fremont, CA; San Jose–Sunnyvale–Santa Clara, CA.

First-Line Supervisors/Managers of Construction Trades and Extraction Workers

Directly supervise and coordinate activities of construction or extraction workers.

Personality Code: ERC

College Majors: Blasting/Blaster Training; Building/Construction Site Management/Manager Training; Building/Home/Construction Inspection/Inspector Training; Building/Property Maintenance and Management; Carpentry; Concrete Finishing; Drywall Installation; Electrical and Power Transmission Installation, General; Electrician Training; Glazier Training; Lineworker Training; Masonry; Painting; Plumbing Technology; Roofer Training; Well Drilling.

Median Annual Earnings: $55,950

Highly Paid Workforce: Out of a total salaried workforce of 577,130, 57,713 people (10%) earn more than $90,220.

Annual Job Growth Through 2016: 9.1%

Average Annual Job Openings Through 2016: 82,923

© JIST Works

Best-Paying Metro Areas: Chicago-Naperville-Joliet, IL-IN-WI; Detroit-Warren-Livonia, MI; Honolulu, HI; Milwaukee–Waukesha–West Allis, WI; New York–Northern New Jersey–Long Island, NY-NJ-PA; Philadelphia-Camden-Wilmington, PA-NJ-DE-MD; San Francisco–Oakland–Fremont, CA; San Jose–Sunnyvale–Santa Clara, CA; Santa Rosa–Petaluma, CA; Seattle-Tacoma-Bellevue, WA.

First-Line Supervisors/Managers of Mechanics, Installers, and Repairers

Supervise and coordinate the activities of mechanics, installers, and repairers.

Personality Code: ECR

College Majors: Operations Management and Supervision.

Median Annual Earnings: $55,380

Highly Paid Workforce: Out of a total salaried workforce of 443,790, 44,379 people (10%) earn more than $84,930.

Annual Job Growth Through 2016: 7.3%

Average Annual Job Openings Through 2016: 24,361

Best-Paying Metro Areas: San Francisco–Oakland–Fremont, CA; San Jose–Sunnyvale–Santa Clara, CA.

© JIST Works

Chapter 15

The $100,000 Job Hunt

As you've seen in the previous chapters about career tracks, the road to a six-figure job can sometimes be very long. Many of the jobs covered in this book require years of preparation. Often you must complete four years of college, pursue graduate or professional studies, and get work experience before the job is open to you.

But even after you have completed the entry requirements for the jobs in this book and get hired, you are not guaranteed to be in a six-figure job. **Remember that, for the great majority of the occupations in this book, the average income is less than $100,000.** Many of the jobs are listed as "six-figure niche jobs," meaning that as few as 10 percent of the workers earn $100,000. Among the "six-figure occupations," as few as 25 percent of the workers earn $100,000. When you read the descriptions of the jobs, be sure to observe the size of the "Highly Paid Workforce." It can give you an understanding of how much competition you'll face to earn six figures.

Look at the median incomes listed for the jobs in this book and you'll note that several are below $50,000. And keep in mind that the median figure means half the workers earn more, half earn less, so even if the median income is $100,000 (as it is for Pharmacists, for example), half of the workers are earning less than six figures. Beginning workers, in particular, are likely to be earning below the midpoint. So even after you have entered one of these jobs, you may not earn six figures until after you get several years of experience or find some special, high-paying niche.

The good news is that this chapter will show you strategies for any career track or personality type that can increase your chances of earning six figures.

Focusing on Your Goal

To get hired in a six-figure niche job, you need to be highly focused on your goal. Colin Frager, an executive recruiter and CEO of the Colin Phillips Group, says that the key to success is a combination of preparation and motivation. From his many years of experience in helping people land six-figure jobs, he has learned that most people begin the job hunt without giving sufficient thought to *what they want* and *what they can bring to the table.*

Employers who hire people for high-paying positions want workers who will hit the ground running and perform a very specific set of job tasks. That means these employers are not interested in job candidates who have only a general notion of what kind of work they are looking for. Understanding your personality type is a first cut; identifying and preparing for a suitable occupation narrows the field further; getting experience in a high-paying industry clarifies your goal still more; reviewing your experiences and deciding which work tasks you have enjoyed most is also helpful. But you need to figure out your intended job in much greater detail before you are ready to compete successfully in the job market. Informational interviewing (discussed later in this chapter) can help.

The other part of preparing for the job hunt is being able to explain coherently what you have to offer the employer and what qualifies you to hold this specific job in the context of their business. Some people have difficulty talking about their skills and experience out of fear of appearing boastful. As Colin Frager observes, it helps to think of yourself not as a person, but as a product or service that you're selling to the employer. This allows you to be objective about your strengths and also helps guide your research into employers' needs.

Ideally, you'll be able to think of yourself as a brand. Just as it's easy to summarize Volvo as the really safe car or Wal-Mart as the store with the low prices, you should be able to think of yourself as having some special attribute or record of achievement that defines what you have to offer an employer. Okay, what's *your* brand? What is going to make the employer want to hire you instead of dozens of other people with impressive resumes?

This process of focusing on your goals and your brand can take hours or even months, but it is much more productive than sending off nontargeted resumes like a dandelion puff scattering its seeds. You wouldn't think of entering an athletic competition without months or years of preparation. What makes you think you can compete in the job market without preparing first?

© JIST Works

Finding Jobs

You may have already heard about the "hidden job market." Studies have revealed that most jobs are found not by answering an advertisement in a newspaper or by waiting for a Web site to match you to an employer, but rather through personal contacts. This is true for all kinds of jobs, but especially for high-paying jobs. In practice, the higher the job pays, the less likely it is to be advertised. You also should consider that advertisements may not provide useful information on how much a job will pay, as salary is often negotiable. Even a Web site claiming to list only six-figure jobs may actually list some jobs at lower levels of pay. Finally, some jobs are advertised just to meet a legal requirement, although a candidate has already been selected.

There are two basic strategies for finding out about unadvertised jobs: **cold-calling** employers who hire people like you or **networking** so that you hear about potential job openings. The two overlap to some extent: through a cold call to an employer, you may hear about a possible job elsewhere, and through your network, you may hear about employers who are most likely to be worth cold-calling. You can pursue both strategies simultaneously.

To pursue either strategy, you need to have your resume in good shape so you can send it off on short notice. The resume needs to show the tight focus you have achieved through the preparation process outlined in the previous section. Your focused thinking should be visible in what the resume says about your career goal as well as what it says about your qualifications for that goal. The cover letter also should be based on this focused thinking.

A multi-page resume that reflects a lot of work experience can blur your focus and probably needs a one-page executive summary so readers can quickly identify what you seek and what you have to offer. Conversely, the resume may benefit from an additional detailed document, headed something like "Key Initiatives and Successes," that highlights your record of achievement for those readers who want more specifics. (Some even include graphs.)

This book does not have room for examples of these documents, but here are some JIST books about resume writing that should prove helpful:

- *Résumé Magic: Trade Secrets of a Professional Resume Writer,* by Susan Britton Whitcomb

© JIST Works

- *The Quick Resume & Cover Letter Book: Write and Use an Effective Resume in Only One Day*, by Michael Farr

- *Sales and Marketing Resumes for $100,000 Careers*, by Louise M. Kursmark

- *Executive's Pocket Guide to ROI Resumes and Job Search*, by Louise M. Kursmark and Jan Melnik

The last two books listed are especially targeted at people seeking high-paying jobs.

Whether you use networking or cold-calling, you also need to have an "elevator speech" prepared and rehearsed. This is a brief statement of who you are, what kind of job you're seeking, and why you qualify for this kind of job. Like the resume, it distills what you learned in your goal-focusing process. No matter where you use this speech, it must be concise enough that you could say it to someone on an elevator and get all your points across before the elevator has stopped. You can practice using this speech, or at least parts of it, whenever anyone asks you what you do for a living (which is a very common question). Instead of giving merely a job title and letting the other person assume that you fit various stereotypes about that occupation, say things about your background and aspirations.

Both networking and cold-calling require you to move outside your comfort zone. Your problem is that you don't know about these hidden job openings. You won't learn about them by talking only to your friends, because your friends tend to know most of the same things you know. The principle behind networking is that by connecting to *the people your friends know* you can learn information (in this case, about jobs) that ordinarily would not be available to you. The principle behind cold-calling is that by talking directly to *the people who make hiring decisions*, you can learn about jobs that may never be advertised.

Networking

Make a list of everyone you know. Include people you went to school with years ago, people you used to work with, relatives you don't see very often, the person who cuts your hair, people in your faith group, the real estate agent who sold you your house, and so forth. Join a professional association, go to meetings, and make contact with people in your field. All of these people have connections to people you don't know, people who may know about jobs. Give them your elevator speech and make it clear to

© JIST Works

them what sort of work you're looking for. You may also find it useful to ask them for advice and look on this as a final stage of career exploration. For example, you might ask them what industries or businesses need people like you, or you might ask whether they know anyone who does this kind of work and what that person's experiences have been. Conversations like this plant a seed: These people now think of you as a job-seeker in this field and may later relay to you news of a job opening. More likely, they will be able to tell you the name of someone who is more knowledgeable about the field, and *that* person may be your actual lead for a job opening. Make a point of asking for the name of someone who knows lots of people in the field you're targeting. Studies of networks show that most contacts are made through a small number of very well-connected people.

Cold-Calling

Someone in your network may mention your name to a manager who is hiring, and that person may give you a call. But, in many situations, the person in your network will give you the name of someone who is hiring, and it will be up to you to make the call. In that case, you are shifting to the cold-calling strategy.

You don't have to wait for your network to turn up likely employers to call. The most effective way to conduct a cold-calling campaign is to research the businesses that hire people for the kind of position you seek. Business directories such as the Yellow Pages can help, but for six-figure occupations, a more productive source for learning about employing businesses is a professional association. If the association has a membership directory, note which companies employ a lot of members. Another clue is to observe which businesses sponsor the association or its activities.

When you have identified a likely business, don't contact the human resources department; they know only about the part of the job market that isn't hidden. Instead, find the name and phone number of someone who has the power to make a hiring decision. In a small company, this may be the CEO or other top manager; in a large company, it may be a department head. Telephone this person. If you call between 8 and 9 in the morning or 5 and 6 in the evening, you may improve the odds that the phone will be answered by the person you seek rather than by a secretary. If you get the person's voice mailbox, hang up and try again at another time; cold calls are unlikely to be returned. E-mail takes less courage than the telephone, but it is too easily lost in the pile of messages cluttering your target's inbox and may automatically be flagged as spam. Still another

© JIST Works

way to make contact is to drop in on the business in person. This tends to work best at small businesses, where you can ask to speak to the person in charge; at a large organization, you are likely to be sent to the human resources department, where your job application and resume will be tucked into a file drawer and probably never be read again.

Once you are talking to a person who can make a hiring decision, you have two tactics open to you: direct and indirect. The direct method is to give your elevator speech, make it clear that you are interested in a job, and ask for an interview. Be prepared to ask several times, because this shows your interest and determination. Don't ask whether the business has job openings, but perhaps ask if the business is likely to have openings in the future. If the person on the other end says that the company is not hiring now, ask for a get-acquainted interview—maybe a lunch date. At the very least, ask for leads to people who might be hiring elsewhere, call those leads, and tell them who referred you. Expect a lot of rejection, but keep in mind that these calls take only a few minutes, so you can cover a large number of employers in one afternoon.

The indirect method is similar—it uses an elevator speech about your background, and aims for an interview—but it stops short of asking for a *job* interview. Instead, you treat the person like a highly targeted networking contact; the goal is an interview that will focus on *learning more information* rather than on being hired. For example, you might say that you are thinking of specializing in the kind of work that goes on in that person's business and you want to learn more about the pros and cons of that specialization. If the person on the other end tries to cut you off by saying that the company is not hiring, make it clear that you are not asking for a job interview—you want information or perhaps advice. The informational interview may not, in fact, lead to a job at that company—at least not at present—but it may lead to a future job offer, and at least it has a good chance of taking your networking campaign to a higher level. This person is much more likely than your second cousin or your high school friend to know someone in another department or a similar business who has a job opening.

Fields That Still Use Traditional Job-Hunting Methods

A few fields have no hidden job market, or only a very small one, so most job-seekers in these fields find openings through traditional methods such as advertisements and human resource departments, rather than through networking and cold-calling.

First-Line Supervisors/Managers of Police and Detectives and First-Line Supervisors/Managers of Fire Fighting and Prevention Workers advance from lower-level positions in their department based on their job performance and their scores on competitive exams. Openings usually are posted. All positions for Air Traffic Controllers are advertised.

Maximizing Your Salary

In the chapters on the career tracks, you've seen suggestions for how to improve your earnings, and almost every case involved acquiring additional skills—managerial or technical, learned in a degree program or on the job. For example, if you're an accountant, you might be able to earn big bucks because of your mastery of obscure knowledge—say, if you were thoroughly familiar with the accounting methods appropriate for international investments, spoke a Middle Eastern language fluently, and thus landed a job with a company that frequently dealt with a stock exchange in that part of the world. Of course, with such specialized knowledge, you would be able to find work in only a limited number of companies. And if business relations with your country of expertise were cut off because of a political crisis, your high-paying job might come to a sudden end.

So remember that flexibility, just like specialized knowledge, is also a useful skill. As work tasks change, or as the work environment undergoes changes, you need to be able to adapt to the new realities. This is especially true for technology, which affects so many work tasks and is constantly evolving, but it also applies to the regulatory environment, fickle popular tastes, foreign competition, and countless other fluid factors that can affect the way your job gets done and therefore your income—and ultimately your ability to stay employed.

On the other hand, flexibility does not mean trying to be all things to all employers. A generalist may be able to fill many different jobs, but employers pay the most to someone who is the perfect fit for a highly specific job function. The best strategy is to have targeted skills but continue to grow and acquire new skills as the environment changes.

In addition to concentrating on their skills, workers in search of improved earnings can use other strategies, such as relocating, working longer hours, and negotiating pay effectively.

© JIST Works

Relocating to Boost Earnings

Some of the jobs included in this book offer six-figure salaries primarily in a few geographical locations; elsewhere, the workers earn considerably less. You'll find these locations identified for "Six-Figure Occupations" and "Six-Figure Niche-Location Jobs" in chapters 5 through 14.

You may wonder why some localities pay much better than others. In some cases, the high wages go hand-in-hand with a high cost of living, meaning that your improved earnings in such a location will put you into a higher tax bracket without buying you a more comfortable lifestyle. In the new community, you may face keener competition for jobs. Also, for a few jobs, different communities have different licensing requirements. So relocating for higher pay is not always a good idea.

But in other cases you can genuinely improve your circumstances by relocating. For example, for industries that involve a lot of collaborative work, businesses tend to cluster in certain geographical areas (think of Hollywood for Film and Video Editors or Silicon Valley for Computer and Information Scientists, Research). Workers who live in such hubs of collaborative activity often can be more productive and thus more able to achieve an affluent standard of living than workers who are located elsewhere. On the other hand, for jobs where people tend to work solo or with assistants rather than peers (think of Dentists), the reverse is often true—workers can earn more if they move to a region where there are few colleagues and therefore little competition.

Industry

People in the same occupation often earn very different amounts in different industries, and sometimes the six-figure positions are clustered in certain industries. In chapters 5 through 14 you'll notice these industries identified for "Six-Figure Occupations" and for "Six-Figure Niche-Industry Jobs."

It's usually easiest to target the high-paying industries while you are preparing to enter the occupation—that is, while you're getting your education or training. You can select a college, a college major, a concentration within a major, an internship, or a training program that aims for the industry you have as your goal. After you have been in the workforce for many years, it is usually difficult to move to a very different industry because your work experience is not particularly relevant, even when the occupational title is the same. You may need to take classes or get informal training to learn the skills required in the better-paying industry.

© JIST Works

When thinking about shifting industries, you also need to consider whether work conditions in the new industry will be to your liking; for example, longer work hours or more frequent travel may be expected. Also, competition is likely to be greater where the salaries are higher.

Most occupations have a professional association that can inform you of the different requirements and conditions across the nation and in various industries. With this information, you can make an informed choice about whether aspiring toward a particular industry would be a good opportunity for you.

Gender

You can't control your gender, but you can take steps to avoid being penalized for it. In 2006, the Census Bureau found that women earned about 75 percent of what men working in the same occupation earned. They also found only 2.8 percent of women earning six figures or more, compared to 9.2 percent of men. Many labor economists argue that this disparity is not always the result of discrimination, but it probably still is in many cases.

If you're a woman, there are strategies you can use to try to maximize your chances of receiving a fair wage. Some occupations have a better ratio of female-to-male wages, and you can compare earnings figures by gender as reported by the U.S. Department of Labor at www.bls.gov/cps/wlf-databook.htm. Some employers have programs in place to recruit women for positions where they have been underrepresented. In other cases, a manager who is a determined and inspiring mentor can accomplish as much for your career as a formal program might. When you research possible employers, try to find out whether they have a record of such efforts. Sometimes they do not publicize these efforts, but you may learn about their reputation for fairness by speaking with women who work for the employer. Also remember to consider the availability of female-friendly fringe benefits, such as paid maternity leave.

Work Hours

Some jobs offer opportunities for you to earn extra income by working longer or unusual hours. For example, in 2006, the highest-paid New Jersey state employee was not the governor, but rather a clinical psychiatrist at a state psychiatric hospital who earned about $277,000, of which $116,500 was earned from working extra shifts. The availability of extra

© JIST Works

pay for shift work or overtime varies partly among occupations and partly among employers. Keep in mind that a policy of extra pay for overtime or shift work does not guarantee that these work hours will be available to you. Businesses that are prospering or that experience busy seasons (for example, tax-preparation services) are more likely to offer overtime work.

Of course, many of the jobs in this book are typically not paid by the hour. For some jobs, especially in sales, commissions can be a big part of the pay package and can produce great rewards for extra hours of work.

Noncompetition Agreements: A Possible Barrier to Job Mobility

Your plans to improve your earnings by moving to a new employer may be thwarted if you have signed a noncompetition agreement with your present employer. For example, if you are working in sales, your employer may ask you to sign a "noncompete" that says you will not take your current clients with you if move to another employer. The agreement usually specifies a time period and in some cases a geographical area where you cannot compete during this period. Enforcement of these agreements varies among states; some states do not enforce them unless the restrictions are very narrow, but before signing anything you should assume that it will be binding. People working at $30,000 jobs rarely encounter these agreements, but at the six-figure level they are much more common, especially if you are working in a highly specialized industry, and they can be particularly burdensome if later you want to go into consulting or entrepreneurship.

The time to negotiate such an agreement—when you have some leverage in the discussion—is when you are hired, not when you are preparing to leave. You may not be able to get the employer to drop the clause entirely, but you may be able to get the terms narrowed so they apply only to conditions that truly are necessary to protect the employer. You also may counter by asking the employer to promise severance pay in the event of a termination that is not for cause; this means that if you are downsized at a later date, you will have income for at least part of the time in which the "noncompete" is still in force. An employer who really needs protection from competition should be able to pay for it, and the courts usually demand that the employer offer something in exchange for its restrictions. However, if you are an at-will employee, your continued employment may be considered sufficient compensation for the employer's demands.

Negotiating Your Pay When You're Hired

Academic degrees, exceptional skills, living in a high-wage area, finding a high-paying job specialization—these factors are supposed to boost your earnings, but none will result in earnings until an employer *makes a salary offer*. In most cases the employer will have a salary figure in mind but also will have some freedom to offer more or less. This is especially true for hiring negotiations for unadvertised jobs, but it also is true even for the less common situation in which the employer has included an expected salary offer in an advertisement for the job.

Therefore, to get the best possible salary offer, you need a strategy for negotiating your pay. Keep in mind that the following suggestions cover only salary-related issues; this book does not have room to cover other issues related to interviewing successfully and evaluating a job offer wisely.

Your Strategy: Save Salary for Last

The most important principle to remember is to save discussion of salary for the very end of the interview and hiring-decision process. Employers often ask for your salary expectations (or perhaps your salary history) very early, perhaps even as part of the job application form or letter. This makes it easy for them to screen out a large number of applicants who don't match the salary figure they have in mind.

Don't screen yourself out by giving this information. Tell them that your salary expectations depend on the specific features of the job, and you need to know more about this job to decide what a reasonable salary figure would be. If there's a blank on the job application demanding a figure, write "Negotiable." As for your salary history, say that the job in question may not be totally comparable to your past jobs, and you need to discuss the similarities and differences so that both you and the employer can decide what pay is appropriate. Note that these arguments contribute to your pitch for why they should interview you. If the employer refuses to interview you unless you indicate your salary expectations, give only a large ballpark estimate and make clear that you expect both parties will be flexible as you learn more about each other.

Useful Information to Have at the Interview

At the interview, information is your strongest weapon. Some of the information that can boost your pay has to do with your own background: your

© JIST Works

skills, your demonstrated work ethic, and ideally your specific contribution to your former employers' earnings. ("I developed a method to cut costs by 5 percent and brought in 50 new clients, thus boosting annual earnings by 10 percent.") Show-and-tell can be very helpful; you don't have to be an artist to have a portfolio. Any tangible representation of your work output will be useful. If it's too big to bring along, bring photographs; if it can't be photographed, use testimonial letters, news clippings, or excerpts from business reports.

Another important kind of information is your knowledge about the business that has the job opening. The more you know about your prospective employer, the better you'll be able to show how your skills match the company's needs. If you know they're prosperous, you can expect to have less difficulty asking for a high salary. If you know they're going through hard times, you can argue that they need your skills to change their fortunes and you can ask that your starting salary be reviewed once you start contributing to their success.

The third kind of information you need is about the labor market. All decisions about pay are made in the context of a market in which employers make offers and workers make demands. You need to know the going rate for this occupation in this industry, in this location, in this kind of business, and for a person with your kind of skills as indicated by your background. Some Web sites claim to provide this kind of information, but it rarely is specific enough for your location and your background. Your best bet is to use personal contacts in your targeted business (or one similar to it) to learn the earnings of workers like you. It is not considered polite to ask people what they're earning, but you may specify a pay figure and ask your contacts whether they think the figure is too high or low. If you have been working with a recruiter—an outside recruiter or "headhunter," not a recruiter at the company where you're interviewing—that person should be able to tell you what range of salary is appropriate to expect.

Your past earnings may or may not be relevant. Your prospective employer may be in a different industry or a different location and therefore not pay at the same rate as your past employers. In addition, the duties expected of you in the prospective job may not be identical to those in your past positions.

Negotiating During the Interview

The purpose of the job interview is to allow you and the employer to gather enough information to decide whether you're a good fit. Only *after* that decision is made—when they're offering you the job—should the issue of salary come up or get specific.

While the interviewer is gathering information about your background and skills, you need to use every opportunity to explain how you can improve the organization's bottom line, because that is what justifies better pay. You may even be able to point out ways in which you can do a bigger job than what the employer originally had in mind. For example, because of your background you may be able to take on technical duties, design tasks, or managerial roles not normally associated with the job. If you and the interviewer agree on pay early in the interview, all of this discussion will be wasted. By postponing talk about pay, you allow this information to influence the salary offer.

The interviewer may steer the conversation toward pay early in the interview, not so much to lock you into a certain level of pay as to simplify the interviewer's task of screening you out of the job. Be prepared with some responses that can shift the conversation back to your qualifications for the job. For example, if the interviewer asks what pay you expect, you might answer, "I'm sure you pay your employees fairly, and I expect you to pay me a fair wage for a person with my background. So let's discuss my background and what I can do for your business." Or you might say, "Let's save that discussion for when we're ready to close the deal. If you're ready to offer me the job now, okay, but I think you need to know more about me and what I can do for your organization." If the interviewer asks about your salary history, be prepared to offer some of the arguments mentioned in a previous paragraph: "This job is not identical to my previous job, so we need to work out fair compensation for the knowledge and skills I'm bringing to this position." Still another tactic is to throw the salary question back at the interviewer: "Why don't you tell me what range of salaries you pay for this position?" Ask a friend to sit down for a practice interview and try out responses similar to these so you can get comfortable with this strategy and achieve a tone that is not evasive or off-putting.

If this strategy does not work and you feel you must specify your salary expectation early in the interview, give a rather broad range, make clear that it is based on research rather than on wishful thinking, and suggest that its relevance to your case depends on further discussion. For example, in an interview for a job as a computer systems manager you might say,

© JIST Works

"I've investigated what computer systems managers are earning in this area. The average is about $105,000, but of course many of them have degrees only in their technical field, whereas I have an MBA, and that can make a 20 percent difference in earnings. That would put the figure at about $125,000, but then again, it's going to depend on what I'll be doing for you. With my background in your industry, I think I can do more for you than most other applicants you're going to interview." Then you would discuss how your skills match the company's needs as you understand them. You might also mention that your salary expectations depend on the overall compensation package.

Although you should try to avoid discussing salary, it's a good idea to ask the interviewer what fringe benefits are typical at the company. Usually there's a standard set of benefits, and the interviewer may even offer you a printed summary. This is not the time to negotiate these benefits, but you may want to do so later, so it is helpful to learn in advance what the baseline benefits are. Find out whether any benefits require you to pay part of the costs.

You also need to understand other factors that may affect your paycheck. Is the pay rate determined by a union contract? (If so, you will not be able to negotiate your pay or benefits, but both probably will be better than they would be otherwise.) Does the company pay commissions or performance-related bonuses? Are you eligible for overtime pay and, if so, what work hours can you expect?

Another piece of information that is useful to know is how much competition you're facing. Ask the interviewer how many people are being interviewed for the position. If you're the only job candidate remaining, you'll be able to negotiate from a stronger position.

Negotiating After the Job Offer

You may be offered the job at the interview, but more likely the offer will come afterward. Let's assume that you want the job if it pays well enough. Based on your research, you should have a figure in mind that you consider fair.

Ideally, the employer will make you a salary offer, and you can decide how to react. If the offer is more than you expected, congratulations! But you may get an even better offer if you don't jump at the first offer. Pause long enough to give the employer the impression that you may be expecting more. You may even ask for time to think over the offer.

© JIST Works

Asking for time is especially important if the offer is less than the figure you had in mind. Use that time to plan your negotiating strategy. If possible, do all your negotiating face-to-face, rather than by telephone, because you can gauge another person's reactions better in person.

Some of the following strategies may help you build a case for a better salary when you make a counteroffer. You also may choose to mention some of them when they make their initial offer, giving them something to think about at the same time that you're considering their offer:

- If another employer has made a better offer, that's the most powerful argument you can use.

- If you have no other offers, but your research tells you the going rate is higher than what they're offering, tell them so. Keep in mind that they probably also have researched the employment market, so be sure you have very good sources to point to.

- If they won't raise their offer enough to suit your expectations, ask them to agree to review your salary sooner than they normally would.

- Employers who won't budge on salary offers sometimes are willing to make concessions on benefits or perks that you want. Maybe you can get stock options, extra vacation, use of a company car, or the ability to work at home part of the week. Sometimes you can argue that you both will gain from the benefit; for example, if the company pays your tuition expenses for night classes, they will profit from your improved skills.

- You may also be able to get concessions on certain work responsibilities you either want or want to avoid. For example, you might ask to be given a managerial task that's not normally part of the job, and this eventually could lead to a higher-paying position. Any tasks you ask to avoid should be lower-level so that ruling them out would not interfere with your growth in the job.

It's possible that the employer, when offering you the job, may ask *you* to specify the level of pay you expect. The arguments you might have used during the interview are no longer relevant, so you'll need to quote a figure—or, better, a range—based on your understanding of the going rate. If the employer makes a lower counteroffer, use some of the preceding arguments to try to sweeten the deal.

© JIST Works

When you and the employer agree on the salary and on any benefits that go beyond the standard package, get the details in writing. The best way to do this without appearing to question the employer's trustworthiness is to jot down *your* understanding of the compensation package, initial it, and ask for the employer's initials. (Initials are less threatening than a signature.)

If the employer cannot offer a level of pay that you have reason to consider fair, say that the job is one you would like if the salary were appropriate, and thank them for their time and consideration. It is possible that they will not find someone else to fill the position and will reconsider hiring you at the salary you asked for.

Negotiating a Raise

Getting a raise is different from negotiating starting pay and therefore calls for different strategies. Negotiations for a raise are easier on all parties concerned. You are more of a known quantity (or should be) than when you were hired, you have become familiar with your boss, and you now have inside knowledge of the business. You also have more control over the timing of the negotiations, and it's important that you choose a time when the business is not in trouble, when your boss's budget for the coming year is still fluid, and when you have some recent accomplishments you can point to. Set up a meeting specifically for this purpose (you might say the topic is "my compensation"). If you have a regularly scheduled annual performance-appraisal meeting, you might use that occasion if you are very confident that the appraisal will be positive, but you should alert your boss ahead of time that you intend to include compensation in the discussion. You should have a specific figure in mind, but you must be prepared to be flexible about it.

Most important of all, be prepared to justify your request for a raise with something more relevant than your desires or your needs. The cost of living may be going up, but everyone else in the company is equally affected by that. You need to be able to argue that you are worth more to the business than your current rate of pay.

The *fairness strategy* is to point out that other workers like you, with a similar level of skill and productivity, are being paid more than you are. To make this argument, you need to prepare for the interview by researching the going rate of pay for workers in your position, in your industry, in your area, and with your credentials and skills. Admittedly, that information

© JIST Works

may be difficult to obtain, but perhaps you can contact workers in another company and ask whether they would consider a certain ballpark figure high, low, or average. As in a hiring interview, the strongest card you can hold is a salary offer from another employer (or another department in your company), but good knowledge of going rates inside and outside your business is the next best card to hold.

The *merit strategy* is to point out that you are working at a higher level than when your pay was set or last adjusted; you now perform what is in effect a new job but are being paid at the rate of your old job. If this is literally true—that is, if you can point to a matching job description for a higher-paid job—you may want to argue for a promotion rather than a raise. But even if you're not asking for a change of job title, you may be able to point to specific work tasks and indicators of skill and productivity that put you at a higher level than you were before. If you can take credit for cost savings, new revenue streams, faster or better output, or higher profit margins, you will have a strong case, especially if you can point to specific measures of these achievements. A newly acquired degree or certification may serve as an indication of improved skills; indeed, in some work situations it automatically produces a raise. With most employers, mere seniority does not merit a raise; if you are simply doing your job as required, you deserve continued employment but no raise.

Have a response prepared in case your boss turns you down. Your boss may concede your arguments based on fairness or merit but still be unable to grant you a raise because of a tight budget or concerns about the future. In that case, it is fair for you to ask when you can bring up the issue again and what the chances are that you will get a positive answer at that time. A good general response to a rejection is to say, "I understand your position." This implies that your boss wants to give you a raise but is unable to, and thus both you and your boss save face. It also leaves open your subsequent course of action. By contrast, a response such as "That's not fair" or "I deserve better" amounts to a criticism of your boss and implies that you're going to look for work elsewhere or scale back your work effort. Unless you are ready to quit or be fired, that is not a helpful strategy.

As with negotiations for starting salary, if your boss cannot offer your desired level of pay, you may ask for extra fringe benefits or perks instead. Still another recourse is to ask to be paid a commission or bonus for the new business or savings you generate; this pay arrangement is feasible only if you can quantify exactly how much revenue you bring in or save.

© JIST Works

Highlights of Chapter 15

- Because six-figure jobs are the exception rather than the rule, for most of the jobs in this book, you need strategies for commanding exceptional earnings.

- To land a high-paying job, you have to identify precisely what work you intend to do and why you are qualified to do it.

- Most job openings are not advertised, especially for high-paying positions, but you can find out about them through networking and cold calling.

- You can maximize your salary by choosing the right industry or location or through a strategy of well-informed and well-timed negotiations.

Index

© JIST Works

© JIST Works

© JIST Works

© JIST Works

P–Q

R

© JIST Works

© JIST Works

© JIST Works

© JIST Works